Journal of Pentecostal Theology
Supplement Series
1

Editors
John Christopher Thomas
Rick D. Moore
Steven J. Land

Sheffield Academic Press
Sheffield

Pentecostal
Spirituality
A Passion for
the Kingdom

Steven J. Land

 Sheffield Academic Press

To Peggy
Alanna, Laura, Jonathan

First published by Sheffield Academic Press 1993
Reprinted 1994, 1997

Copyright © 1993, 1994, 1997 Sheffield Academic Press

Published by Sheffield Academic Press Ltd
Mansion House
19 Kingfield Road
Sheffield S11 9AS
England

Printed on acid-free paper in Great Britain
by The Cromwell Press
Melksham, Wiltshire

British Library Cataloguing in Publication Data

A catalogue record for this book is available
from the British Library

ISBN 1-85075-442-X

CONTENTS

PREFACE

This work is of, by and for the Pentecostals who have nurtured, exasperated, challenged and encouraged me for the past forty years. I hope they recognize themselves and also find some new perspectives in this interpretation and re-vision of our tradition. I have sought to be controversial in the best sense of the word. This is almost assured by juxtaposing words like 'holiness', 'Pentecostal', 'affections' and 'ecumenical'.

Because I believe that the whole church is Pentecostal, this study is also, I hope, ecumenical in a sectarian sense. By going deeply into the Pentecostal affections, I hope that other Christians will be able to distinguish themselves from and to identify with Pentecostals.

The polemical irenic edges are there, to be sure. I very much want to speak for *rapprochement* between Pentecostal and Holiness bodies, for a deeper appreciation by Pentecostals of their own heritage, for the crucial importance of religious affections for all Christians (especially Pentecostals), and to put forward a trinitarian re-vision that will provoke and encourage a more socially, missionally, ecumenically and theologically responsible Pentecostalism. I hope that my liberal Protestant (in the tradition of Schleiermacher) and fundamentalist friends (in the tradition of Warfield and the Scottish Common Sense philosophy) will find things to aggravate and engage their interest in these pages. Pentecostals have much reason to learn from both, embrace neither and to expand, if not radically alter, the label 'evangelical' as a self-designation. The antinomy of reason and 'feelings' must be transcended; I have tried to show one way of doing that.

There are so many persons who have contributed to this work, but I must begin with those who taught me the most fundamental and continually significant theological discipline—prayer. My parents, Jack and Mary Land, have given of themselves to me and many others for over four decades now. My wife Peggy and I served with my parents for twenty years in an urban Atlanta Pentecostal ministry which demanded constant spiritual renewal and theological work.

The members of the Society for Pentecostal Studies have through conversation, sharing of ideas, and provocative research, stimulated my development and thought. By their work and example, Leonard Lovett and David Daniels have reminded me of the crucial importance of the black roots and spirituality for a Pentecostalism that would be a folk-liberation movement of the Spirit. Mel Robeck, Jerry Sandidge, Harold Hunter, Vinson Synan and Dan Albrecht have all urged me on and their work is reflected in this study. Donald Dayton, who has pioneered in both theological and historiographical fields of inquiry, has freely shared research materials and has chided me and other members of the Society concerning our sometime 'theological inferiority complex'. I hope I have neither neglected nor proven his point. William (Bill) Faupel, in addition to sharing a great amount of historical data, arranged for an interview with Dr Walter Hollenweger for which I am deeply grateful. Bill's careful and extremely valuable work undergirds my own and is a prerequisite for understanding North American Pentecostalism. He read a rough draft and made comments which were deeply appreciated. David Bundy, bibliophile and linguist *extraordinaire*, and Frank Macchia have taught and encouraged me much concerning the Holiness–Pentecostal connections and the larger, deeper meaning of glossalalia.

I must thank all Pentecostal leaders who so generously gave of their time, perspectives, homes and hearts over the past fifteen years. Special thanks to Yung-Chul Han in Korea, Margaret Gaines in Israel, the late J. Herbert Walker, Jr and his dear wife, Lucille, in Europe, Andre Weber in France, José Minay (a South American Pentecostal bishop), Rick and Jan Waldrop, David Munguia, Roberto Aldana and Rudi Giron in Guatemala, Miguel and Mireya Alvarez in Honduras (now in the Philippines), Reverend Enrique Guerra in Costa Rica, Reverend and Mrs Pedro Pablo Castillo in Nicaragua, Arthur Naidoo, James Seekola, Reuben Timothy and Wynand de Kock in South Africa, Neil and Leslie Morrison in Scotland, Brian Robinson, Steve and Kathleen Hall in England, Ivan and Valentina Fedotov of Russia, Hong Yang of China, and a host of international students whom it has been my privilege to teach and from whom I have learned much.

President Cecil Knight, Dean Robert Crick, Dr James Beaty one of my copyeditors, the faculty and students of the Church of God School of Theology in Cleveland, Tennessee have understood, encouraged and supported me and my family during these past twelve years. Dr Crick especially has encouraged me in my Pentecostal pursuits and deepened my pastoral care perspective. Rick Moore, Chris Thomas, Jackie and Cheryl Johns have been important dialog partners and friends.

Several libraries have assisted me during the past ten years. Barbara McCullough at The William Squires Library in Cleveland, Tennessee and Valerie Watkins of the Woodruff Library of Emory University were especially helpful. The staff of the Pentecostal Research Center and Charles Towler of the Church of God Publishing House, both in Cleveland, Tennessee, helped me track down some of the early Pentecostal hymnody.

I owe special thanks to the editors and staff of Sheffield Academic Press for initiating this series of monographs and to Steve Barganski, whose editorial work has helped to make this manuscript presentable.

Several years ago my dissertation advisor, Don Saliers, assigned to me a chapter on 'Pentecostal Spirituality' in a book he was editing for Crossroad Press in New York. That became the seed of and impetus for this work. As teacher, mentor and friend Dr Saliers has influenced me deeply. I look forward to future collaboration. He has been an excellent mentor-director.

Theodore Runyon, a member of my Dissertation Committee, along with my wife, encouraged me to enter the doctoral program in the late 1970s. I have known Theodore and Cindy Runyon for over twenty years now. Their ministry to me and other students has been consistently helpful and always encouraging. Cindy Runyon, Periodicals Librarian at Pitts Theology Library, Emory University, has, by her personable and professional assistance to me and other students at Emory, made the research seem more bearable and the completion that much more enjoyable. Dr Runyon's Wesleyan studies, liberation interests and ecumenical spirit have significantly shaped my theology. He is a friend and colleague, and one of the most challenging professors I have had!

Also on my committee were Dr Richard Bondi, Dr Hollis Gause and Dr Hal Knight. Dr Bondi's background in narrative theology and his extremely insightful critique of the dissertation proved most helpful. His wife Roberta Chesnut prepared one of my doctoral exams. They are both valued colleagues. Dr R. Hollis Gause has taught theology and biblical studies for over thirty years. For the last ten years we have taught together. He and his wife Beulah are adopted grandparents in my family. His criticisms, questions and comments made this a much clearer work. Though I am sure this monograph still needs much more polishing, it is not for lack of laboring on Dr Gause's part. He has lectured for me and assisted in many other ways during this endeavor. Dr Hal Knight, the last person on the Committee, has done more than anyone else to see that I completed this task. He has been friend, copy editor and dialog partner from start to finish. I deeply appreciate all that he has contributed to me personally and professionally.

Next to my family, the members of the Mission Church of God in Atlanta, Georgia have borne the most with me during the gestation and delivery of this work. Their kind understanding, patient endurance, and sincere prayers and encouragement bore me along when the going was tough. My sister Rosemary and her husband, Steven Lester, have called and urged me on regularly. Susan Harper, a member of the church, one of my former students, and a ministerial colleague has decoded my writing and typed this manuscript. She has sacrificed much time and worked hard to make this a presentable piece while completing her own graduate theological studies.

But the ones who have given the most are the ones who know me best—Alanna, Laura, Jonathan and my wife, Peggy. The children have missed their dad. They have made me tell them over and over why and what I was doing...until I finally understood it myself! They are glad to have their father back. My children have taught me much about Pentecostal spirituality by their questions, doubts, fears, beliefs, prayers and example. They learned this, largely, from their mother. Peggy Goude Land has been a spiritual example, a companion in ministry, and my best friend for twenty-one years. We have 'talked out' this research on many long walks and through many late night conversations. The faith and perseverance in her parents Liston and Eunice Goude has come to mature expression in her, and the chief beneficiaries have been myself and our children. With her I give thanks for a work begun, completed and unfinished.

ABBREVIATIONS

AF	*The Apostolic Faith* (September 1906–May 1908) reprinted by F.T. Corum (ed.), *Like As Of Fire* (Wilmington, MA, 1981)
DPCM	S.M. Burgess and G.B. McGee (eds.), *Dictionary of Pentecostal and Charismatic Movements* (Grand Rapids: Zondervan, 1988)
HBT	*Horizons in Biblical Theology*
HTR	*Harvard Theological Review*
JES	*Journal of Ecumenical Studies*
JPT	*Journal of Pentecostal Theology*
JPTSup	*Journal of Pentecostal Theology*, Supplement Series
JSNTSup	*Journal for the Study of the New Testament*, Supplement Series
NASB	Unless otherwise stated all Scripture quotations are from the New American Standard Bible (LaHabra, California: The Lockman Foundation, 1960)
Pneuma	*Pneuma: The Journal of the Society for Pentecostal Studies*
RSR	*Religious Studies Review*
SJT	*Scottish Journal of Theology*
TTod	*Theology Today*

An Analysis and Re-vision of Pentecostal Spirituality

In this work I attempt a fresh and constructive, if somewhat contro-versial, interpretation and re-vision of the Pentecostal tradition. In the first chapter—the theoretical, methodological section—the funda-mental relationship between theology and spirituality takes a distinctively Pentecostal but interestingly Barthian turn, especially with regard to the role of prayer in the theological task. Agreeing with Walter Hollenweger that the first ten years of the Pentecostal movement form the heart not the infancy of the spirituality, I go on to assert the crucial importance of the Wesleyan, Holiness and nineteenth-century revivalist-restorationist roots. Spirituality is defined as the integration of beliefs and practices in the affections which are them-selves evoked and expressed by those beliefs and practices.

The second chapter is a running narrative analysis of certain Pentecostal beliefs and practices using songs, testimonies and early eyewitness accounts to tell the story. The apocalyptic nature of the spirituality is analyzed, critiqued and developed to show the relation of revelation, history and the kingdom of God.

The third chapter shows how Christian affections integrate and undergird Pentecostal beliefs and practices. A mutual conditioning is noted among orthodoxy (right praise/belief), orthopraxy (right practice) and orthopathy (right affections). Thus the analysis of Pentecostal spirituality is taken to a new level, transcending in the process the outdated and fruitless antinomy of reason and 'feelings'. Pentecostal affections are correlated with certain divine attributes, the kingdom of God and Pentecostal testimony to ·suggest a kind of Pentecostal faith development characterized by a crisis—development dialectic.

The fourth and final chapter offers a trinitarian re-visioning of Pentecostal spirituality, arguing that a passion for the kingdom of God is ultimately a passion for God. Drawing upon the construction and

re-vision, certain internal issues and external criticisms of the movement are noted; further research needs are briefly discussed in the
afterword.

In summary, this study moves through four stages: (1) the
relationship between spirituality and theology, (2) a description-
analysis of certain beliefs and practices which characterize Pentecostal
spirituality, (3) a demonstration of the integration of the beliefs and
practices in Pentecostal affections, and (4) a trinitarian re-vision.

Chapter 1

PENTECOSTAL SPIRITUALITY AS THEOLOGY:
A THEORETICAL INTRODUCTION

The Pentecostal Movement Then and Now

'Back to Pentecost': The Fall of the Latter Rain
Jesus Christ, in the midst of the intense apocalyptic expectations of his
disciples, commanded them to wait for the 'promise of the Father'.
This baptism in and filling of the Holy Spirit was the fulfillment of the
prophecy of Joel[1] and empowered Christ's witnesses to the end of the
age and the ends of the earth. The coming and mission of Jesus and
that of the Spirit was couched in the language of promise and fulfillment in such a way that fulfillment carried an overflow or residue of
promise which had personal and global historical implications. Each
'already' of fulfillment carried within it the 'not yet' of consummation. The waiting for Christ became waiting in Christ for his return.
The waiting for the promised Spirit became waiting in the Spirit for
the time when, by the Spirit, God would be all in all.

This 'promise-fulfillment, already-not yet' is a tensed dynamic
which characterizes Christianity's eschatological passion. From time
to time when the tension is resolved prematurely—either in the
direction of an other-worldly, 'not yet' escapism or a this-worldly,
'already' accommodation—there arise movements of restoration,
revival, awakening and renewal to remind the church that it is the
'eschatological mother'[2] whose sons and daughters are meant to
prophesy. Pentecostalism was and is such a movement. Pentecostal
spirituality sprang forth in North America from eighteenth century
Wesleyan and nineteenth century Holiness roots. It embodied all the
eschatological tensions, turmoil and blessings of the premillennial

1. Acts 1–2.
2. E. Käsemann, *New Testament Questions of Today* (London: SCM Press,
1969), p. 100.

revivalism that had swept across the nation in the latter half of the nineteenth century. It was seen as the answer to the earnest prayers of thousands of believers who through global networks of personal associations, periodicals, camp meetings, etc. prayed for a renewal of Pentecost. In 1856 William Arthur, an English Methodist, expressed this longing in the following prayer:

> And now, adorable Spirit, proceeding from the Father and the Son, descend upon all the churches, renew the Pentecost in this our age, and baptize Thy people generally—O, baptize them yet again with tongues of fire! Crown this nineteenth century with a revival of 'pure and undefiled religion' greater than that of the last century, greater than any 'demonstration of the Spirit' even yet vouchsafed to men.[1]

Throughout the nineteenth and into the beginning of the twentieth century Pentecostal fires were kindled in England (Irvingites), Germany, India, Russia, Wales and North America (Finney, Moody, the Palmers, and so forth).[2] But it was in the Bible School of Charles Fox Parham in 1901 that Agnes Ozman was 'baptized in the Holy Spirit' with the 'evidence of speaking in other tongues'. This insight of Parham and his students was carried by William J. Seymour to Los Angeles in 1906. Seymour, a humble one-eyed black Holiness preacher who had been Parham's student, published the first issue of *The Apostolic Faith* newspaper in 1906. The motto on the masthead of every issue read, 'Earnestly contend for the faith which was once delivered to the saints—Jude 3'. The first article announced that Pentecost had come to Los Angeles and that there was a 'revival of Bible salvation...as in the Book of Acts'.[3]

Seymour joyously reported that

> The power of God now has this city agitated as never before. Pentecost has surely come and with it the Bible evidences are following, many are being converted and sanctified and filled with the Holy Ghost, speaking in tongues as they did on the day of Pentecost. The scenes that are daily

---

1. W. Arthur, *The Tongue of Fire; or the True Power of Christianity* (New York: Harper, 1856), pp. 189-227.

2. M.E. Dieter, *The Holiness Revival of the Nineteenth Century* (Metuchen, NJ: Scarecrow Press, 1980); D.W. Dayton, *The Theological Roots of Pentecostalism* (Grand Rapids: Zondervan, 1987); D.W. Faupel, 'The Everlasting Gospel: The Significance of Eschatology in the Development of Pentecostal Thought' (PhD dissertation, University of Birmingham, England, 1989).

3. W.J. Seymour, *AF* 1.1 (1906), p. 1.

enacted in the building on Azusa Street and at missions and churches in other parts of the city are beyond description, and the real revival is only started, as God has been working with His children mostly, getting them through to Pentecost, and laying the foundation for a mighty wave of salvation among the unconverted.

The meetings are held in an old Methodist church that had been converted in part into a tenement house leaving a large, unplastered, barn-like room on the ground floor...

Many churches have been praying for Pentecost and Pentecost has come. The question is now, will they accept it? God has answered in a way they did not look for. He came in a humble way as of old, born in a manger.[1]

Seymour noted that this 'Holy Roller', 'Colored Church', as some locals referred to it, was

in the vicinity of tombstone shops, stables and a lumber yard... You would hardly expect heavenly visitations there unless you remember the stable at Bethlehem... But here you find a mighty revival going on from ten o'clock in the morning till about twelve at night.

In commenting further on the fact that they were meeting in a barn Seymour speculates as to why God chose this place:

If it had started in a fine church, poor colored people and Spanish people would not have got it, but praise God it started here. God Almighty says He will pour out His Spirit on all flesh... It is noticeable how free all nationalities feel. If a Mexican or German cannot speak English, he gets up and speaks in his own tongue and feels quite at home for the Spirit interprets through the face and people say amen. No instrument that God can use is rejected on account of color or dress or lack of education. This is why God has so built up the work.[2]

It was said that 'the color line was washed away in the blood' at Azusa Street. And, remarkably, this was also the case for a short while in the South as evidenced in the reports of white evangelist G.B. Cashwell and the ministry of black Pentecostal Bishop C.H. Mason who was to become the spiritual leader of the Church of God in Christ. Mason ordained white and black ministers and the first Pentecostal seminary, located in Atlanta, Georgia at the Interdenominational Theological Center, bears his name.

But the breaking down of social barriers and beginnings in a

1.   *AF* 1.1 (1906), p. 1.
2.   *AF* 1.3 (1906), p. 1.

humble stable (they also had an 'upper room' at Azusa!) were not the
only parallels with the New Testament church. This event was
interpreted by its adherents as the latter rain restoration of apostolic
faith and power for the last days' evangelization of the world.
Everything was determined by the overall expectation of the imminent
parousia of Jesus Christ.[1]

The 'full gospel' for the fullness of times was needed for the filling
of saints with the Holy Spirit, so that they could fill the earth with the
apostles' doctrine. This 'full gospel' was comprised of five theological
motifs:

1. Justification by faith in Christ.
2. Sanctification by faith as a second definite work of grace.
3. Healing of the body as provided for all in the atonement.
4. The pre-millennial return of Christ.
5. The baptism in the Holy Spirit evidenced by speaking in
    tongues.

It was the fifth motif that, more than anything else, served as a 'sign'
that the 'evening light'[2] was shining before the darkness when no one
could work.[3]

The movement was simultaneously restorationist and eschatological.
The participants believed that God was restoring the apostolic faith
and power for the end times through signs and wonders. God had
restored justification by faith through Luther, sanctification by faith
through Wesley, divine healing through Dr Cullis and many other
nineteenth-century ministers,[4] the blessed hope of Christ's premillennial second coming through the prophecy conferences of the
latter half of the nineteenth century, and lastly the baptism in the Holy
Spirit as power for last-days world evangelization. In their view God
was calling upon all saints to be godly witnesses in the power of the
Holy Spirit. Now the prophethood of all believers could be added to
the priesthood of all believers.

There were other analogies to the New Testament church. There
was an aversion to creeds which divide and thus hinder the mission of

---

1.   D.W. Faupel, 'The Function of "Models" in the Interpretation of Pentecostal
Thought', *Pneuma* 2.1 (Spring, 1980), pp. 47-49.
2.   A.J. Tomlinson (ed.), *The Evening Light and Church of God, Evangel.*
3.   Jn 9.4.
4.   P.G. Chappell, 'Healing Movements', *DPCM*, pp. 353-74.

the Church. There was a suspicion of organizations which ran by mechanisms and political schemes instead of gifts of the Spirit. In fact the early movement was suspicious of anything which did not have direct biblical precedent or hindered the work of the sovereign Spirit of God. Christ ruled the church tangibly though the 'whole Bible rightly divided' and intangibly by the Holy Spirit's gifts and guidance.

There was no single founder of the movement. Like the New Testament days, communication and instruction were carried on through letters, tracts, testimonies and, most importantly, through an ethos growing out of and centered in revivalistic, participatory, populist-oriented worship. All those who had 'gotten their Pentecost' were witnesses, tellers of good news.[1] So there were no systematic treatises; that would be a kind of second-order activity removed from the atmosphere of prayer, praise and witness. Though most of the people were literate—some at Azusa even 'highly educated'—they were overwhelmingly oral in their worship, witness and work.

As in the New Testament, the sense of urgency to warn the church and to witness to the nations colored all understanding, activity and affectivity. Now was the time for 'the everlasting gospel' (Rev. 14.6, 7), the 'gospel of the kingdom' (Mt. 24.14), to be proclaimed in power and demonstration of the Holy Spirit.[2] The Bride must be prepared for the Bridegroom. The lost must be brought into the ark of safety before the coming Great Tribulation. This sentiment is captured by Frank W. Sandford, Charles F. Parham's mentor from Shiloh, Maine, in the change of the title of his periodical from *Tongues of Fire* to *The Everlasting Gospel* in 1901. This was to be 'The Last Solemn Message of the Age'. Sandford declared that

> The first gospel message was proclaimed by an angel—'good tidings of great joy to all people, for unto you is born a Savior'.
> The last gospel message will be likewise proclaimed—'I saw another angel having the everlasting gospel to preach unto them that dwell on the earth... to every nation'.
> The first was a message of peace and good will. The latter is to be a message of warning and judgment.
> The first represented 'the acceptable year of the Lord'. The latter, 'the day of vengeance of our God!'

---

1. This is a common designation used throughout the early issues of *The Apostolic Faith*.
2. Faupel, 'The Function of "Models"', pp. 87-99.

> The first brought the glad tidings to a world lost in sin, the 'whosoever believeth in Him might be justified freely through the redemption that is in Christ Jesus'. The latter warns that same world that it is speedily to give an account for the use or abuse of its privilege, and prepares the way for the time when 'The Lord shall be revealed from heaven with His mighty angels, in flaming fire taking vengeance on them that obey not the gospel'. The former prepared the way for 'a Man of sorrows'. The latter for the 'King of kings'.
>
> The first represents the voice of song singing joyfully over the hills of Bethlehem, 'Glory to God in the Highest!'
>
> The second, the voice of divine authority crying aloud to all lands, 'Fear God and give glory to Him!'
>
> The first heralded One coming meek and lowly, riding on an ass into Jerusalem to die for men.
>
> The latter heralds One coming in 'great power and glory' to the City of the King to reign 'From the river to the ends of the earth'. All hail the power of the everlasting gospel.[1]

Christ would not come until this message had been proclaimed to all nations in words, signs and wonders. The pace and focus of individual and world history was now quickened and intensified. This movement spread rapidly through all the pre-established networks of nineteenth-century revivalism and the new fields opened by persons who went out immediately, with little or no formal training, to the four corners of the earth.[2]

The movement grew slowly at first, and within the first fifteen years was influenced by racial, theological and social controversies. Nevertheless, Pentecostal churches today represent the largest Protestant grouping in the world and their spirituality, as transmitted through the Charismatic renewal, has influenced every branch of Christianity. Along with Roman Catholicism, Eastern Orthodoxy and Protestantism it may be regarded as a 'fourth force' (as opposed to the usual 'third force' designation) in Christianity.

The Dimensions of Pentecostal Spirituality
The dimensions of this spirituality's impact provide a good argument for giving it a closer look. More is needed than an apologetic for

---

1. F.W. Sandford, 'The Everlasting Gospel', cited in Faupel, 'Everlasting Gospel', p. 47.
2. Each issue of *The Apostolic Faith* carried news from the mission fields and testimonies of those preparing to go 'into the harvest'.

Spirit baptism or yet another study of behaviors such as glossolalia. The movement will soon be one hundred years old, and with the years has come the development of creeds, institutions of higher education, elaborate ecclesiastical organizations, and tons of publications per year.[1] Nearing the centenary mark the movement has demonstrated staying power.

The dimension of length or longevity is, however, eclipsed by that of breadth. Although it began in North America, Pentecostalism is strongest now in the so-called 'Third World'. David Barrett estimates that over seventy-five per cent of all members of the over one thousand, non-white/Third World indigenous denominations are composed of persons who bear all the phenomenological marks of Pentecostalism. In addition, there are eight hundred explicitly Pentecostal denominations, indigenous to non-white races in the Third World. In addition to the millions of members of the original Pentecostal bodies there are the millions who are part of the charismatic renewal, or the so-called 'third-wavers' who are evangelicals experiencing a renewal of the Spirit but not recognizing it as a separate experience from conversion. 'Third-wavers' emphasize signs and wonders, but stay in their churches and do not organize into distinct renewal groups. The members of all three waves of the renewal are now found in eleven thousand Pentecostal denominations and three thousand independent charismatic denominations. They constitute twenty-one per cent of organized global Christianity.

As of 1988, there were 327 million affiliated church members of which 176 million were Pentecostal, 123 million charismatic, 28 million 'third-wave'. The movement grows at a rate of 19 million new members a year or around 54 thousand per day (two-thirds of which are converts/new members). On a worldwide scale, 29 per cent are white, 71 per cent are non-white. They are

> more urban than rural, more female than male, more children (under eighteen years) than adults, more third-world (sixty-six per cent) than western world (thirty-two per cent), more living in poverty (eighty-seven per cent) than affluence (thirteen per cent), more family-related than individualist.[2]

1.   W.E. Warner, 'Publications', *DPCM*, pp. 742-51.
2.   All the statistics in this discussion are from D. Barrett, 'Statistics, Global', *DPCM*, pp. 810-30.

East Asia, Latin America[1] and Africa are becoming rapidly pentecostalized, whereas Europe remains more charismatic. Some fourteen per cent of all charismatics in mainline churches have 'gone independent' each year since 1970, forming some '100,000 White-led independent Charismatic churches across the world loosely organized into forty or so major networks'.[2]

One fourth of all full-time Christian workers in the world are Pentecostal/charismatic. They are active in eighty per cent of the thirty-three hundred large metropolitan areas of the world. They are 'more harassed, persecuted, suffering, martyred than perhaps any other Christian tradition in recent history'.[3] They are often scorned, imprisoned, tortured and killed by totalitarian dictators or those revolutionaries who oppose such regimes. They usually seek a 'third way' of peace in the Third World, and have been characterized as a 'haven for the masses'[4] who do not engage in direct socio-political action; nevertheless, they have created alternative communities of caring, respect and empowerment and thus developed their own programs of 'affective conscientization' toward liberation.[5]

Although it is impressive that this movement has achieved such breadth in so short a time, the dimensions of height and depth are probably the most theologically significant. By height is meant the dimension of praise, worship, adoration and prayer to God—this is the most compelling characteristic to most observers and participants. But to this must be added the dimension of depth. This is the reason for the almost century-long sustained growth and breadth of impact. The depth dimension speaks of the 'deep things' of the human heart: the abiding, decisive, directing motives and dispositions which characterize Pentecostals. One cannot read the early accounts of the Azusa Street revival or hear the testimonies of Pentecostals today without being struck by this depth of conviction and passion. It is a steadfast longing for the Lord and the salvation of the lost. It is a continuous, joyous exclamation of the inbreaking presence and soon to

1. See David Stoll's discussion of the current situation in *Is Latin America Turning Protestant?* (Los Angeles: University of California Press, 1990).
2. Barrett, 'Statistics, Global', p. 119.
3. Barrett, 'Statistics, Global', p. 119.
4. C.L. D'Epinay, *Haven of the Masses* (London: Lutterworth Press, 1969).
5. C. Bridges-Johns, *Pentecostal Formation: A Pedagogy among the Oppressed* (JPTSup, 2; Sheffield: JSOT Press, 1993).

be consummated kingdom of God. I have observed this on five continents over the last fifteen years. To that extent there is a remarkable continuity from Azusa to Seoul, to Glasgow, to Managua, to Santiago, to Durban, to Moscow. A spirituality of these dimensions demands a closer theological look; it needs an examination of the inner logic of this passion for the kingdom.

Approaching Pentecostal Spirituality

Thesis: The Integration of Holiness and Power
It is part of the unfinished theological task of Pentecostalism to integrate the language of holiness and the language of power— languages spoken by the Holiness and Pentecostal movements respectively. It is a theological and pastoral mistake to dichotomize, confound, or simply to identify love and power. Indeed, in keeping with the earliest Pentecostal soteriology of justification, sanctification, and Spirit baptism, the basic theological challenge and most pressing pastoral need is to show the integration of righteousness, love and power in this apocalyptic movement of spiritual transformation.

My thesis is that the righteousness, holiness and power of God are correlated with distinctive apocalyptic affections which are the integrating core of Pentecostal spirituality. This spirituality is Christocentric precisely because it is pneumatic; its 'fivefold gospel' is focused on Christ because of its starting point in the Holy Spirit. Underlying this correlation is a soteriology which emphasizes salvation as participation in the divine life more than the removal of guilt.

Indeed, Jesus Christ is the center and the Holy Spirit is the circumference of a distinctive Pentecostal spirituality whose lineaments it is the task of this work to trace. The distinctive apocalyptic affections of Pentecostalism will be shown to be the integrating core for its narrative beliefs and practices. But the decisive context and ever-present horizon for most usefully and comprehensibly displaying those beliefs, practices and affections is eschatological: the presence of God who, as Spirit, is the agent of the inbreaking, soon-to-be consummated kingdom of God.

Justification: The Distinctiveness of this Study
There is a present need for a comprehensive, theological analysis and constructive explication of Pentecostal spirituality. Until recently most

studies of Pentecostalism have been concerned with an apologetic defense of Pentecostal particularities, especially those associated with Spirit baptism,[1] or with an analysis of some Pentecostal behavior, especially glossolalia. The former was done by Pentecostals and charismatics whereas the latter was usually done by someone outside the movement.[2] More comprehensive theological works by Pentecostals are essentially traditional outlines of evangelical fundamentals with a few extra chapters on Spirit baptism and gifts.[3]

In recent years Pentecostals have focused on such things as visions and testimonies,[4] particular historical figures,[5] branches of the movement, worship, footwashing, and missiology.[6] Gordon Wheelock

1.   The two most able assaults on the Pentecostal doctrine have come from F.D. Bruner, *A Theology of the Holy Spirit: The Pentecostal Experience and the New Testament Witness* (Grand Rapids: Eerdmans, 1970) and J.D.G. Dunn, *Baptism in the Holy Spirit* (Philadelphia: Westminster Press, 1970). Dunn's work is the most inviting, understanding and helpful.

2.   Faupel ('Everlasting Gospel', pp. 6-13) terms the two approaches the 'doctrinal' and the 'behavioral'.

3.   One of the best known and widely used has been M. Pearlman, *Knowing the Doctrines of the Bible* (Springfield, MO: Gospel Publishing House, 1937). A more recent work, which includes, in addition to all the usual systematic loci, a long chapter on divine healing, is G.P. Duffield and N.M. Van Cleave, *Foundations of Pentecostal Theology* (Los Angeles: L.I.F.E. Bible College, 1983). A holiness-Pentecostal approach is taken in N.D. Sauls, *Pentecostal Doctrines: A Wesleyan Approach* (Dunn, NC: The Heritage Press, 1979), I.

4.   A theologically and philosophically informed hermeneutical investigation is found in J.-D. Plüss, *Therapeutic and Prophetic Narratives in Worship: A Hermeneutic Study of Testimony and Visions* (Bern: Peter Lang, 1988).

5.   *Pneuma* contains short articles on various historical figures which have been or are about to be the subject of dissertations or theses. W.J. Seymour and C. Fox Parham, for example, are treated in recent dissertations. See D.J. Nelson, 'For such a Time as this: The Story of William J. Seymour and the Azusa Street Revival' (PhD dissertation, University of Birmingham, England, 1981). The *DPCM* contains articles on all the prominent early pioneers.

6.   In addition to the standard denominational histories for groups such as the Pentecostal Holiness, Assemblies of God and Church of God, Oneness Pentecostalism has been studied by D.A. Reed ('Origins and Development of the Theology of Oneness Pentecostalism in the United States' [PhD dissertation, Boston University, 1978]) and J.H. Howell ('The People of the Name: Oneness Pentecostalism in the United States' [PhD dissertation, Florida State University, 1985]). The roots of Black Holiness Pentecostalism are discussed in W.C. Turner Jr, 'The United Holy Church of America: A Study in Black Holiness Pentecostalism' (PhD dissertation, Duke

considered Spirit baptism in North American Pentecostalism and offered a restatement of that doctrine in dialog with the charismatic and mainline challengers. Leonard Lovett considered black-Holiness Pentecostalism and put it into dialog with black liberation thought.

There are a few chapters in books, some journal articles, and dictionary entries that deal directly with Pentecostal spirituality,[1] but none that do so with an analytical, constructive theological intent. These works are more descriptive and suggestive. Williams's book was an early neo-Pentecostal expression of the general characteristics of the spirituality which centered on Spirit baptism. He touched on historical precedent and discussed the contemporary significance of the movement. Spittler's article in *DPCM* went into more detail

University, 1984); L. Lovett, 'Black Holiness-Pentecostalism: Implications for Ethics and Social Transformation' (PhD dissertation, Emory University, 1979); and J.M. Shopshire, 'A Socio-Historical Characterization of the Black Pentecostal Movement in North America' (PhD dissertation, Northwestern University, 1975). E.L. Waldvogel traced the roots of the 'baptistic' Pentecostals in her 1977 Harvard University dissertation, 'The "Overcoming Life": A Study in the Reformed Evangelical Origins of Pentecostalism'. E.M. Crews, Jr has looked at the effects of 'redemption and lift' (upward social mobility) in his 1988 Harvard University dissertation, 'From Back Alleys to Uptown: A History of the Church of God (Cleveland, Tennessee)'. See the article and bibliography in J.W. Shepperd, 'Worship', *DPCM*, pp. 903-905. J.C. Thomas, *Footwashing in John 13 and the Johannine Community* (JSNTSup, 61; Sheffield: JSOT Press, 1991). This is a carefully and persuasively argued proposal for the sacramental legitimacy of the footwashing rite in today's church. Two of the more prominent contemporary Pentecostal missiologists are L.G. McClung (*Azusa Street and Beyond: Pentecostal Missions and Church Growth in the Twentieth Century* [South Plainfield, NJ: Bridge Publishing, 1986]) and P.A. Pomerville (*The Third Force in Mission* [Peabody, MA: Hendrickson, 1985]).

1.   Brief, general treatments of Pentecostal spirituality are found in J.R. Williams, *The Pentecostal Reality* (Plainfield, NJ: Logos, 1972), esp. pp. 57-84; R. Spittler, 'Pentecostal and Charismatic Spirituality', *DPCM*, pp. 804-809; and W.J. Hollenweger, 'Pentecostals and the Charismatic Movement', in C. Jones, G. Wainwright and E. Yarnold (eds.), *The Study of Spirituality* (New York: Oxford University Press, 1986), pp. 549-53.

See also the excellent brief comments of K. McDonnell in 'The Distinguishing Characteristics of the Charismatic-Pentecostal Spirituality', *One in Christ* 10.2, (1974), pp. 117-28. McDonnell makes much of the categories of 'presence' and 'crisis' which I also emphasize while seeing the crisis as an important category not only for Pentecostals but also for all Christians (though I do use it in a slightly different way than McDonnell).

concerning Pentecostal Charismatic practices and defined spirituality as 'pietistic habits of ordinary individuals' while theology was 'systematized, usually written, reflections on religious experience'. His approach, while suggestive and complementary to the one taken in this study, emphasizes, by way of contrast to my work, individual experience with experience being understood primarily as emotions or feelings. He sees spirituality as a 'cluster of acts and sentiments that are informed by the beliefs and practices that characterize a specific religious community', while my study has emphasized the integration of narrative beliefs and practices in the affections.

Chapter 3 of this study will carefully delineate the meaning of 'affections'. The implicit 'values' (experience, orality, spontaneity, otherworldliness and biblical authority) which characterize Pentecostal practices are cited by Spittler and found earlier in Hollenweger. The latter's work is especially important for this study in that we are in agreement that the first ten years represents the 'heart' and not the infancy of the movement. Hollenweger also has a great appreciation of the orality (I would say 'narrativity') of Pentecostal spirituality as well as its Black (via Azusa Street) and Catholic (via J. Wesley) antecedents. Hollenweger and I, as over against Spittler and Williams, make more of these points and, as a result, tend to see theology and spirituality in less rationalistic terms. We both have a great appreciation for the older critical tradition of Pentecostalism.[1]

Spittler and Williams also have appreciation for these aspects of spirituality but have been more concerned to provide a cognitive structure for Pentecostal experience. This dissertation also provides a 'cognitive structure' but with an affective base which would in turn produce a different theological construction. Carl Henry has been a significant, though by no means exclusive, influence upon Spittler's early theological development. Williams's work, while clearly and faithfully delineating Pentecostal themes in volume 2 of his *Renewal Theology*,[2] nevertheless does not show the influence of a Pentecostal hermeneutic throughout. In addition, while going further than many Pentecostals to interact with Wesleyan perspectives, the treatment is extremely brief and not central to his more Reformed roots and interest. He still operates out of the notion of perfection as a kind of

---

1. See W.J. Hollenweger, 'The Critical Tradition of Pentecostalism', *JPT* 1 (1992), pp. 7-17.
2. Grand Rapids: Zondervan, 1990.

philosophical 'perfectus'. He sees the biblical relations of perfection to blamelessness, righteousness and maturity but, like so many other writers since Warfield who fail to interact with Wesleyan scholarship, seems to equate entire sanctification with 'perfectionism' or to confound it with glorification.

Williams's view is preferable to the traditional Lutheran approach and his work is the best attempt to date at a charismatic systematic theology. Whatever comes later will have to take him into account and build upon his work. He makes more of Spirit baptism and tongues than many classical Pentecostal scholars! While benefitting much from Williams, Hollenweger and Spittler, the approach taken here differs in terms of the view of theology, spirituality and, most especially, the significance of the religious affections.

Although several articles in *Pneuma* (the journal of the Society for Pentecostal Studies) have discussed hermeneutics, eschatology, missiology and a wide range of historical concerns,[1] there have been none which sought to address directly the fundamental theological issue of the relationship between spirituality, theology and method (with the possible exception of the articles of Michael Dowd and Mark McClean).[2] Grant Wacker's bibliographical work and historical articles do the best job of giving a sense of the milieu and faith of early Pentecostals.[3] While most recent efforts have focused on biblical, historical, practical and ecumenical[4] concerns, this work, seeks to offer an analysis, integration, and re-vision of Pentecostal spirituality in a manner not attempted until now.

1. Two of the more noteworthy recent approaches are M.D. McClean, 'Toward a Pentecostal Hermeneutic', *Pneuma* 6.2 (Fall, 1984), pp. 35-36; and G.T. Sheppard, 'Pentecostalism and the Hermeneutics of Dispensationalism: Anatomy of an Uneasy Relationship', *Pneuma* 6.2 (Fall, 1984), pp. 5-34.

2. See McClean, 'Pentecostal Hermeneutic', n. 35 and M.B. Dowd, 'Contours of a Narrative Pentecostal Theology and Practice' (unpublished paper, Society for Pentecostal Studies, 1985).

3. G. Wacker, 'The Functions of Faith in Primitive Pentecostalism', *HTR* 77 (July/October, 1984), pp. 353-75.

4. *Pneuma* 9.1 (Spring, 1987) was devoted to Pentecostals and ecumenical dialogue. J.L. Sandidge and C.M. Robeck, Jr have been especially active in this important work, whereas several Pentecosal churches from the Third World have joined the World Council of Churches.

Resources: The Historical Foundations of this Study
There is an abundance of bibliographical resources for the study of
Pentecostalism today. The best place to get in touch with this quickly
is the bibliographical essay by Grant Wacker in *The Dictionary of the
Pentecostal and Charismatic Movements*.[1] There one finds such indispensable sources as Charles Edwin Jones's massive two volumes, the
bibliographies of Watson Mills and, of course, the dated but still valuable and encyclopedic survey of Walter Hollenweger. Hollenweger, in
commenting on his research some twenty years after his ground-
breaking dissertation, examines certain phenomenological characteristics of the movement and lifts up the crucial importance of the shift
of Pentecostalism and Christianity in general to the Third World
majority as we approach the twenty-first century.[2] His work remains
important for its comprehensive, global and Third World advocacy.

But by far the most influential works in relation to this study are
those of Donald Dayton and William Faupel. Dayton's ongoing effort
to recast the historiography and definitions of evangelicalism so that
Holiness and Pentecostal paradigms are not assimilated into Reformed-
fundamentalist categories provides a crucial standpoint from which to
consider Pentecostal spirituality today. Dayton was one of the first to
assert that Pentecostalism is a distinctive theological development and
not merely an experiential episode in twentieth-century Christianity.
His analysis of a Pentecostal gestalt of theological motifs set a new
tone for Pentecostal studies.[3] William Faupel's work, like Dayton's, is
heavily supported by historical research. Indeed, there is no more
clear, complete, meticulously documented work on North American
Pentecostalism available anywhere.[4] It is the most significant and
careful historical work to be produced on North American Pentecostalism. It surpasses Hollenweger and Anderson and is more deeply in
touch with the Pentecostal ethos. It offers a clear insight into the
various streams and eddies of North American Pentecostal development, while giving nuanced analyses of the major figures and issues.
The theological interpretation of Dayton and the historical

1.   G. Wacker, 'Bibliography and Historirgraphy of Pentecostalism (U.S.)',
DPCM, pp. 65-76.
2.   W.J. Hollenweger, 'After Twenty Years' Research on Pentecostalism',
International Review of Mission 75.297 (January, 1986), pp. 3-12.
3.   Dayton, *Theological Roots*.
4.   Faupel, 'Everlasting Gospel'.

investigation of Faupel will be the basis for future Pentecostal self-criticism and construction. Faupel's thesis, in accord with that of the social-historical approach of Robert Mapes Anderson,[1] is that 'American Pentecostalism can best be understood as the emergence of a millenarian belief system that resulted from a paradigm-shift which took place within nineteenth-century Perfectionism'. Faupel's massive account concludes by demonstrating 'that a recovery and reflection of the initial expectations are necessary if Pentecostalism hopes to enter into meaningful dialog with other theological traditions'.[2] His work affords the critical-historical foundation for my own.

The foregoing discussion demonstrates that there is nothing in the literature which seeks to analyze Pentecostal beliefs and practices as integrated in the affections—showing the crucial role played by eschatology. But in addition to formal justification, there are purposes which are at the heart of the personal motivation for such a work.

Purposes: The Motivation for this Study
Those who see Pentecostalism as essentially fundamentalist Christianity with a doctrine of Spirit baptism and gifts added on will be disappointed, as will those who see Pentecostalism as an experience which fits equally well in any spirituality or theological system—perhaps adding some needed zest or interest. Thus, I argue persistently, if occasionally indirectly, that Pentecostalism cannot and should not be simply identified with a rationalist or scholastic type of evangelicalism. Further, it cannot, without fundamental alteration and accommodation, be assimilated into any and every Christian denomination without eventually bringing fundamental changes. Though recognizably Christian, it is in a period of theological adolescence where decisions are being made about how to use the parental inheritance, whom to court, marry and befriend, what vocation to pursue, and which kind of training and communication is most important for its future. Nevertheless certain aspects of a distinctive Pentecostal self-understanding are emerging already.

Pentecostalism flows in paradoxical continuity and discontinuity with other streams of Christianity. Insofar as it retains similarity to the first ten years of the movement, it is more Arminian than Calvinist

---

1. R.M. Anderson, *Vision of the Disinherited: The Making of American Pentecostalism* (New York: Oxford University Press, 1979).
2. Faupel, 'Everlasting Gospel', p. 17.

in its approach to issues of human agency and perseverance. It is more Calvinist than Lutheran in its appreciation of the so-called 'third use of the Law' to guide Christian growth and conduct. It is more Eastern than Western in its understanding of spirituality as perfection and participation in the divine life (*theosis*). In this regard it has much to learn from persons like Gregory of Nyssa, Macarius the Egyptian and St Symeon, the New Theologian. It is both ascetic and mystical. These treasures could naturally and fruitfully be mined as the line of Wesleyan continuity is traced backwards and forwards. Pentecostalism is more Catholic than Protestant in emphasizing sanctification-transformation more than forensic justification, but more Protestant than Catholic in the conviction that the Word is the authority over the church and tradition for matters of faith, practice, government and discipline. In its origins Pentecostalism was more Anabaptist than the magisterial Reformation in its concern for peace and a covenanted believers' church where discipleship and discipline are essential features of congregational life. Pentecostalism has a more Holiness-evangelical hermeneutic than the fundamentalist-evangelical tradition in terms of its actual use of Scripture and understanding of the role of reason.[1] Finally, it is more liberation-transformationist than scholastic-fundamentalist in its way of doing theology as a discerning reflection upon living reality. (This will be explained in greater detail later in this chapter.) Pentecostalism, therefore, exists in continuity but differentiating discontinuity with other Christian spiritualities. To the extent that it has a distinctive spirituality and theology, it may not be seen, used or identified with an experience or experiential episodes. There may be Pentecostal-like experiences but Pentecostal spirituality is another matter.

Other motives for this study have formed in response to fifteen years of contact with Pentecostals from five continents in classes, mission endeavors, prayers and interviews. They were asking for more Pentecostal literature that was distinctive and integral to their praxis. They were seeking a theological clarity and grounding to serve better the interrelated pastoral, mission and ecumenical concerns. Mission success has brought in millions of new converts and transfers from other Christian groups. The question arises, 'How can we

1. D.N. Dayton, 'Yet Another Layer of the Onion or Opening the Ecumenical Door to Let the Riffraff in', *The Ecumenical Review* 40.1 (January, 1988), pp. 87-110.

disciple such a mass of people?' Further and in keeping with the 'experiences of salvation' (regeneration, sanctification, Spirit baptism, healing, and so on), what daily disciplines and ways of approaching personal and social crises grow out of and are congruent with this ethos? How must the present approach be supplemented or changed? On what basis? In addition to the dialogue with liberation practitioners in Latin America, Pentecostals have been carrying on their own dialogs and engaging in painful but persistent self-examination concerning the context and extent of mission.[1] All this is occurring as a greater number of liberationists begin to construct a liberation spirituality and to recognize the importance of the doctrine of the Holy Spirit.

These pressing and painful matters must be addressed in a way that does not compromise the fundamental spirituality but addresses these new challenges, needs and opportunities. This is especially so in those areas of Latin America and other Third World locations where Pentecostals have a greater and greater influence and responsibility by virtue of the sheer size of the movement.[2]

Third World Pentecostals are not as preoccupied with the fundamentalist-modernist, personal versus social, conservative versus liberal controversies as are North Americans. This is not to say that they are unaware of liberalism or radicalism, but they are more open to finding ways to incorporate valid insights and make changes that will help the people. Pentecostals have been 'Base Communities' for decades as they have networked and survived in very repressive environments. Theirs is a grass roots ecumenism born of immediate missionary and pastoral concerns.

It is the purpose of this study, then, to explicate a Pentecostal spirituality which is apocalyptic, corporate, missional and essentially affective. After the analysis and integration of Chapters 2 and 3, a constructive 're-vision' is offered which attempts to address some of the Third World challenges, internal problems and external criticisms. As Chapters 2 and 3 unfold, the contours of the response should become clearer. It is hoped that the re-vision will advance the cause of

---

1. J. Sepúlveda, 'Reflections on the Pentecostal Contribution to the Mission of the Church in Latin America', trans. J. Beaty and S.J. Land, *JPT* 1 (1992), pp. 93-108. G. Vaccaro, *Identidad Pentecostal* (Quito: Consejo Latinoamericano de Iglesias, 1988). See also the entire December 1975 issue of *Pastoralia* 7.15.

2. Stoll, *Latin America*.

unity and missionary effectiveness in the body of Christ, and that
Pentecostals will begin to see liberals as well as conservatives as
important dialog partners.[1]

Perspectives on Pentecostal Spirituality

There are certain presuppositions, convictions and theological
commitments which constitute a standpoint from which to approach
Pentecostal spirituality. It is not claimed that this is the only basis for
such an analysis but only that this one is an especially appropriate
methodology for this particular subject matter. The elements of this
perspective, this Pentecostal view of the theological task, are discussed
under three heads: (1) Spirituality and Theology, (2) Origins and
Continuity, and (3) Eschatology and Coherence.

Spirituality and Theology

Theological science is basically a construal of the relationships
between God and the world. For Pentecostals, the starting point for
such an undertaking is the Holy Spirit who is 'God with us'. The God
who was present among Israel and in Jesus Christ is now present as
the Holy Spirit. The God who will one day be 'all in all'[2] is at work
now in all things, working there together for the good of those who
love him.[3] The Holy Spirit brings the Father and the Son who,
together with the Spirit, abide with and in the believer.[4]

To start with the Holy Spirit is not necessarily to become unitarian,[5]
but indicates a theological, practical concern. This can be seen when
the New Testament baptismal order of Father, Son, Holy Spirit in
Mt. 28.19 is changed so that the Son is mentioned first in the benediction of 2 Cor. 13.14 ('The grace of the Lord Jesus Christ, the love of
God, and the communion of the Holy Spirit'). The order of this
benediction is usually followed in the gospel proclamation. However,
when discussing life and service in the church (1 Cor. 12.4-6) Paul's

1. See P. Valliere, *Holy War and Pentecostal Peace* (New York: Seabury
Press, 1983), esp. Ch. 1.
2. 1 Cor. 15.28.
3. Rom. 8.28.
4. Jn 14.16.
5. H.R. Niebuhr, 'Theological Unitarianisms', *TTod* 40.2 (July, 1983),
pp. 150-57.

order is Spirit, Lord, God. The alternating order in these three scriptural contexts is not meant to imply a lack of full equality among the three divine persons (as we shall see in Chapter 4).[1] Indeed, just the opposite is true.

The Pentecostal concern is that of Paul in 1 Corinthians 12: to emphasize the lived reality of the faith, the life and service of the people of God who are organically constituted as the body of Christ by the indwelling of the Holy Spirit. As Newbigin has observed, the Pentecostals focus neither on right structure (Catholic) nor right message (Protestants). Instead, they emphasize that the 'Christian life is a matter of the experienced power and presence of the Holy Spirit today...neither orthodoxy of doctrine nor impeccability of succession can take the place of this'.[2] In seeking to safeguard the uniqueness, sufficiency and finality of Christ the Roman Catholic and Protestant approaches often result in 'a church which is a shell'[3] or, as Pentecostals (with Wesley) would say, 'a form of godliness denying the power thereof'.[4] With the Protestants there is agreement on the priority of Scripture over the church and a neglect of visible order and structure. With the Catholics there is a recognition of the Christian life as 'an actually experienced and received reality, something involving an ontological change in the believer'.[5]

In commenting on the first outpouring of the Spirit upon the Gentiles of Cornelius's household (Acts 10) Newbigin asserts that

> Nothing could be more plain or unambiguous. The gift of the Spirit was a visible, recognizable, unquestionable sign that God had accepted these Gentiles as His own people, and before that fact the most massive and fundamental theological convictions simply had to give way. The Holy Spirit may be the last article of the Creed, but in the New Testament it is the first fact of experience...The Spirit is God's recognizable witness (e.g. Acts 15.8) to His own presence, and therefore is entitled to right of way before all arguments based on *a priori* reasoning.[6]

It was out of a concern for this 'right of way' of the Spirit that early Pentecostals disdained and eschewed 'man-made Creeds'. It was

1. T.F. Torrance, *The Trinitarian Faith* (Edinburgh: T & T Clark, 1988).
2. L. Newbigin, *The Household of God* (London: SCM Press, 1953), p. 87.
3. Newbigin, *Household*, p. 87.
4. 2 Tim. 3.5
5. Newbigin, *Household*, p. 88.
6. Newbigin, *Household*, p. 88.

not that they had no fundamental beliefs—their periodicals and testimonies make it obvious that they did— rather, the objection was to a creedalism which they believed brought disunity and rejected the new blessing that the sovereign Spirit was restoring among them. Their primitivism was born out of a desire for apostolic faith, power and manifestations of the Holy Spirit among ordinary believers. The presence of the Holy Spirit constituted the church. As on the day of Pentecost, the message, structure, faith and order might all be in place; but it took the power of the new age, the last days' outpouring of the Spirit, to constitute the church a missionary fellowship which would witness in words, power and demonstration of the Holy Spirit. The church lives from the Spirit in Christ unto the glory of the Father.[1] Creeds must guard the faith not limit the sovereign leading of the Spirit.

If God is the living God, the God who in Trinitarian communion is spirit; if the church is a living organism of charisms and signs; and, if salvation is a living relationship with this God among these people who live in last days' expectancy and urgency—if all this is the case, then theology must be a discerning reflection upon this living reality, these divine–human relations.[2] Theology requires not only discursive reasoning but also the engagement of the whole person within the communion of charisms. The community of the Spirit and Word functions as a worshipping, witnessing, forming, reflective whole; but at the heart of all this is the liturgical life of the community. Ranaghan has concluded that the birth of Pentecostalism cannot be attributed to only the two works of grace theology. He finds that too 'narrow and incomplete'. Rather,

> From the field preaching of Wesley to the tents of Aimee Semple McPherson, it has been this one way of worship which has made the theology come alive and given it experiential validity. The worship has provided the vehicle for the theology. One can say further and maintain that the theology has served basically as a commentary on the worship which has always been the central reality.[3]

1.   K. McDonnell, 'The Experiential and the Social: New Models from the Pentecostal/Roman Catholic Dialogue', *One in Christ* 9 (1973), pp. 43-58.
2.   M.W. Duggan, 'Implications for Pentecostal-Charismatic Theology' (presented at the fifteenth annual meeting of the Society for Pentecostal Studies, Gaithersburg, MD, 1985).
3.   K.M. Ranaghan, 'Rites of Inititation in Representative Pentecostal Churches

Wheelock believes that Pentecostal 'theology as a whole seeks to convey that an arid, rationalistic, formalistic, unemotional, non-experiential and non-charismatic approach to religious life is unacceptable'. He sees much of this vitality coming from the African-American culture's emphasis on the

> nonconceptual aspects of life generally and religion specifically... The whole man should be caught up in the process... the experiential component is viewed as a 'natural' element and enthusiastic involvement as a fitting modality of religious expression. It was much of this expectation and practice that was transmitted at Azusa.[1]

In the context of American restoration-revivalism, it was the 'black spirituality of the former slaves in the United States' encountering the specific Catholic spirituality of the movement's 'grandfather', John Wesley, that produced Pentecostalism's distinctive spirituality. Neither Wesley nor the African-Americans did theology in the traditional, scholastic way. Sermons, pamphlets, hymns, testimonies, conferences, spirituals—these were the media of this movement.

But this is not so unlike the first hundred years of Christianity. Though some were 'well educated', there were not many mighty or wise or noble among them.[2] Letters, testimonies, epistles, Gospels, songs, a brief history and an apocalypse— these were the tools of the first-century house churches. 'Folk religion' and 'populist theology' carry all the dangers of fanaticism and all the promise of continual renewal in the church. Pentecostalism has experienced and manifested both tendencies. But it is important to see that theology is not to be identified solely or even primarily with systematic treatises, monographs and scholarly apparatus in centers of academia. Theology begins in the prayerful response of persons to God.

If, then, the Holy Spirit is taken as a starting point and the centrality of worship is given due place of primacy, it must be acknowledged that prayer—individual and corporate, human and 'angelic', with sighs and groans, praise and petition—is at the heart of this spirituality. But if it is the heart of the spirituality, it must also figure centrally in the

in the United States, 1901–1972' (PhD dissertation, University of Notre Dame, 1974).

1. D.R. Wheelock, 'Spirit-Baptism in American Pentecostal Thought' (PhD dissertation, Emory University, 1983), p. 334. See also Nelson, 'For such a Time as this'.

2. 1 Cor. 1.26.

understanding of the theological task. The language of the vocative and the indicative, of prayer and belief, must be seen together. For Pentecostals it is impossible to know God and the things of God without prayer, because in prayer one responds to the Spirit of truth. When one ceases to be prayerfully open, even the light of truth or belief that one has becomes dark, distorted and may soon be forgotten.

Theology thus conceived is no mere speculative enterprise; it is urgent, last-days work. With Karl Barth Pentecostals can affirm that 'Prayer is an eschatological cry based on acknowledgement of God's name, will and reign...it is the actualization of our eschatological reality that is possible here and there...'[1]

Barth discussed the relation of prayer and theology in his *Evangelical Theology: An Introduction*.[2] Four related claims concerning this relation are discussed by Don Saliers in the introduction to the second edition of Barth's 1949 book, *Prayer*.

1. The first and basic act of theological work is prayer. Theology itself, while demanding historical knowledge and conceptual reasoning, is radically dependent upon having been addressed by God in such a manner as to respond freely in return... The conception of God must be congruent with the nature of address to the self-revealing God, whose revelation is accompanied by the command and invitation to share in the divine life... The essence of prayer and worship, then, is acknowledgement of God and God's gracious turning in mercy and judgment toward all creation. This response arises from the capacity of the creature, through grace, to love and rejoice in gratitude for who God is...

2. The second claim is that the object of theological reflection is a 'Thou' encountered, not an idea to be grasped as the 'Ultimate God' or the 'Ground of Being', for instance. Doctrinal language about God must be in response to something actually discerned in God. But this means to thank, to praise, to invoke, and to petition God. This is why Barth can say, 'Theological work must really and truly take place in the form of a liturgical act'. This is implicit in Barth's reflection on the fact that we are not only to speak the words Jesus gives us, but we must also receive him and the life of service he confers in and through the words...

1.   K. Barth, *Prayer* (ed. D.E. Saliers; trans. S. Terrien; Philadelphia: Westminster Press, 1985), p. 18.

2.   K. Barth, *Evangelical Theology: An Introduction* (New York: Holt, Rinehart and Winston, 1963), pp. 160-64.

3. Thirdly, since theological reflection about God is itself dialogical, we cannot rest content with building upon the certainties of previous systems of thought... To conceive God as living and redeeming the world is humanly possible only by receiving anew through grace the present activity of God. *Theology itself becomes an offering to God*, and a continuous petition that this offering may be acceptable [emphasis mine].

4. Finally, theology cannot guarantee truth, because it cannot in itself guarantee the grace of God... Certainty in our knowledge of God lies not in formulated doctrines, according to Barth, but in acknowledging, invoking, and petitioning that God will truly make the divine Word and being accessible to us.[1]

Upon reading this one is reminded of Barth's life-long appreciation and sharp disagreement with the theology of Schleiermacher, whom he believed had blurred the distinction between the human and divine by collapsing the Holy Spirit into the human spirit. But Barth thought he might begin his own theological work again, and this time start with the Holy Spirit. There is in the immediately foregoing discussion of prayer and theology the seeds of such a beginning.

Pentecostals would find much to recommend Barth in this respect. There is in the first point the recognition of the initiative of God; in the second, an acknowledgment of the personal address (God is Spirit!); the third might serve as a basis for rejection of creedalism, though not of creeds themselves; and, finally, the fourth point emphasizes the sovereignty of the Holy Spirit.

For Pentecostals, to know God is to be in a right relation, to walk in the light and in the Spirit. To know and not to do the truth is a lie, to exist in contradiction. In that case even the light one has will become darkness. For example, to say 'God is with us' without being with God is to lie or merely to speculate. Christian theology as spirituality must be consistent with, appropriate to and responsive to its source and object, the living God.

This is very much like the theology of the Apostolic Fathers who were 'essentially practical, unconcerned with speculative theology, unaware of cultural matters...' But it is also much like the later patristic-monastic theology in which there was no distinction between prayer and theology.

---

1. Saliers, in Barth, *Prayer*, pp. 17-19.

> Up until the twelfth century theology was not a manner of knowing but
> a manner of praying. Theology was not a doctrine to be analyzed
> intellectually or discussed in school. The purpose of theology was not to
> explain God, but to know Him in contemplation, adoration, praise and
> thanksgiving. If theology was a science, it had to do with affections. This
> prayer conception of theology obtained until the first half of the twelfth
> century... [1]

Therefore, to do theology is not to make experience the norm, but it
is to recognize the epistemological priority of the Holy Spirit in
prayerful receptivity. Speaking of a pneumatic epistemology, Howard
Ervin

> posits an awareness that the Scriptures are the product of an experience
> with the Holy Spirit which the biblical writers describe in phenomeno-
> logical language... the interpretation of this phenomenological language is
> much more than an exercise in semantics or descriptive linguistics. When
> one encounters the Holy Spirit in the same apostolic experience, with the
> same charismatic phenomenology accompanying it, one is then in a better
> position to come to terms with the apostolic witness in a truly existential
> manner... in the sense that a vertical dimension to man's existence is
> recognized and affirmed. One then stands in 'pneumatic' continuity with
> the faith community that birthed the Scriptures. [2]

In addition to a distinctive epistemology, other Pentecostal scholars
are calling for an ontology and hermeneutic with which to construct a
systematic theology 'worthy of the name Pentecostal'.[3] For David
Nichols such an approach would involve a 'spiritual' ontology with its
analogy of love as opposed to analogy of faith or being.[4] This
ontology would take seriously the transcendent presence of God as the
fourth dimension of reality. God who is 'other' is not outside the
world of time, space and matter.[5] Nichols believes that it is time for
Pentecostal theologizing to 'shake free from the shackles of exclusive
rationalism, (adaptations of Hodge, Shedd, Warfield, etc.) and from

---

1. McDonnell, 'The Experiential', p. 48.
2. H.M. Ervin, 'Hermeneutics: A Pentecostal Option', *Pneuma* 3.2 (Fall,
1981), p. 22.
3. D.R. Nichols, 'The Search for a Pentecostal Structure in Systematic
Theology', *Pneuma* 6.2 (Fall, 1984), pp. 57-76.
4. Nichols, 'The Search', pp. 68-75.
5. Nichols, 'The Search', pp. 68-69.

irrationalism, and to stand on its own two feet with a dimensional understanding of spiritual truth'.[1]

All of this serves to emphasize the importance of the Holy Spirit as a starting point for a distinctive Pentecostal approach to theology as spirituality. Does this, however, mean that Pentecostals place the Spirit above the Word and thus elevate experience from the category of source for theology to that of norm? The answer is 'Yes' and 'No'. Yes, the Spirit is prior to the written Word of God, but the Spirit inspires, preserves and illumines that Word within the communion of those who are formed, corrected, nurtured and equipped by that Word. Yes, the Spirit does not exist only to illumine Scripture and apply the benefits of salvation to the believer. The gifting and guiding of persons in community and the community as a whole is the ongoing, daily task of the Spirit. The signs and power of the Spirit are not an optional addition for a church that would engage principalities and powers and suffer unto death.

However in a consideration of the relationship of Word and Spirit, the Word as living Word of God in Jesus is, of course, equal with the Spirit. The person and work of the Spirit is in salvific continuity with the person and work of Christ, but it is not exhausted therein. The recovery of dialectical balance or of a proper integration of the Spirit-Word addresses the crisis of authority in the church today and also expresses a central feature of Pentecostal theology. This integration is violated in various ways by differing Christian traditions.

Roman Catholic theology, even since Vatican II, still tends in practice to place the church over the Word and then further to place tradition on a level with Scripture. Protestant fundamentalist scholasticism has so subjugated Spirit to the Scriptures that the only significant function of the Spirit is to witness to the Bible which is interpreted by human reason. Other groups which place Spirit over Word and develop private 'revelations' beyond and over Scripture—contradicting or correcting Scripture!—clearly err on the other side. Then there is the subtler, supposed subjugation or domestication of the Holy Spirit in which the Spirit serves only to provide zest for ecclesial undertakings, becomes another word for the grace of the sacraments (so that one receives grace and not God the Holy Spirit) or is identified with the light of reason or common human experience as in some

---

1.   Nichols, 'The Search', p. 73.

more liberal versions of theology. All of these ways of subsuming the Spirit are correlated with an improper understanding of the relationship of Spirit and Word. Agreeing with Calvin and Luther, James Jones in a neglected but important work, states that

> the Bible is of little value without the sovereign work of the Holy Spirit. The Bible has no significance when ripped from the context of the experience of the Spirit. Refusing to subsume the Spirit under the Word frees the Spirit to do more than confirm the text and shut up.[1]

We might also add that this also frees the Spirit to do more than assure the believer and then shut up. But Jones continues by pointing out that

> The Spirit does not contradict the Scriptures but his job is more than just repeating what we can find by reading there... John indicates that the Lord expected the Spirit to direct the church in those areas not covered by Jesus' teachings (John 15.7-12)... The first apostolic council went back to the Old Testament covenant with Noah but justified their decision by saying 'it seemed good to the Holy Spirit and to us' (Acts 15.28; 11.15-17).[2]

Jones further maintains that the polemics of the past have separated the Bible from the Spirit in community, and therefore destroyed any valid basis for Christian faith.

> Protestants have the Bible, but the Bible without the Spirit and the community is a dead letter giving rise to arid scholasticism. Catholics have the community, but the community without the Bible and the Spirit becomes only an institutional shell. Pentecostals have the Spirit but the Spirit without the Bible and the community inevitably leads to subjectivism and fanaticism... In the complete Spirit-filled body of Christ, as Paul portrays it, these three partial authorities complement each other. The Spirit inspires the Word and builds up the community; the Word enables us to understand our experience of the Spirit and teaches us the form of our common life; the community forms the context in which the Word is understood and the Spirit encountered. Using the Bible to tear down rather than build up the church, using the church to squelch the Spirit, using the Spirit as a pretext to go beyond the perimeters of the Gospel have destroyed the foundations of Christianity in the modern world more than any external attacks by atheists and skeptics.[3]

1. J.W. Jones, *The Spirit and the World* (New York: Hawthorn Books, 1975), p. 99.
2. Jones, *The Spirit*, pp. 98-99.
3. Jones, *The Spirit*, pp. 100, 106.

The wholeness of the body of Christ given in the proper relation of Spirit, Word and community has as its corollary a view of spirituality which is the integration of beliefs, affections, and actions (of knowing, being and doing). Indeed for a Pentecostal theology-as-spirituality, with a starting point in the Holy Spirit, it is a necessary correlation. Mark McClean insists,

> It is simply time to admit that the Pentecostal understanding of the mode of God's presence among His people in conjunction with our use of Scripture in the common life of the Church results in a Pentecostal hermeneutic and theology, that at major points is different from an orthodox non-Pentecostal hermeneutic and theology. The task before us now is to realize and explore the implications of that fact for our understanding of God's continued activity in the world, and for our understanding of our self-identity and tasks given to us by the living, acting and speaking Creator of all things.[1]

This theological task demands the ongoing integration of beliefs, affections and actions lest the spirituality and theology fragment into intellectualism, sentimentalism and activism respectively. When *theologia* is restored to its ancient meaning, the dichotomization that too often occurs or is perceived between theology and spirituality can be overcome. Experience of the Spirit, who is the agent of mutuality and interrelatedness in the Trinity and the church,[2] drives toward and requires this integration of belief, affections and practice which is at once the definition of spirituality and of the theological task.

To state this claim in a more formal way: orthodoxy (right praise-confession), orthopathy (right affections) and orthopraxy (right praxis) are related in a way analogous to the interrelations of the Holy Trinity. God who is Spirit creates in humanity a spirituality which is at once cognitive, affective and behavioral, thus driving toward a unified epistemology, metaphysics and ethics. To speak of and long for the full realization of this reality is the privilege and pain of Christian theology. It is in a sense to long for the eschatological Trinitarian realization of the kingdom of God which Jürgen Moltmann has so eloquently described in his *Trinity and the Kingdom*. Dialog partners in the development of a sense of this realization have been Karl Barth, John Wesley and Jürgen Moltmann in their

1. McClean, 'Pentecostal Hermeneutic', *Pneuma* 6.2 (Fall, 1984), p. 50.
2. J. Moltmann, *The Trinity and the Kingdom* (New York: Harper & Row, 1981).

distinctive contributions to an understanding of orthodoxy, orthopathy and orthopraxy, respectively.

Karl Barth's development of the relation of prayer and theological vocation has already been referred to above. However, while insisting that all action must proceed from and be judged by some cognitive awareness of the 'facts' of divine revelation, Barth nevertheless indicates something of his wholistic view of 'knowledge' and 'orthodoxy' in the following discussion:

> We cannot impress upon ourselves too strongly that in the language of the Bible knowledge (*yada, gignoskein*) does not mean the acquisition of neutral informatioh, which can be expressed in statements, principles and systems, concerning a being which confronts man, nor does it mean entry into a passive contemplation of a being which exists beyond the phenomenal world. What it really means is the process of history in which man, certainly observing and thinking, using his senses, intelligence and imagination, but also his will, action and 'heart', and therefore as whole man, becomes aware of another history which in the first instance encounters him as an alien history from without, and becomes aware of it in such a compelling way that he cannot be neutral towards it. . . [1]

This statement was put to use by Jürgen Moltmann who, though differing with Barth from time to time, nevertheless remains his student in many ways. In *The Trinity and the Kingdom* Moltmann develops the doctrine of the Trinitarian history of God in the direction of an eschatological Trinitarian realization of the kingdom. Moltmann sees history in God and God in history without dissolving God into history or leaving history without significant freedom and responsibility. His goal is to enable the church to join God in an orthopraxy (right action) which seeks to be an anticipation, represent-ation and/or resistance in the light of the kingdom that is coming and now is.[2] Truth is to be done as well as believed, and this requires a passionate commitment to the messianic community of the crucified and risen Lord who, by the Spirit gives a sustaining, mobilizing, living hope.

If Barth emphasized evangelical faith and Moltmann radical hope, John Wesley could be described as the theologian of the love of God.

1.   Barth, *Church Dogmatics* (Edinburgh: T. & T. Clark, 1961), IV.3.1, pp. 183-84, cited and discussed in Nichols, 'The Search', p. 67.

2.   Moltmann, *Trinity and the Kingdom*, pp. 124-28, 209-22; *The Church in the Power of the Spirit* (New York: Harper and Row, 1977), pp. 189-96.

He and Jonathan Edwards represent a deep stream of evangelical thought which has yet to be fully integrated into the North American evangelical establishment. His concern for what contemporary Methodist theologian Theodore Runyon has called 'orthopathy' was borne of his years of personal struggle, study and practice in and among the Methodist societies, bands and classes which were at the forefront of awakening, renewal and reform in eighteenth-century England. Runyon sees this orthopathy as providing 'a necessary but currently missing complement to orthodoxy and orthopraxy'. For him orthopathy is 'religious experience as an event of knowing between the Divine Source and human participant' involving four interrelated factors:

1. The divine source of experience who makes impressions on the spiritual senses of the human beings.
2. The *telos* of experience: the intention of the source, the purpose and goal for the human being.
3. The transformation brought about through experience.
4. The feelings that accompany experience.[1]

His description of these essential components of experience recognizes

> the important, powerful, and absolutely necessary contribution which experience has to make to the identity, mobilization and mission of the Church; and at the same time the checks and balances necessary if experience is to be guided into the most productive channels... experience needs the word of orthodoxy if it is to communicate rightly and the actions of orthopraxy if it is to be the instrument of the sanctification of the world. But both words and deeds need to be fulfilled with the divine power and impact of the motivating Spirit, mediated, received and communicated further through experience... [It is] feelings that focus our energies, enlist us, motivate us and give us passion. Who will fight against injustice, prejudice and corruption who does not have feelings of justice and outrage against injustice? Who will sacrifice for others and engage in acts of mercy who does not feel compassion? Who will spend long hours over a microscope or poring through books who does not know the feelings of joy and satisfaction that come with discovering a new truth or finding new

---

1.   T.H. Runyon, 'The Importance of Experience for Faith' (Ministers' Week Address, Emory University, 1988), p. 4; the address is revised and appears in R. Maddox (ed.), *Aldersgate Reconsidered* (Nashville: Abingdon Press, 1990), pp. 93-108.

confirmation of an old truth? Who will work hard at great emotional cost putting a marriage back together who does not feel the importance of those relations to all who are touched by them?[1]

Building on but going beyond the perspective of Runyon, this study uses 'orthopathy' to refer to the affections which motivate the heart and characterize the believer. As shown by Saliers, Clapper and Knight,[2] the Christian affections are the heart of the spirituality of Edwards and Wesley. They are likewise the heart of Pentecostal spirituality.

The personal integrating center of orthodoxy and orthopraxy is orthopathy, those distinctive affections which are belief shaped, praxis oriented and characteristic of a person. Affections are neither episodic, feeling states nor individualistic sentiments. There are, of course, attendant feelings or emotions that come and go and intermingle in the affections over time. Unlike 'feelings' these affections are distinctively shaped and determined by the biblical story and evidence the marks of particular communal and historical location.

In Chapter 3 I will analyze three Christian affections in their distinctively Pentecostal configuration. This will, however, be no mere attempt to balance reason and emotion. Balance is a term often used in the general culture and evangelical mainline churches to refer to a certain kind of mental health or mean of normality. Balance speaks of equal weight given to reason and feeling. Those who speak this way often see the religion of the lower classes, the disinherited, the African-Americans and Pentecostals as being merely 'emotional' and filled with psycho-motor manifestations. Although recognizing the value of feeling as motivation and excitement, they fail to see the crucial and fundamental role of affections in salvation and, therefore, in the theological enterprise in general. Hence, the word 'integration' is deliberately chosen as being preferable to 'balance'.

Integration in certain crises of oppression, domination and breakthrough may be more like the fusion of a hydrogen bomb. Western

1. Runyon, 'Experience', p. 16.
2. See D.E. Saliers, *The Soul in Paraphrase* (New York: Seabury Press, 1980), *Worship and Spirituality* (Philadelphia: Westminster Press, 1984); H.H. Knight, III, *The Presence of God in the Christian Life* (Metuchen, NJ: Scarecrow Press, 1992); G.S. Clapper, *John Wesley on Religious Affections: His Views on Experience and Emotion and their Role in the Christian Life and Theology* (Metuchen, NJ: Scarecrow Press, 1989).

society, especially in its white, middle and upper classes, values control and quietness in matters of religion (though not, of course in sports, political campaigns, discotheques, rock concerts and so on). In contrast, when those oppressed by demonic forces and/or violated and defiled by humanity catch the vision of a kingdom that liberates, sanctifies and empowers a new existence, there is often, indeed almost inevitably, intensity of response. The joy and exuberance, the depth of sorrow and longing, the courageous witness of millions of such persons cannot simply be written off as hysteria, mass psychosis or cheap escapism.

It is crucial for Pentecostals to consider carefully their beliefs, affections and practices before they uncritically accommodate to culture, are assimilated into mainstream denominations, or are co-opted by socio-political ideologies. In the words of the Chilean Pentecostal pastor Juan Sepúlveda:

> We do not propose to reject theological reflection in the Pentecostal context (we are, in fact, reflecting theologically here), but rather we are attempting to repair the road for a form of theological reflection which assumes the richness and specificity of the Pentecostal experience. It is the emphasis on doctrines which has created the idea that Pentecostalism proposes an other-worldly salvation, when what the testimony of the Pentecostal experience shows us is, above all, the opportunity of a salvation here and now.[1]

Or again, as Peruvian Pentecostal pastor Bernardo Campos has said recently,

> We Pentecostals have always done theology... and as we understand it today it is the living experience and reflection (method) which the Church as a community of faith does (subject), in a social space and a given time (context), concerning the action of God in the world in Jesus and by His Holy Spirit (object, content), with two fundamental purposes to experience and to give account of:
>
> 1. The evangelization and reconciliation of the world with God, in the dynamic of the creation and growth of the new person.
> 2. The creation of a new society (new earth) in the dynamic of the advance of the kingdom of God in history...

> The Christian Church has experienced two theological traditions worthy of being taken into account: a systematizing tradition (Aquinas, Calvin, Barth) and an experienced, non-systematic tradition (Müntzer,

1.   Sepúlveda, 'Reflections', p. 1.

Kierkegaard, Unamuno, etc.). One must ask, 'What are the advantages
and risks of a systemization and what are the advantages and risks of a
theology of experience without divorcing them'.[1]

Campos describes Pentecostal experience as being first of all the
'community's mode of being, of doing, and of living'.[2] It is a means
of understanding that moves from experience to testimony to doctrine
to theology and back again in an ongoing dynamic that is more implicit
than explicit, more oral than written, more affectively-rational than
principled-rational, more narrative than strictly propositional. The
affective integration which comprises the Pentecostal affections is the
experiential center of a distinctive theology which in less than a century has impacted every continent and every Christian denomination.

Perhaps it is the failure of the more Reformed (and especially
Lutheran) approaches to appreciate salvation as affective integration
('the faith that works through love') that makes it difficult for them to
understand and theologically adjust to Pentecostals, Wesleyans,
African-Americans and whole multitudes of Third World indigenous
churches. There are, of course, notable exceptions to this;[3] but, on the
whole, the major contemporary criticisms have come from fundamentalist dispensationalists like John MacArthur[4] and the much more
informed and nuanced critics such as James Dunn and Frederick Dale
Bruner.[5] While it is not the task of this study to offer a direct rebuttal,

---

1.   B.L. Campos, 'From Experience to Pentecostal Theology' (trans. J. Beaty
and S.J. Land, paper presented to the Encuentro Pentecostal Latinoamericano,
Buenos Aires, Argentina, 1989), pp. 1, 4, 5.

2.   Campos, 'Experience', p. 1.

3.   Synan surveys the charismatic movement in the various 'mainline' churches
in *The Twentieth Century Pentecostal Explosion* (Altumante Springs, FL: Strang,
1989), esp. pp. 109-20, 159-72. See also the excellent Lutheran charismatic
theology of L. Christenson (ed.), *Welcome Holy Spirit* (Minneapolis: Augsburg,
1988).

4.   J. MacArthur, Jr, *The Charismatics: A Doctrinal Perspecitve* (Grand Rapids:
Zondervan, 1978) and *Speaking in Tongues* (Chicago: Moody Press, 1988).

5.   Bruner, *A Theology of the Holy Spirit*; J.D.G. Dunn, *Jesus and the Spirit*
(Philadelphia: Westminster Press, 1970). See the Pentecostal responses in
H.M. Ervin, *Conversion-Initiation and the Baptism in the Holy Spirit* (Peabody,
MA: Hendrickson, 1984); *idem*, *Spirit Baptism: A Biblical Investigation* (Peabody,
Massachusetts: Hendrickson, 1987); and H.D. Hunter, *Spirit Baptism: A
Pentecostal Alternative* (Lanham, MD: University Press of America, 1983); and
R. Williams, *Renewal Theology* (3 vols.; Grand Rapids: Zondervan, 1993).

thus adding to and building upon those already offered by Pentecostals, it is hoped that this approach will make clear some of the reasons for misunderstanding and talking past one another.

Spirituality as primary theology forms the theoretical standpoint for an analysis of Pentecostalism which will prove recognizable to Pentecostals and afford a basis for revision and dialog. But before that analysis proceeds it is necessary to offer two further observations which are of substantial importance to the development of the thesis. One relates to a limitation and the other to the overall context.

Origins and Continuity

With Walter Hollenweger this study will accept as a historical limitation the first ten years of the twentieth century as the heart and not the infancy of Pentecostal spirituality.[1] Dr Hollenweger, one of the leading, if not foremost, authorities on world Pentecostalism's variety and dynamics, takes 'the early Pentecostal spirituality as the norm by which I measure its subsequent history'.[2]

The streams of Pietism, Puritanism, Wesleyanism, African-American Christianity and nineteenth-century Holiness-Revivalism form a confluence which has today become a sea of Pentecostal believers.[3] Therefore, though there is an incredibly diverse array of Pentecostal denominations as the twenty-first century approaches, yet the original or essential spirituality has left its mark on them all and remains to be re-visioned if the movement is to have theological coherence and continuity. This historical focus or bracketing captures what is perhaps the two most important spiritualities which formed the originators of Pentecostalism: Wesleyan and African-American.[4]

The Wesleyan spirituality embodied a specific catholic tradition of transformation which included Western and Eastern figures. Wesley

1. W.J. Hollenweger, 'Pentcostals and the Charismatic Movement', in Jones, Wainwright and Yarnold (eds.), *The Study of Spirituality*, pp. 549-53.

2. Hollenweger, 'Pentecostals', p. 551.

3. For a broader historical perspective consult S.M. Burgess, *The Spirit and the Church: Antiquity* (Peabody, MA: Hendrickson, 1984); R.A.N. Kydd, *Charismatic Gifts in the Early Church: An Exploration into the Gifts of the Spirit during the First Three Centuries of the Christian Church* (Peabody, MA: Hendrickson, 1984); S.M. Burgess, 'The Doctrine of the Holy Spirit: The Ancient Fathers', *DPCM*, pp. 417-32; 'The Doctrine of the Holy Spirit: The Medieval Churches', *DPCM*, pp. 432-44.

4. Hollenweger, 'Twenty Years' Research', p. 4.

translated and abridged many of these sources in a Christian library which he produced for the edification of his lay leaders.[1] He taught a second-crisis experience, both preceded and followed by a development, beginning in new birth and maintained only through moment-by-moment abiding in Christ.

Following Wesley such nineteenth-century Holiness leaders as Finney, Moody, Hannah Whitall Smith, Asa Mahan and Phoebe Palmer—though from both Wesleyan and Reformed backgrounds—were all in agreement that there was a subsequent 'sanctification', 'baptism in the Holy Spirit' or 'overcoming life' which is the purchased possession of Calvary for every believer.

It is generally recognized that the early Pentecostal revival built on this Wesleyan-Holiness foundation in embracing the 'fivefold' or 'full gospel' of justification, sanctification, Spirit baptism, divine healing, and premillennial return of Jesus; all of these were to be definite experiences flowing from the atonement. That is to say, the Christian could by faith receive the full blessing and benefits, a five fold blessing, if trusting in Christ he or she sought the Lord and 'paid the price' of asking, seeking and knocking. The following song quoted in *The Apostolic Faith* in 1906, illustrates this desire:

> 'Baptized with the Holy Ghost'
> (By F.E. Hill)
>
> Do you long to be full of joy and free,
> To be strong in God and His glory see,
> Then obey His word and you shall be,
> Baptized with the Holy Ghost.
>
> CHORUS
> 'Ye shall be baptized', Jesus said,
> Baptized with the Holy Ghost.
> Tarry then until with power endued,
> Baptized with the Holy Ghost.
> Yes, I'll be baptized with His power,
> Baptized with the Holy Ghost,
> 'Tis the gift I see, the Father's promise to me,
> Baptized with the Holy Ghost.
>
> Will you consecrate to Him now your all,
> Let Him have His way while to Him you call,

---

1. Hollenweger, 'Twenty Years' Research', p. 4.

As in faith you wait, the power will fall,
Baptized with the Holy Ghost.

'Tis the gift of God to the sanctified,
He will comfort, lead and will be our guide,
And will dwell in us, coming to abide
Baptized with the Holy Ghost.

Will you gladly fall at the Savior's feet,
Give your doubtings o'er and be made complete,
There to dwell in peace and communion sweet,
Baptized with the Holy Ghost.

You can sing God's praises now, and by and by,
You shall speak with tongues, and shall prophesy,
In the power of God ye shall testify,
Baptized with the Holy Ghost.[1]

Had there been no eighteenth-century Wesleyan and nineteenth-century Holiness movements there would have been no twentieth-century Pentecostalism; and Pentecostalism is at any rate inexplicable without this theological heritage. Even researchers of the 'non-Wesleyan' roots of Pentecostalism acknowledge its Wesleyan lineage. As Edith L. Blumhofer, whose doctoral dissertation dealt with the non-Wesleyan antecedents of Pentecostalism, has said, 'Until 1910, most Pentecostals accepted without question the insistence that an experience of Christian perfection preceded Spirit baptism'.[2] Non-Wesleyans in the nineteenth-century Oberlin and Keswick movements were 'Wesleyanized' and thus 'Arminianized'. William Menzies, the Assemblies of God historian, has studied the non-Wesleyan roots of the movement but nonetheless has noted that Wesleyanism via the Holiness movement was the cradle of Pentecostalism.[3]

The importance of the Wesleyan origins of the movement for the understanding and re-visioning of the spirituality cannot be overstated. It is discussed in detail by historians Vinson Synan[4] and

1. *AF* 1.4 (1906), p. 2.
2. E. Blumhofer, 'Purity and Preparation', in S.M. Burgess (ed.), *Reaching Beyond: Chapters in the History of Perfectionism* (Peabody, MA: Hendrickson, 1986), p. 275.
3. W.M. Menzies, 'The Non-Wesleyan Origins of the Pentecostal Movement', in V. Synan (ed.), *Aspects of Pentecostal-Charismatic Origins* (Plainfield, NJ: Logos, 1975), p. 97.
4. V. Synan, *The Holiness-Pentecostal Movement in the United States* (Grand Rapids: Eerdmans, 1971).

Melvin Dieter[1] and by historian-systematician Donald Dayton.[2]
Donald Wheelock in his 1983 dissertation on 'Spirit Baptism in
American Pentecostal Thought' concludes that

> Wesleyan and non-Wesleyan Pentecostals agree that personal holiness
> precedes Spirit baptism. For the former it is the definite crisis experience
> in which the 'root' of sin is plucked up, while for the latter it is a matter of
> victorious consecration which is maintained and deepened by the
> assistance of the Holy Spirit.[3]

Further, Wheelock states that almost all American Pentecostals state
the following 'conditions' for Spirit baptism: obedience to God
through separation from all known sin, a request for prayer and unity
with others, a praise-filled worship and a faith-filled expectation.

Melvin Dieter, aware of the past intense conflict between the
Holiness and Pentecostal churches, nevertheless observes that this was,
to a large extent, a family dispute between fraternal, if not identical,
twins. He concluded that even the largest and more 'baptistic'
Pentecostal body, the Assemblies of God, has a spiritual dynamic
that is

> at least equally or even more strongly derived from the historical camp-
> meeting perfectionism as it is from any classical Reformed categories. The
> theological and experiential wineskins of the Keswick low-church
> Anglicans and others through whom the higher-life message came back to
> its American home have... been hard put to contain the holiness wine. To
> use another metaphor, the dominant genes of the vigorous Christocentric
> pneumatology residing in our common parent, the holiness revival, have
> left on all the progeny such a unified imprint of spirituality and experience
> that each of us will be the loser if we fail to recognize... the ultimate
> charge that Warfield and his friends leveled against the movement [New
> School revivalism of Finney, Mahan, *et al.*] was that it was really
> 'Methodist'. The holiness connection is important for Pentecostals
> because it carries with it the nineteenth century concern for abolition,
> prohibition, women's rights, and the reform of society according to the
> righteous standards of God. When Pentecostalism and the holiness

---

1.   Dieter, *The Holiness Revival*; and 'The Development of Nineteenth Century
Holiness Theology', *Wesleyan Theological Journal* 20.1 (Spring, 1985), pp. 61-77;
and 'The Wesleyan Holiness and Pentecostal Movements: Commonalities,
Confrontation and Dialogue' (unpublished paper, Society for Pentecostal Studies,
Asbury Theological Seminary; Wilmore, KY, 1988).

2.   Dayton, *Theological Roots*.

3.   Wheelock, 'Spirit Baptism', p. 210.

churches were impacted by the aftermath of the Civil War, Reconstruction, the new higher criticism of the Bible, the 'liberal' social gospel and the increasing 'embourgeoisement' of Methodism, they were forced to choose between fundamentalism and modernism. By choosing fundamentalism the Wesleyan agenda for 'spreading scriptural holiness throughout the land' was reduced to rescue missions, storefront churches, soup kitchens and other kinds of person- to-person involvement. A further result of this alliance has been the presence of both movements at the founding of the National Association of Evangelicals in the 1940's, in spite of the fact that the word 'evangelical' in North America usually excludes or redefines the holiness Pentecostal paradigm in favor of the more Presbyterian-fundamentalist paradigm. This drew both movements into battles concerning inerrancy and drew them away from rethinking and further application of their fundamentally transformationalist heritage.[1]

All of these characteristically Wesleyan concerns can be heard in the words of Frank Bartleman, who was an eyewitness and participant in the 1907 Azusa Street revival.

> We need deliverance from strife and confusion, a deeper consecration and death to self... God's fire falls on sacrifice, as in Elijah's case. The greater the sacrifice, consecration, the more fire. But Ananias and Sapphira are in the mission work today. They are striking the Peters dead with their money and influence. The man who is paying the full price in consecration has very little voice in the meetings... Preach not to please a 'party' but to raise a standard... God gathered a lot of seasoned saints together at 'Azusa' in the beginning. They were subdued and purified through months of prayer, and years of experience with God. We live in a light jazzy age... They refuse the fires of purifying, holiness of heart. We have an atmosphere of confusion. There is too much 'professional' work, railroading seekers through, like a 'quack' doctor's office. This produces a 'fake' Pentecost, with spurious 'tongues'. The 'singing in the Spirit' is also imitated. Men have learned to do these things without the Spirit, and suggest them to others for their imitation. We have even heard leaders call for any demonstration they wanted from the people. What would Peter say to such a demonstration?... We advertise 'miracles', wonderful preachers, etc., and have crowds following bill-board 'signs' to the next big meeting. But are the 'signs following'? Men love the spectacular. What we do not understand is the 'wonderful'.[2]

---

1. Dieter, 'The Wesleyan-Holiness and Pentecostal Movements', pp. 2-4.
2. F. Bartleman, *Azusa Street* (South Plainfield, NJ: Bridge Publishing, 1980), pp. 164, 166.

Dieter and Bartleman, each in his own way, show why the taking into account of the Wesleyan roots is vital. But so is the other stream, black spirituality, because this spirituality was the immediate mediator of Azusa in the person of William Seymour. One of the largest North American Pentecostal bodies today, the Church of God in Christ is predominately African-American. It was founded by C.H. Mason, whose name is given to the first Pentecostal seminary in the world in Atlanta, Georgia. This black spirituality was represented by scores of others who were hymn writers and evangelists. Hollenweger says that the reason for the growth of Pentecostalism lies in its African-American roots which he summarizes by listing the characteristics of black spirituality.

—orality of liturgy;
—narrativity of theology and witness.
—maximum participation at the levels of reflection, prayer and decision-making and therefore a form of community that is reconciliatory;
—inclusions of dreams and visions into personal and public forms of worship; they function as a kind of icon for the individual and the community;
—an understanding of the body/mind relationship that is informed by experiences of correspondence between body and mind; the most striking application of this insight is in the ministry of healing by prayer.[1]

It was the confluence of African-American and Wesleyan spiritualities, which gave rise to this movement of participation in the Spirit.

A very significant part of the Wesleyan-Holiness inheritance was the ministry of women;[2] already in the nineteenth century the language of sanctification as Spirit baptism had proven to be inclusive of women as prophets. Sons and daughters were to prophesy. Women testified, preached, founded churches and witnessed in the power of the Spirit.[3]

---

1. Hollenweger, 'Twenty Years' Research'. See also L. Lovett, 'Black Origins of Pentecostalism', in *Aspects of Pentecostal-Charismatic Origins* (Plainfield, NJ: Logos, 1975), pp. 145-58. See also W.J. Hollenweger, 'The Black Pentecostal Concept: Interpretations and Variations', *Concept* 30 (1970); and S.S. Dupree (ed.), *Biographical Dictionary of African-American, Holiness-Pentecostals 1880–1990* (Washington, DC: Middle Atlantic Regional Press, 1989).

2. D.W. Dayton, *Discovering an Evangelical Heritage* (Peabody, MA: Hendrickson, 1976).

3. R.M. Riss, 'Role of Women', *DPCM*, pp. 893-99.

More will be said about this later, but again the importance of the Wesleyan roots cannot be overestimated.

An eschatological equality seemed to bloom wherever the vision and reality of the kingdom of God was experienced in missionary urgency and spiritual zeal. The major metaphor for the church of the last days was the 'Bride'; she was being prepared for the Bridegroom. This 'feminization' of the church by the Holy Spirit was a further affront to society and a warning to the church at large that God was doing a new thing. If the church was going to witness to all nations before the soon coming of the Lord, it appeared that the Spirit's strategy was to enlist everyone—male and female—in the army. Again, a discerning reflection upon the living reality of the outpouring of the Spirit upon sons and daughters led the Pentecostals to see that the Scriptures concerning 'silence' of women in the church had to be reinterpreted. That reinterpretation had already begun in the Holiness movement, as in Phoebe Palmer's *The Promise of the Father*,[1] but was given fresh impetus in the new 'Pentecostal reality'.

Eschatology and Coherence

For Pentecostals, the Holy Spirit is the agent of the kingdom of God. Christ is the king or regent, and the Holy Spirit is the active reigning presence. It is the Spirit who makes Christ and the Father known. It is in the Spirit that believers are presented to the Father through Christ. The kingdom of God is already present, but not yet consummated. Unlike the dispensationalism of fundamentalism which draws a sharp line between Kingdom Age and Church Age, Pentecostals testified to and rejoiced in the inbreaking of the kingdom of God. Therefore the so-called sign gifts of the Apostolic Age had not disappeared. Augustine and subsequent dispensationalists had been wrong. With Wesley the Pentecostals affirmed that if the gifts had been withdrawn or were not as much in evidence, it was due not to a divine dispensational bracketing but to the fall of the church under Constantine and the love of many 'waxing cold'. Pentecostals would have no problem with Barth's assertion that God would once again bestow his lights and wonders wherever the Spirit is 'cried and sighed'.[2] So when the Pentecostals spoke of restoration, it was not primarily a restoration of this or that outward characteristic of the

1. P. Palmer, *The Promise of the Father* (Boston, MA: H.V. Degen, 1859).
2. Barth, *Evangelical Theology*, p. 58.

early church, but primarily the apostolic power and expectancy.

Indeed the transcendent presence of God among the people in an outpouring seen as the 'restoration of Pentecost', is that which gives coherence to the Pentecostal testimony, practice and affections. The Latter Rain restoration of Pentecostal power was for last-days evangelization. Their mission was to warn the church to repent, consecrate, put on the robes of white, and get oil in the lamp before the Bridegroom appeared. The everlasting gospel, the gospel of the kingdom was to be heralded by witnesses whose mouths had tasted the powers of the age to come and whose eyes had seen evidence of that power at work among them.

It was urgent that men and women be called from darkness into light, because the kingdom age was already dawning. Believers were to be entirely sanctified. With Wesley they could agree that faith in Jesus Christ 'qualified' them for heaven and entire sanctification made them 'fit' for heaven.[1] If believers regarded iniquity in their hearts, they would not be ready for the Rapture; and would go through the Great Tribulation. Furthermore, those resistances and hold-outs in their personal lives would hinder their receptivity to the Holy Spirit and they would be poor witnesses for the Lord. The 'law of love' required that believers wash their robes and make them white in the blood of the Lamb. Willful refusal to do so could lead ultimately to one's name being blotted out of the 'Lamb's book of life'.

The baptism in the Holy Spirit was to be upon the sanctified life. The same Spirit who would resurrect the dead and rapture the Bride would fill every hungry, obedient seeker. This filling seemed to be a further step toward the realization of the resurrection hope in that yet more power was bestowed and one was 'sealed' and made 'rapture ready'.

Healing was in anticipation of the final healing of all things. The material was meant for the spiritual and vice-versa. Healing anticipated a millennial restoration of all things: heaven come to earth and no more sickness or sorrow. This longing for universal healing is expressed in the words of a popular gospel song 'Our Lord's Return to Earth' (based on Acts 2.9, 10, 11):

---

1.   J. Wesley, 'On the Wedding Garment', in A.C. Outler (ed.), *The Works of John Wesley: Sermons IV* (Nashville: Abingdon Press, 1987), pp. 139-48.

I am watching for the coming of the glad millennial day,
When our blessed Lord shall come and catch His waiting Bride away.
O my heart is filled with rapture as I labor, watch and pray,
For our Lord is coming back to earth again.

Jesus' coming back will be the answer to earth's sorrowing cry,
For the knowledge of the Lord shall fill the earth and sea and sky;
God shall take away all sickness and the sufferer's tears will dry,
When our Savior shall come back to earth again.

Yes, the ransomed of the Lord shall come to Zion then with joy,
And in all His holy mountain nothing hurts or shall destroy;
Perfect peace shall reign in every heart, and love without alloy
After Jesus shall come back to earth again.

Then the sin and sorrow, pain and death of this dark world shall cease,
In a glorious reign with Jesus of a thousand years of peace;
All the earth is groaning, crying for that day of sweet release,
For our Jesus to come back to earth again.

CHORUS
Oh! our Lord is coming back to earth again,
Yes, our Lord is coming back to earth again;
Satan will be bound a thousand years, we'll have no tempter then,
After Jesus shall come back to earth again.[1]

Already the Bride was being prepared; already hearts were filled with 'rapture' as they labored, watched and prayed. The saints 'groaned' with the Spirit and all the earth for the 'day of sweet release'. Already, many sicknesses were being healed, sins forgiven, sorrower's tears dried. The peace born in yielded hearts filled with love 'without alloy' was already reigning in believers. The faith, worldview, experience and practice of Pentecostals was thoroughly eschatological. They lived within the tension of the already but not yet consummated kingdom. If the Holy Spirit was at the heart of this tension, He was also the bridge or bond between the ages.

As was true for John Wesley, so too Pentecostals traveled in the Spirit forward or backward in time—back to Sinai, back to Calvary, back to Pentecost—forward to the Armageddon, the Great White Throne Judgment, the Marriage Supper of the Lamb. Time and space were fused and transcended in the Spirit, and at the heart of the testimony expectation and worship was Jesus the Savior, Sanctifier,

1.   *Church Hymnal* (Cleveland, TN: Tennessee Music and Printing Co., 1951), p. 327.

Healer, Baptizer with the Spirit and coming King. God the Father received all prodigals through Jesus in the Spirit. And then he sent them out in Jesus' name and the power of the promised Spirit, to preach the gospel of Christ to all nations...and then would be the end.

Taking due account of this eschatological context renders the spirituality comprehensible and useful for analysis and revision.

An Overview

The thesis of this study will be developed in two interrelated chapters. First, taking into account the theoretical, historical and personal concerns of Chapter 1, the distinctive blend of narrative beliefs and worship-witness practices is analyzed in Chapter 2, as the ethos of Pentecostal spirituality is displayed. It is argued that the 'already–not yet' tension characteristic of the eschatological vision is decisively important for understanding the shape and power of this spirituality.

The heart or integrating center of the spirituality is located in the affections. Chapter 3 attempts to show how three essential affections— gratitude as praise-thanksgiving, compassion as love-longing, and courage as confidence-hope—are ingredient in the Pentecostal understanding and experience of salvation, worship, witness and, most importantly, prayer. These affections operate by a certain 'grammar' and exist in a reciprocally conditioning mode with the beliefs and practices. They may be legitimately termed 'apocalyptic affections' since they are constituted by the distinctive eschatological reality and vision of Pentecostals.

Having displayed these central beliefs, practices and affections, Chapter 4 offers a re-vision of Pentecostal spirituality which remains in continuity with the original spirituality of the movement. Certain internal tensions and external criticisms are noted and briefly responded to in the light of the development in the foregoing chapters. These tensions and criticisms also serve as part of the motivation for the re-vision. The construction offered seeks to ground a vision of the Christian life, history, church and mission in an explicitly Trinitarian spirituality which is historically consistent, in keeping with the roots of the movement, internally healing of some of the major divisions, ecumenically responsive, and missionally deepened.

Thus the structure of this monograph moves from a distinctive formulation of spirituality and the theological task I have just articulated to an analysis of the constituative beliefs and practices in Chapter 2, to the integration of the beliefs and practices in the affections in Chapter 3, and finally, to a revision of the spirituality using a Trinitarian hermeneutic in Chapter 4.

Chapter 2

PENTECOSTAL SPIRITUALITY AS APOCALYPTIC VISION:
A NARRATIVE-PRAXIS ANALYSIS

Early Pentecostals understood the outpourings of the Spirit in the first
century at Pentecost and at the inception of the twentieth-century
Pentecostal movement as the fulfillment of divine promises, especially
Joel's prophecy concerning the last days.[1] In these instances the
fulfillment contained at the same time an 'overflow' of promise yet to
be fulfilled, and, on both occasions, the interpretation of the event was
the proclamation of the gospel which was at once about Jesus and the
end. Pentecostalism's reason for existence was the carrying out of a
last-days, global, missionary mandate by those who were Christ-like
witnesses in the power of the Holy Spirit. The kingdom of God was at
work among God's people, and the evidence was much the same in the
twentieth as in the first century. The wonders and gifts of the Holy
Spirit in the ministry of Jesus were being repeated,[2] but these were
not the only signs observed by the early Pentecostals. The following
early testimony and song indicate the 'signs of the times' and the
appropriate response.

> The Lord's coming is no doubt drawing near. Many signs are now being
> seen which are in perfect accord with the prophecy of Scripture, but two
> signs are indeed prevalent just now, and can be noticed by any one who is
> on the look out. The love of many is waxing cold because iniquity is
> abounding. Mt. 25.12.

> By actions, if not by words, many are saying, 'My Lord delayeth His
> coming. Lk. 12.45. In their testimonies they used to express themselves
> with a glow of heavenly luster beaming forth from their countenance, that
> they believed Jesus was coming so soon, and were so happy because they

---

1. Joel 2.28-32. See R. Stronstad, *The Charismatic Theology of St Luke*
(Peabody, MA: Hendrickson, 1984).
2. Mt. 11.4-6; Lk. 11.20.

felt they were ready to meet Him. Today many of these same voices are silent on that line. Wake up, loved ones, your Lord will come while you are sleeping, if you do not stir yourselves and watch. He will come at an hour that you think not. Come! Awake! Be Ready! You can be ready if you will. Stir up the gift that is in you, by prayer and fasting if needs be, and testimony and praise, until you are all aglow and overflowing with His love again.

No matter what the rest may do, no matter what they say,
Keep the fire burning in your soul, fire up!
Be true to God, and He'll reward you at the judgment day,
Keep the fire burning in your soul, fire up!

And when your heart is growing cold, you'll need to fire up.
Keep the fire burning in your soul, fire up!
Just tarry in the upper room until your heart is stirred,
Keep the fire burning in your soul, fire up![1]

The urgent fervency issuing from the apocalyptic vision of Pentecostals is evidenced by a worship and witness which is crucially dependent upon the witness of the Spirit and therefore constantly concerned with the presence and parousia of Jesus Christ. Though Pentecostalism is often written off as mere emotionalism or an experience safely transplanted into various Christian gardens, this chapter shows the distinctive logic of Pentecostal beliefs and practices as they both express and confirm the apocalyptic reality which did and still does suffuse and inform the corporate life of the community. After a consideration of the original apocalyptic vision and the three-fold Pentecostal experience, I examine this spirituality more analytically by means of four formal categories. Testimonies, songs, articles, pamphlets and books will be woven into the fabric of this running narrative-praxis account.

Pentecostal Presence: The Inbreaking of the Spirit in the Last Days

God, who is spirit, is present in triune fellowship by virtue of the activity of the Holy Spirit, in and among the believers. The 'natural' person cannot know, love or follow God.[2] It is the spiritual responsive person who can walk in the light, walk in love, and walk in the power of the Spirit as a witness. It is the Spirit who brings the Son and the

1. *The Evening Light and Church of God Evangel* 1.1 (March 1, 1916), p. 8.
2. 1 Cor. 2.14-16.

Father to abide in the believer.[1] The church is made a habitation of
God through the Spirit.[2] By the Spirit the believers taste the powers of
the age to come[3] and receive the down payment or pledge of the
promised redemption.[4] The Spirit is the effective reigning power and
sovereign agent of the kingdom whose king is Jesus.[5] The Spirit is the
'finger of God' who drives out demons, cleanses lepers and empowers
gospel proclamation.[6] According to the early Pentecostals, it was this
concrete, visible work of the Holy Spirit in worship and witness which
was being received in these last days.

Apostolic Faith: Recovering the Eschatological Vision
Pentecostals referred to themselves as an apostolic faith movement due
to their desire to recover for the present age the faith and the power
of the apostolic church. Paradoxically, it was this primitivistic,
backward-looking concern with the early church which was responsible for their passion for the coming of Christ. For them a restoration of primitive faith was a prelude to the restoraiton of all things.

They exhibited three kinds of primitivism, two of which were
carried over from the nineteenth century. Their ecclesiastical primitivism led them to be suspicious of 'man made' creeds and institutions.
Their ethical primitivism called them to an all-consuming passion for
holiness. God's people, the Bride of Christ, must wash their robes and
make them white in the blood of the Lamb. But it was the experiential
primitivism which catalyzed the other two and directed everything
toward the soon coming of the Lord. Believers today, they reasoned,
can, should and must evidence the same longing and power as the first
Christians, if they are to be in eschatological continuity with the
beginning and end of the church of Pentecost. To recover the
apostolic faith meant to live in expectation of the coming of Christ in
the time of the Latter Rain.

Thus, the outpouring of the Spirit at Pentecost constituted the
church as an eschatological community of universal mission in the

1.   Jn 14.16.
2.   Eph. 2.22.
3.   Heb. 6.1-6.
4.   2 Cor. 1.23; Eph. 1.14.
5.   Jn 3.8.
6.   Lk. 11.20; Mt. 11.4-6.

power and demonstration of the Spirit.[1] The tongues at Pentecost and Peter's subsequent sermon meant that the church in general and each Spirit-filled individual are to be and to give a witness to the mighty acts of God in saving humanity. This witness centers in Jesus Christ and must therefore be given in the power of the Spirit if it is to have continuity with his ministry and fulfill the promise of the Father through Christ. The 'full gospel' of the Jesus who is Savior, Sanctifier, Healer, Baptizer in the Holy Spirit and coming King can and should be proclaimed in the fullness of the Spirit so that the kingdom will be manifested in the midst of the world in words and deeds.

When men and women came into Pentecostal services and experienced this eschatological power, this restoration of apostolic age, they saw the Scriptures, themselves and the world differently: the resurrection of Jesus as their own resurrection, the first Pentecost as their own 'Pentecost', the crucifixion of Jesus as their own crucifixion—all these events were telescoped, fused and illumined by the expectation that became the message of the entire Pentecostal movement: 'Jesus is coming soon!' And how did they know that this outpouring of the Spirit was the Latter Rain, the sign of the imminent arrival of the king? Because they, like those with Peter in Cornelius's household, heard them speak with other tongues.[2] Signs and wonders, even outbreaks of tongues, had occurred throughout history but never as part of such a large-scale restoration of apostolic faith and power.

Outsiders focused quickly on the tongues as indicative of a whole movement of irrational, revivalistic, hysterical protest by the disinherited and illiterate. If it was not evidence of demonization, which some fundamentalists still maintain, then it was, at best, proof of derangement. The reactions of those who came into direct contact with the movement went from one extreme to the other—from the 'last vomit of Satan' to regressive gibberish.[3]

But this eschatological key, this apocalyptic revelatory experience, was seen by the Pentecostals as the driving force and galvanizing vision of the entire movement. This is beginning to be appreciated today outside the movement also. In addition to the massive, carefully crafted

1. H.R. Boer, *Pentecost and Missions* (Grand Rapids: Eerdmans, 1961).
2. Acts 10.46-47.
3. H. Ward, 'The Anti-Pentecostal Argument', in Synan (ed.), *Aspects*, pp. 99-111.

and overwhelmingly persuasive dissertation of William Faupel,[1] there
are those like the Dominican John Orme Mills who understand that

> what made the Pentecostal revival in the United States at the beginning of
> this century important, what set it against the world and much contempor-
> ary religious practice as if it were something startlingly new, something
> that could transform men's lives, was not (to take the most obvious
> example) that people 'spoke in tongues'. After all, if considered apart
> from its Christian context, speaking in tongues is not a particularly
> interesting or unusual phenomenon, let alone something to astonish or
> disconcert the Christian world.
>
> No, what was arresting about those first twentieth-century Pentecostals
> was their conviction (a conviction tongue-speaking and the other gifts they
> had been given irrefutably confirmed, in their opinion) that the new
> pouring-out of God's Holy Spirit on them had empowered them to share
> fully the life of the church of the apostles, the 'church of Pentecost'.
> And—so alive was their vision of the New Testament church—this meant
> that they experienced a fresh, urgent sense of expectation which they
> could identify with that known by the first generation of Christians. The
> charismatic manifestations emerging among them—tongues, healing,
> exorcism, prophecy—they interpreted as signs that they were bringing in
> the 'last times'. The Scriptures were being fulfilled: here was the 'latter
> rain' spoken of by Joel and James, portending the coming of the Lord in
> glory at the world's end. Is it surprising then, that they had such confi-
> dence, such hope? Were they not already seeing around them indications
> that all things were being made new, as told in the book of Revelation?[2]

Although Mills may not assign as much significance to the sign of
tongues as some early Pentecostals, he nevertheless is on the opposite
side from those observers and commentators who classify this as a
'tongues-movement'. It is only within the gestalt of the apocalyptic
narrative, the narrative of which the Pentecostals now saw themselves
as being a significant part, that the meaning of the spirituality can be
known. To locate the theological center of Pentecostalism in Spirit

1.   Faupel, 'Everlasting Gospel'.
2.   The first three chapters of the book of Revelation reveal Jesus Christ and the
state of the church as known by him and addressed by the Holy Spirit. Revelation is
thus an unveiling of the meaning of history in Jesus Christ by the Holy Spirit and the
progressive and particular dealing of God with the church and world in the light of
the end. See J.O. Mills, 'New Heaven? New Earth?', in S. Tugwell, G. Every,
P. Hocken and J.O. Mills, *New Heaven? New Earth?* (London: Darton, Longman
& Todd, 1976).

baptism, as Bruner does,[1] or to see tongues as the only thing that distinguishes the spirituality from that of the Holiness or evangelical movements is to miss the point altogether. It is the eschatological shift within the Holiness movement toward premillennialism that signals what is decisive. Dayton and Faupel have described this shift; however it is crucial to note that this is not a shift away from Christ to the Spirit, from love to power, or from gradual to instantaneous change of persons and society.[2] These realities are more fused together than split apart or even prioritized. It is an infusion—because of the Spirit's effusion—of apocalyptic vision and power which alters the way in which Christ, church, the Christian life and change are seen. As Käsemann said of 'all Christian theology' so it can be said of Pentecostal theology, 'Apocalyptic was the mother...'[3] Pentecostals were adopted by and adopted this 'mother' and became sons and daughters, prophets and prophetesses of a new order of the Latter Rain of the Spirit.

The social deprivation and functional adaptation to psychosocial strain models of analysis, used to great and informative advantage by someone like Robert Mapes Anderson (*Vision of the Disinherited: The Making of American Pentecostalism*), tell only the most obvious and superficially interesting part of the story. Grant Wacker, in reviewing Anderson's book, underscores the point made here as to the importance of apocalyptic discontinuity for understanding the pneumatic continuity of the Pentecostals with the early church. He asserts that

> Long after the computers have shut down and the behavioral scientists have gone home, the real work of the 'new' social historian remains to be done: somehow to understand the dialectic between social forms and the private lives inside. This means, among other things, that the historian who seeks to untangle the origins of a religious movement like Pentecostalism is charged with the task of showing how plain men and women, locked into a particular position in the social system, paradoxically invested their lives with significance by discerning chaos in order as well as the reverse. It may well turn out that the enduring significance of the vision of the disinherited is that it flourished precisely because it was so desperately out of step with the times...[4]

1. Bruner was the first to use the term 'pneumatobaptistocentrism'. See his *A Theology of the Holy Spirit*, esp. p. 337, index entry, 'Christocentricity'.
2. Faupel, 'Everlasting Gospel', pp. 134-95.
3. Käsemann, *New Testament Questions of Today*, p. 102.
4. G. Wacker, Review of *Vision of the Disinherited* by R.M. Anderson,

They would have said that the movement flourished because it afforded an
exhilarating vision that life on earth could be a foretaste of heaven. And a
warning of the wrath to come.[1]

The outpouring of the Spirit in the post-Easter community created
and sustained that eschatological tension and vision which characterized the early church and the early Pentecostals. Now everything was
considered from the standpoint of the imminent parousia. In the
transcendent presence of God categories of time and space were fused;
and, since Jesus was near, so was the end. The Spirit who raised Jesus,
made him present in salvation, signs and wonders, and showed things
to come. The Spirit who burned as intense hope and energized
witness, superintended the ongoing mission. To live in the Spirit was
to live in the kingdom. Where the Spirit was present in eschatological
power, there was the church of Pentecost. In concluding his treatise
on *The Spirit and the Bride*, Revd G.F. Taylor offered the following
advice to those who wanted to be equipped for service and ready for
the appearance of the Bridegroom:

> While you may be greatly helped by following these directions, yet you
> must avoid all formality. You cannot bring God down to any special form
> in any matter. The best advice after all is, Get in the Spirit, stay in the
> Spirit, and follow the Spirit at any cost.[2]

This means that eschatology (and especially the apocalyptic vision)
is neither an introduction nor a postscript to theology but a constituent
part of the whole. It is 'a conceptualization which is prescribed by
Jesus' proclamation of the kingdom and his appearances after the
resurrection'.[3] It is an apocalypticism which 'begins with the special,
contingent history of Jesus Christ, the resurrection of the crucified
and his Easter appearances, and aims at the universal deity of this
God. It inquires after the future of God and proclaims his coming in
proclaiming Christ'.[4]

Pneuma 4.2 (Fall, 1982), pp. 53-62.
    1.   G. Wacker, 'The Functions of Faith', pp. 353-75.
    2.   G.F. Taylor, 'The Spirit and the Bride', in D.W. Dayton (ed.), *Three Early
Pentecostal Tracts* (repr.; New York: Garland Publishers, 1985).
    3.   J.R. Drayer, 'The Significance of Apocalypticism in Contemporary British
Eschatology' (ThD dissertation, Southern Baptist Theological Seminary, 1970),
p. 242.
    4.   J. Moltmann, 'Theology as Eschatology', in F. Herzog (ed.), *The Future of
Hope* (New York: Herder & Herder, 1970), p. 7.

In his recent work *Holiness in Israel* John Gammie has found that the apocalyptic writers catch up the themes of the priests, prophets and sages, but integrate them into their own eschatological concerns. The holiness of God as well as the end itself is not capable of being co-opted or manipulated by the present. But this very distance creates a new history, new possibilities that are announced and moved forward by God and those who live in the divine Spirit by the Word.

Apocalyptic Faith: Living in the Last Days
Just as Pentecost was added to the teachings of Jesus in the experience of the early church, the baptism in the Holy Spirit was added to the fourfold gospel (Jesus as Savior, Sanctifier, Healer, coming King) of the Holiness movement. The baptism in the Spirit was a break, a discontinuity, a definite definable, ineffable turning point in the history of the church and the early Pentecostals. It was a break that signalled God's intervention in and sufficiency for the missionary task of announcing the gospel of the kingdom to all nations before the end. This meant that the nexus of socio-political cause and effect, of demonic and even religious opposition and hindrances—none of this could stop the fulfillment of God's plan.

This gave a new sense of hope to each believer. It was the Father's will to give them the kingdom.[1] This hope would keep them pure, utterly sincere and devoted to the mission. The outpouring of the Spirit made them primary and not secondary witnesses of the risen Lord. They could say what they had seen and heard concerning the ongoing work of Jesus Christ to save, to heal, to deliver and so forth. Hope is not given by and in and for the present world order that is passing away. This does not mean they demeaned this world. It was a hope which had continuity—a new body, a new earth, a new heaven. But this hope was at the same time discontinuous because it is new—a new creation. With one foot in creation and the other in the age to come, the Pentecostals hoped for the salvation of the lost and longed for Jesus to come.

His coming was imminent, but no date could be set. Everyday life and events became invested with cosmic significance because God was at work in all things. There were not many *adiaphora* for Pentecostals; indeed this was not a time for silly, foolish jesting or

1. Lk. 12.32.

taking chances with the ways of the world. The Lord was near. The holiness practices and restrictions from the nineteenth century were retained by most North American Pentecostals for almost half a century. Even today they remain conservative on most issues, though of course now that certain luxuries are more affordable they are not seen as quite the compromise with the world that they once were.[1] However, with regard to the sense of break, a new hope and the awareness of being involved in a cosmic struggle with powers and principalities—in all these respects Pentecostalism lived and lives in an apocalyptic existence made existentially palpable by the presence, manifestations and power of the Holy Spirit.[2]

This longing for the Lord to come, for the Holy Spirit and for the kingdom of God are part of the same thing: it is one passion. And for Pentecostals it is a passion that can change everything. The baptism in the Holy Spirit was the gateway into this eschatologically oriented vocation of witness. Entrance through that gateway might be very forceful, as in the case of university-educated N.J. Holmes, or very gentle, as in the case of Joseph H. King, one of the early leaders of the Pentecostal Holiness Church. Holmes reports that he

> fasted for three days, without eating or drinking anything... At times everything was dark, so dark that everything in my experience seemed to go away... One night as my heart was going up for the Holy Ghost, it seemed that the whole room was filling with a mist of heaven, and my whole body was being permeated by it. And a great roll of mist above my head as a waterfall... I felt my tongue slightly moving up and down, the motion growing stronger and stronger. I was conscious that it was not I, that did it, and I was sure it was the Holy Ghost, and immediately my teeth began to chatter without my effort or control... I recognized the presence and power of the Holy Ghost in all this, and as soon as I discovered the control of my mouth I testified and praised God for Pentecost.[3]

---

1. The Church of God, Cleveland Tennessee, for example, no longer has bans on jewelry, movies, etc. Now that more is affordable, it seems that more has become permissible. The ethical statements are no longer short, blunt prohibitions; now they are principles and propositions with appropriate Scriptures correlated to each. As the story changed so did the ethic. But no new unifying story has emerged to guide ethical behavior, and 'affordability' is clearly neither a biblical nor a particularly theologically satisfying ethical stance.

2. J.O. Mills in Tugwell, *et al.*, *New Heaven? New Earth?*, pp. 69-118.

3. N.J. Holmes and L.S. Holmes, *Life Sketches and Sermons: The Story of*

Holmes's journey from Presbyterianism to the Holiness movement to Pentecostalism is fascinating in itself, but what is really significant for our purposes is the intense longing for God and the deep satisfaction that obtained when he was visited with his 'Pentecost'. Changes of denomination were common and so it is no surprise that creeds were not given ultimate authority (a misunderstanding of creeds to be sure). The point, however, is that the coming of the Spirit was so definite and so deep that any change was possible if necessary to obtain the blessing, the equipment, the 'Pentecost'. Some were like the Methodist minister in Kansas who objected that Pentecostals failed to keep 'the niggers in their place'. But before he could have his baptism in the Spirit he had to wade through a whole camp meeting made up of mostly African-Americans. He subsequently testified, 'God surely broke me over the wheel of my prejudice'.[1]

Continuity with one's racial, cultural and/or denominational identity might be disrupted and altered by the discontinuous Spirit baptism. In establishing experiential, pneumatic continuity with the first-century church of Pentecost one was forced to consider conformity with the church of the end, the holy Bride made up of all races, tongues and nationalities. The early Pentecostals, though noting previous revivals of the Spirit and charismatic manifestations throughout history, did not do so to establish or to legitimate their practice. Rather Pentecostals leap

> the intervening years crying, 'Back to Pentecost'... They do not recognize a doctrine or custom as authoritative unless it can be traced to that primal source of church institution, the Lord and His apostles... If we can so order our lives that they shall fit the New Testament, we care no more for a lack of evidence that the majority of professors of religion did so in the past than we do for the overwhelming evidence that the majority of them are not doing so today.[2]

In this passage B.F.Lawrence, a Pentecostal pioneer, illustrates what some have called the ahistorical character of the movement—or a desire to leap the ages back to Pentecost. But seen in another way it is

Pentecostal Pioneer N.J. Holmes (Royston, GA: Press of the Pentecostal Holiness Church, 1920), pp. 139, 140, 143, 144.

1. *Pentecostal Evangel* (March 22, 1924), 6, 7, cited in Wacker, 'The Functions of Faith', p. 155.

2. B.F. Lawrence, 'The Apostolic Faith Restored', in D.W. Dayton (ed.), *Three Early Pentecostal Tracts* (New York: Garland Publishers, 1985), p. 12.

a prophetic concern to return to the root, the original covenant, as the prophets of Israel were constantly saying to the religious establishment of their day. The future can only become the promise of God if there is first a word, an apocalyptic convincing of sin, righteousness and judgment, which gives voice to and makes a space for the cry of the dispossessed, the languishing mass who feel removed from the immediacy of God and victimized by cultural and ecclesiastical forces which tend to shut down their historical process.[1]

A relativizing of the establishment and its processes is necessary in order to break through, to give voice to the pain of those longing for God and the world that is lost. For thousands of the participants in the more radical Holiness groups, being born again, and receiving a sanctifying filling of love intensified this longing. Back to Pentecost meant back to the Holy Spirit and then forward to the future that God will give soon—not the product of the predict-and-control technology from the culture of evolutionary optimism, critical realism and 'embourgeoised' elitism. The Pentecostals were committed to the fundamental beliefs of Christianity but, in the words of B.F.Lawrence again, were

> laboring to obtain that supernatural character of religion which was so pre-
> eminently a mark of it in the old days. We do not mean to say that others
> who believe in the new birth have wholly lost this, but we desire a return
> to New Testament power and custom along all those lines of activity
> which made evident beyond controversy that the church was the living
> body of a living Christ. We believe that healing for the body, expulsion of
> demons, speaking in other tongues, were in early times the result of an
> activity of the Holy Spirit in direct harmony with, nay, stronger still, a
> direct result of the divine attitude toward the church and world. Further,
> we hold that this attitude was the only one consistent with the divine
> nature. If this is true, then with the writer of the Letter to the Hebrews we
> say, 'Jesus Christ, the same yesterday, today and forever,' and expect the
> immutable nature to maintain an unchanged attitude accompanied by the
> same glorious results.[2]

God had not changed. The promises were for the children and the children's children—as many as God would call.[3] The recovery of Pentecostal power—a definite, visible historical occurrence—was a

1.   W. Brueggeman, 'II Kings 18, 19: The Legitimacy of a Sectarian Hermeneutic', *HBT* 7 (1985), pp. 1-42.

2.   Lawrence, 'The Apostolic Faith Restored', p. 13.

3.   Acts 2.39.

fulfillment of the promise of the Father which was necessary to carry out the global missionary mandate of the church. That having been accomplished and all the nations having heard the gospel in power and demonstration of the Spirit, the promised coming of the King of Kings to catch away the Bride could occur.

Pentecostals, to repeat an emphasis of Chapter 1 and the beginning of this chapter, were people of the promise. Of course the Holiness movement of the nineteenth century had also spoken much of the promise of the Father. But for Pentecostals the fulfillment of the Pentecostal promise in visible, concrete, global manifestations announced something new that God was doing and about to do. It gave a sense of history and directedness to individual lives. The present was passing away, the future was expected, sought and anticipated. The kingdom of righteousness, peace and joy in the Holy Spirit was already at work and soon to be consummated. Thus the present was to be lived in hope, obedience and holiness. God, who has not changed, will keep the divine promises and give surprises, representations, intimations, glimpses of the future along the way through gifts of the Spirit. Each time a believer was filled with the Spirit, each time the power fell in a new assembly or country, history drew nearer its proper end. The church, the individual, the family—everything had to change in light of the new direction, impetus and focus.

This end had begun with the life, death and resurrection of Jesus. Though elements of apocalyptic faith had been restored after the fall of the church in the Constantinian era, now, with the recovery of the universal 'prophethood' and witness of all believers, the restoration of apostolic gifts and power, and the baptism of the Spirit 'upon the sanctified life',[1] all was in place for the total mobilization of the church. History became mission, and the church was constituted a missionary movement. Believers were agents, not victims; they were harbingers of the coming kingdom. The Bride did not simply wait in the church for the Bridegroom; she went out to invite others to the marriage supper for which each worship service was a rehearsal and anticipation.

---

1.   The phrase baptism of the Holy Spirit upon the sanctified life recurs frequently in *The Apostolic Faith*, and seems to indicate that the earliest Wesleyan-Pentecostals saw sanctification as a transforming, and Spirit baptism as an empowering, work of grace.

The historical event of the twentieth-century restoration of Pentecost and the reality of the not yet fully consummated kingdom of God were united in category of promise. The promised Spirit, the promised kingdom, the promised filling with the Holy Spirit, the promised gifts, all these were promises believed and received by the Pentecostals. By believing these promises the believer became a partaker of God's nature, a citizen of the present and coming kingdom, and a participant in a world-historical process whose end was assured, because God was working in all things for good.

This was no occasion for resignation in the face of the 'fate of God'. Rather one must now walk in the light, walk in love, walk in the power of the Spirit, if one was to walk with God. The kingdom that was coming was one of righteousness, perfect love, fullness of joy in the Holy Spirit, healing for the nations, and a final victory over death and Satan. To believe in that kingdom was to walk according to the nature, will and goal of the king. Salvation was participation in the life of God through transformations by grace through faith. History was God's story and each person had a part to play, a gift to offer, a witness to give. There was something of what Moltmann describes as 'good apocalyptic', that is a 'historifying of the world' and a 'universalizing of history'.[1]

But if there was this 'good apocalyptic' there was also the 'bad' kind. At times, persons who had been so used to being passive would lapse into the view of prophecy as fate. They would see God as only over against the world, especially during times of cultural rejection and persecution. Failing to see prophecy in its historical context they would sometimes develop highly speculative, individualized and fantastic concrete applications which thrilled but did not mobilize. To the extent that they saw themselves as fundamentalist conservatives, as over against the modernist liberals, they forfeited much of the

1. A.J. Conyers, *God, Hope and History: Jürgen Moltmann and the Christian Concept of History* (Macon, GA: Mercer University Press, 1988), p. 77. Conyers is a reliable guide and provides a helpful overview of Moltmann's discussion on 'historifying of the world' and 'universalizing of history'. See Moltmann's comment ('While apocalyptic does conceive its eschatology in cosmological terms, yet there is not the end of eschatology, but the beginning of an eschatological cosmology or an eschatological ontology for which being becomes historic and the cosmos opens itself to the apocalyptic process') on p. 137 and further discussion in his *Theology of Hope* (trans. J.W. Leitch; New York: Harper, 1967), pp. 124-38.

nineteenth-century Holiness birthright of 'spreading scriptural holiness throughout the land'.[1] Soup kitchens, orphanages, rescue missions and so on were all employed, but the broader societal, global and cosmic dimensions of the kingdom were limited to one thing: the preaching of the gospel to all nations.

Initially the realization of apocalyptic spirituality gave a sense of belonging, dignity and power to many who had seen themselves as victims. Although all Pentecostals fall into the category of the oppressed, many, perhaps most, were from among the poor. Yet the majority of those poor who heard the Pentecostal message did not accept it. Thus, social location cannot adequately account for the movement or the motivation of those who became participants then or more recently.

But what is not at issue is that for early Pentecostals the church was to be a witness in the power of the Spirit in the last days. They were a people hungry for God and filled with premillennial expectancy. Today, upward social mobility is clearly affecting the apocalyptic fervor and urgency as the world looks a little better to contemporary, more affluent North American Pentecostals. They often have a guilty conscience and struggle with their roots.[2] The early eschatological expectancy and fervent witness activity are seen more nearly in its pristine state among the burgeoning Third World Pentecostals. They, as the early Pentecostals, keep 'fired up' by means of the narratives and practices which each missionary fellowship employs to explain and demonstrate the kingdom of God in its worship and witness.

Pentecostal Narratives: Participating in the Story of God

The Biblical Drama and the Christian Life
On the first day of Pentecost worship and witness marked the entrance of the church, and thus each believer, into a new phase of the salvation-history drama of redemption. Peter's address to the multitudes who rush together questioning the meaning of this event reveals—in a 'this is that' specification—that this is a specific fulfillment of biblical prophecy requiring obedience to the gospel of Jesus

1. T. Smith, *Revivalism and Social Reform* (Gloucester, MA: Peter Smith, 1957).
2. M. Poloma, *The Assemblies of God at the Crossroads: Charisma and Institutional Dilemmas* (Knoxville: University of Tennessee Press, 1989).

Christ. It is confirmation of the exaltation of the risen Lord and an anticipation of his parousia. The promises of the coming of the Spirit and the coming again of the Savior are part of the one promise of God to redeem his creation. [1]

On the day of Pentecost Peter announced—in the city where Jesus had been crucified, a city dominated by Rome, the city where he had denied Jesus—that a new chapter was being written. Crucifixion, resurrection, Pentecost, parousia, all formed one great redemption, one story in which they were participants with assigned roles to play. Pentecost meant that the victory witnessed in the resurrection of the crucified one and the promised parousia would not simply be told by those who wait passively for the soon coming of the Lord. No, the power of the age to come was being poured out upon the church for the accomplishment of a universal proclamation of the particular redemption in Jesus Christ, a proclamation in word and power and demonstration of the Spirit.

The early Pentecostals saw themselves as recovering and re-entering that Pentecostal reality. The vivid presence of the Spirit heightened expectation, propelled into mission, enlivened worship and increased consecration in preparation for the appearance of the Lord of the

---

1.   The whole context of Acts 1 and 2 is eschatological: it is a salvific fusion of Old Testament prophecies, the life, death, resurrection and parousia of Jesus, and the outpouring of the Holy Spirit. All these themes found expression in the Pentecostals' evangelization, eschatological vision and experience of Spirit-filling. See G.E. Ladd, *The Presence of the Future* (Grand Rapids: Eerdmans, 1974), pp. 322, 324, 327:

> The same God who is now acting in historical events to bring about a fulfillment of the messianic salvation will act out the end of history to bring his kingdom to its consummation... The important point is that these two redemptive acts—the historical and the eschatological—are in fact one redemptive event in two parts... *The eschatological consummation of the kingdom is inseparable from and dependent upon what God is doing in the historical person and mission of Jesus...*
>
> The motif of the apocalypses (IV Ezra 4.25ff.; see also 6.18ff.; 8.63ff.; En.80.2ff.; 99.1ff.; 100.1ff.; Jub. 23.16ff.; Sib.Or. 2.199.; Apoc.Bar. 25.1ff.; 48.31ff.; 70.2.ff.) is that the evil which has dominated the age will become so intense at the end that complete chaos will reign, both in human social relationships and in the natural order. The motif in the Olivet Discourse (Mt. 24.3ff) is an extension of the conflict motif which characterized both Jesus' mission and the mission of His disciples in this age. Jesus agreed with the apocalyptists that evil will mark the course of the age; the kingdom of God will abolish evil only in the age to come. But into this evil age something new has come: the good news (Mark 13.10) about the kingdom of God (Mt. 24.14). This message of God's redemptive acts in history must be proclaimed in all the world before the end comes. Therefore history is not abandoned to evil.

harvest. No one could take for granted her or his place at the marriage supper of the Lamb. The wise virgins would have oil in their lamps, would be filled with the Spirit, watching, waiting, working for the Bridegroom.[1] The paradox of expecting a sudden event and not knowing when it would occur—waiting in readiness and indeterminacy—was paralleled by the vigorous activity in worship and witness (preparing the saints and the world for his coming) and the abiding rest of the saints.[2] Watching and at rest, witnessing and worshipping, seeking the Lord and waiting on the Lord, these were the rhythms of the early revival. And all of this made sense in the light of what God had done, was doing and would finish.

This story of redemption in the Spirit made sense of the 'ups and downs' of the daily life of the participants. In the Spirit they walked with the children of Israel, the prophets, the apostles and early church believers. In the Spirit they anticipated the great marriage supper of the Lamb at the last day. In the Spirit the blessings and trials of each day were interpreted as part of the one story of redemption. Thus, by interpreting their daily life and worship in terms of the significant events of biblical history, their own lives and actions were given significance. Everybody became a witness to Calvary and his or her own crucifixion with Christ, the biblical Pentecost and a personal Pentecost, the healings of the disciples and his or her own healing and so on. The singing reflected this idea of the present normativity of biblical events and therefore, for that very reason, the necessity of existential appropriation and participation.

> At the Cross, At the Cross
> Where I first saw the light
> And the burdens of my heart rolled away.
> It was there by faith, I received my sight,
> And now I am happy all the day.[3]

Thus for them Calvary was not only a specific historical event but also a testimony and focus for daily life. From the blood of Christ's atonement, as it was said over and over, all benefits flow.

These benefits of complete redemption were already present as

---

1. The parable of the wise and foolish virgins was a favorite sermon and article topic in early Pentecostal circles. It served as an apologetic and an exhortation for Spirit filling which was equated with 'oil in the lamp'.

2. Ladd, *Presence*, p. 328.

3. *Church Hymnal*, p. 264.

promise, type and shadow in the Old Testament. *The Apostolic Faith* in September of 1907 proclaimed the 'Old Testament Feasts Fulfilled In Our Souls Today':

> All through the Old Testament we read of the feasts that God appointed to be kept in the worship to Him. There were four feasts: the Passover Feast, Feast of First Fruits, Feast of Pentecost (or Feast of Weeks), and Feast of Tabernacles. They all typify what we get through the cross now, justification, sanctification, the baptism with the Holy Ghost, and then a continual feast. Together they typify a complete redemption.[1]

For those early Pentecostals to abide in the Word was simultaneously to abide in Jesus and the written Word. Seymour stated that 'as long as you live in the Word of God, He will always be present'.[2] The redemption events live in the believers and the believers live in them, because they are in Christ and Christ is in them by the power of the Spirit. The Bible as Spirit-Word is the light that shines upon the path illuminating the journey of life as salvation and mission. The Bible was and is inspired. In the community of worship and witness, of praise and proclamation, the Word is written, living and preached. But it is not so much a textbook of propositions as it is the story of redemption in Christ by the Holy Spirit and the journey in the Spirit through Christ to the Father. The doctrines of verbal inspiration and infallibility are precipitants of a spirituality which practiced a much fuller doctrine of the Word of God.

To abide in the Word was to use it as the norm for evaluating beliefs and practice. As they dealt with fanaticism and speculation there was a strong emphasis on sticking to the biblical story: if it was not in Scripture, then it should not be enacted. This did not mean that there was no daily specific guidance for the church and individuals from the Holy Spirit. It did mean that Scripture would provide the means to test and direct that guidance and provide boundaries. New experiences would often be the occasion for finding new insights into Scripture. Familiar Scriptures would take on a new meaning. But the beliefs, affections and practices would all have to be tested by the Word.

Thus, the point of Pentecostal spirituality was not to have an experience or several experiences, though they spoke of discrete experiences. The point was to experience life as part of a biblical

---

1.   *AF* 1.9 (June–September, 1907), p. 2.
2.   'Christ Abides in Sanctification', *AF* 1.9 (June–September, 1907), p. 2.

drama of participation in God's history. The church was a movement from the outer court to the inner court to the holy of holies; from Egypt through the desert across the Jordan into Canaan; from Jerusalem to Judaea, Samaria and the end of the age (and the uttermost parts of the earth); from justification to sanctification to Spirit baptism, and then in justification, sanctification and Spirit baptism into the harvest.

Whether it was couched in terms of biblical dispensations, discrete personal experiences, or missionary travels, all of this language was meant to speak of the mighty acts of God's story of redemption in Scripture, in their lives and in the world. It was one seamless fabric. In fact, obedient participation in the story was something like a robe of righteousness worn by the saints who would one day walk with Christ in glory, because they walked with him in service now. Thus their concern was not so much with an *ordo salutis* as a *via salutis*. The narrative of salvation provided the structure for formation within the missionary movement.

The whole congregation was involved in the process of formation. The singing, preaching, witnessing, testifying, ordinances (baptism, Lord's Supper, foot washing),[1] altar calls, prayer meetings, gifts of the Spirit, all the elements of corporate worship prepared people for and called them to new birth, sanctification, Spirit baptism and a life of missionary witness. These ways of remembering the biblical Word mediated the biblical realities in a kind of Pentecostal sacramentality[2] in which there was a constant, mutually conditioning interplay between knowledge and lived experience, 'where learning about God and directly experiencing God perpetually inform and depend upon one another'.[3]

This way of knowing, of forming Pentecostal witnesses, is seen in 'the Old Testament word for knowledge, *yada*, which points beyond the conceptualization of an object to the actualization of a relationship. This is why *yada* is used for marital lovemaking (e.g. Gen. 4.1) and

1.   H.D. Hunter, 'Pentecostal Ordinances', *DPCM*, pp. 653-54; P.D. Hocken, 'Theology of the Church', *DPCM*, pp. 211-18.

2.   Ranaghan, 'Rites of Initiation', pp. 688-94.

3.   R.D. Moore, 'A Pentecostal Approach to Scripture', *The Seminary Viewpoint* 8.1 (1987), pp. 1, 2. See esp. his 'Canon and Charisma in the Book of Deuteronomy', *JPT* 1 (1992), pp. 75-92 for an Old Testament theological basis for my use of Spirit-Word in this study.

covenantal intimacy (e.g. Jer. 1.5; 22.16; 31.34)'. The force and power with which this often occurred in Pentecostal services indicated that transformation, not mere information, was the goal of the process. Worship was a crisis encounter, an event of meeting with the living God which precipitated certain crises in the life of the believer according to where she or he was in their salvation journey.

These crises in the life of the believer flowed from the redemptive accomplishment of Jesus Christ toward the parousia and consummation of the kingdom of God. When Jesus said on the cross, 'It is finished', he did not mean that everything that needed to be done by God or believers was over. The 'finished work of Calvary' was the completion of his earthly life, teaching and sacrificial offering. The mission of the Spirit moved within and from that life offering but had its own sovereign purpose. This view is opposed to some more Reformed views which in effect see the 'finished work of Calvary' as an accomplished fact whose benefits are applied through personal identification with Christ. This too is an event but not a particularly transforming one, and certainly not one which presses toward the kingdom.

Though the earliest Pentecostals certainly understood the meaning of imputation and justification, they were more concerned with the impartation of righteousness and sanctification, the transformation of lives and the empowered mobilization of the church. The emphasis of salvation was not so much on 'standing' as it was on 'movement'. It was not primarily a matter of identification with Christ but of conformity to him. It was not so much a 'position' as a 'participation'. This was a direct result of the eighteenth-century Wesleyan perspective which, although diluted and distorted somewhat in its nineteenth-century American adaptations, nevertheless retained the Arminian sense of personal agency and responsibility ('respondability').[1]

The journey toward God was a journey with God in God. It was walking toward the Father with Jesus in the Spirit. But this journey was also fundamentally a journey into God: a kind of mystical, ascetical journey which was ingredient in knowing God and going further, deeper and higher. To know God was to be directed by God's will, motivated by God's love and strengthened by God's power. As Jesus had come to do the will of the Father, so the believer was sent to

---

1. C.E. Jones, 'Holiness Movement', *DPCM*, pp. 406-409. D.D. Bundy, 'Keswick Higher Life Movement', *DPCM*, pp. 518-19.

fulfill righteousness. The point was not only to be declared righteous, pardoned and forgiven initially in new birth and, thereafter, each day; the point was also and simultaneously to declare *for* righteousness. The Father drew believers to himself through Jesus by the Spirit. But he drew them in order to set them on the path of righteousness and life, and off the path of sin and death. They must turn, be born again and set out on the path.

There was constant mention among early Pentecostals of the importance of walking in all the light you had. Other believers (non-Pentecostals) would not be condemned, because they were walking in all the light they had. They would, of course, miss the full blessings of Pentecost; but they were, nevertheless, Christians. Some felt that though they may not go in the Rapture because they did not have the seal of the Spirit in his infilling, nevertheless, they could come through the Tribulation through faith in Jesus.

There was a great inconsistency in the polemical point being made here. The struggle is evidenced in Seymour who, while teaching the necessity of Spirit baptism in order to be a part of the raptured Bride of Christ, also counselled Pentecostals who were tempted to pride and abuse toward other believers in the following manner:

> You cannot win people by abusing their church or pastor. As long as you preach Christ, you feed souls; but as soon as you jump on the preacher, you grieve the Spirit... but if you get to preaching against churches, you will find that sweet spirit of Christ that envieth not, vaunteth not itself, is not puffed up, thinketh no evil, suffereth long and is kind, is lacking and a harsh judging spirit takes its place. If you feed them from Christ, you will find the same Spirit burning in their hearts.
>
> The main thing is, Are you in Christ? The churches are not to be blamed for divisions. People were hunting for light. They built up denominations, because they did not know a better way... we do not have time to preach anything else but Christ. The Holy Spirit has not time to magnify anything but the Blood of our Lord Jesus Christ. Standing between the living and the dead, we need to so bear the dying body of our Lord, that people will only see Christ in us, and never get a chance to see self. We are simply a voice shouting, 'Behold the Lamb of God!' When we commence shouting something else, then Christ will die in us...
>
> When people run out of the love of God, they get to preaching something else; preaching dress, and meats, and doctrines of men, and preaching against churches. All these denominations are our brethren. The Spirit is not going to drive them out and send them to hell. We are to recognize every man that honors the Blood. So let us seek peace and not

confusion. We that have the truth should handle it very carefully. The
moment we feel we have all the truth or more than anyone else, we will
drop.[1]

Seymour, then, urged a concentration upon Christ and indicated that
persons were responsible for the light they had. The 'lighted pathway'
of early Pentecostals was the 'highway of holiness' whose road signs
were clearly marked on the testimony maps so that new sojourners
would know the way. These signs were stages or steps which referred
to the 'experiences' which were to be expected and which in their
cumulative and interacting complexity constituted 'the Pentecostal
experience'.

The observation is made often by insiders and outsiders that
Pentecostals crave personal experience; and, paralleling this either
implicitly or explicitly, is the acknowledgment of the centrality of the
presence of God in Pentecostal worship.[2] The word 'experience' is
used with varying degrees of care, sometimes referring to no more
than certain transient feelings which finally issue in a kind of
emotional catharsis. At best it refers to the importance of the living
God among his people, and some today are saying that Pentecostalism's main contribution lies in the recognition of a certain
charismatic dimension or vocational enablement to enhance what is
already there,[3] or a release of the graces implanted in baptismal
initiation.[4]

Whatever terminology for these experiences is used, for
Pentecostals the category of crisis is important. There is a parallel
between the view of the end as a crisis ushering in a new heaven and
earth and a view of the Christian life as a series of crises. New birth,
sanctification, Spirit filling, healings, prophecies, calls to ministry, all

1.   'The Church Question', *AF* 1.5 (1907), p. 2.
2.   R. Spittler, 'Pentecostal Spirituality', in D.L. Alexander (ed.), *Christianity
Spirituality: Five Views of Sanctification* (Downers Grove, IL: IVP, 1988);
E. O'Connor, *The Pentecostal Movement in the Catholic Church* (Notre Dame: Ave
Maria Press, 1971); McDonnell, 'Distinguishing Characteristics', pp. 117-28.
3.   Lederle and Hunter over against Bruner maintain a second dimension of
experience and second charismatic, vocational work of the Spirit, respectively. See
H.I. Lederle, *Treasures Old and New: Interpretaions of Spirit-Baptism in the
Charismatic Renewal Movement* (Peabody, MA: Hendrickson, 1988) and Hunter,
Spirit Baptism.
4.   McDonnell, 'The Experiential', pp. 43-58.

are definite crises or interventions of God; all are present manifest-ations of the life of the coming kingdom. Of course each crisis exists in some continuity with what has gone before and, most especially, with the eschatological goal of all things. Nevertheless, it is also true that the crisis often makes possible new and/or supplemental insights into the past, new expectations for the future and, hence, a new present self-understanding.

This eschatology is in contrast to that of a traditional fundamentalist dispensationalist who in agreement with Augustine, Warfield and others believed that the gifts of the Spirit, the so-called 'sign gifts', were limited to the Apostolic era. This dispensational bracketing means that one is now in the 'church age' where there is a definite division between the church and the kingdom, between Sermon on the Mount kingdom passages of Scripture and Pauline prescriptions for the church, and between this age and the one to come.

For strict dispensational fundamentalists one age cannot inter-penetrate another. But for Pentecostals the lines of distinction are drawn differently. Though influenced by Scofieldian dispensational-ism,[1] they put a different twist on it. Many Pentecostals operated out of three dispensations, instead of seven or twelve; that is, they saw an age of the Father, one of the Son and one of the Holy Spirit. These three ages roughly corresponded to the history of Israel, the life, ministry, death, resurrection and ascension of Jesus, and Pentecost as the beginning of the present age of the Spirit. There was overlap and interpenetration of these dispensations, and there was a kind of progressive, logical development. The stories told (testimonies) about this development provided continuity not only with what had gone before but, most especially, with the future apocalypse.

Indeed the entire unfolding of events, as was sometimes graphically unfolded in thirty-foot-long and seven-foot-high charts in sanctuaries throughout the world, was one continuous process of divine revela-tion. The last book in the Bible, the Revelation, provided a perspective with which to look back at the whole in much the same way as knowing the last chapter in a mystery novel allows one to read each previous chapter differently. Much mystery remained, but in the end

---

1. For a brief overview of dispensationalism and its continued impact on Pentecostalism with some contemporary Pentecostal dissent (Gause, Horton), see F.L. Arrington, 'Dispensationalism', *DPCM*, pp. 247-48, and P.H. Alexander, 'Finis Jennings Dake', *DPCM*, pp. 235-36.

God, a God of righteous love and power, prevailed along with all those who were right with him, loved him and lived out of his power, while the Beast, False Prophet and Antichrist were defeated. The spirits associated with these eschatological figures were and are already at work and representations or anticipations of them could be identified in the global political arena as well as close to home. The powers of the age to come were already being poured out over the dispensational walls erected by the traditional 'charters' of dispensational history. The church was the new Israel and had a special concern for national Israel because of promises directed to her. However, while there was a difference between national Israel and the church, the spiritual destiny was the same; the promises of God looked forward to the same kingdom and 'throne of David' to be restored when Jesus would sit in the millennial kingdom and rule the nations.

So the kingdom was breaking through from the future and the Spirit was being poured out. The Pentecostals did not sell everything and go up to a mountain to await his appearing. They did not retreat to a prayer cave. They did not set dates for his coming, though they, as the early church, were sure it would be soon. No, what was called for was the preaching of the gospel to the nations and getting the Bride ready for the Bridegroom. The crisis experiences within this eschatologically oriented development process were stages along the way, markers along the aisle, toward the altar and marriage supper. They were not experiences for experience's sake. They were the necessary preparations for a kingdom where all is holiness unto the Lord, a kingdom which even now is righteousness, peace and joy in the Holy Spirit.

There was no consideration of merit or works-righteousness. Faith was the gift of God by grace. But the faith which justified worked through love. In response to the righteousness declared by God for the believer, the believer was to declare for, and walk in, all righteousness. Those who loved Jesus were to love the church and neighbor. Those who were saved by the power of God were to receive power to spread the liberating gospel unto all nations.

This meant that the church became a missionary fellowship where testimonies were given constantly in order to develop in the hearers the virtues, expectancy, attitudes and experiences of those testifying. A typical early testimony (and the services and periodicals were always full of them) would run something like this: 'I'm so thankful the Lord has saved me, sanctified me, and filled me with the blessed Holy Ghost. I'm thankful to be a part of His Church and on my way to heaven'.[1] There would follow then some review of recent or upcoming events which were to be occasions of praise or petition for the body. Healing, trials, temptations and victories could be reflected upon by the body. By listening to and giving testimonies the congregation was involved in a praxis of theological reflection which, though open-ended, produced great uniformity and carried built-in relevance.

There was also congregational control of 'wildfire' or fanaticism.[2] Consider the following excerpt from a letter dated 27 February 1907 from the widely influential evangelist and church leader G.B.Cashwell in Dunn, North Carolina:

> I am receiving letters every day from north, south, east and west from people that have attended my meetings saying that they have received their Pentecost and speak in tongues.
>
> People have been gulled here by take it by faith, reconsecrate, baptism of fire, 'dynamite', and 'lyddite', till the faith of the people is almost gone. Praise God for Pentecost. Get your justified experience all in good shape, then get the sanctified experience of a clean heart. Then when your faith takes hold of the promise of the Father and Son, and the word of God, you will have great joy as they did that went up from Olivet to Jerusalem. Then you can praise and bless God and the Holy Ghost will come in and praise God Himself in unknown tongue [*sic.*] and you will never doubt it any more, if they burn you at the stake or behead you. He will bear witness of Himself. Let us not come short of the promise.[3]

Evangelists and congregations who had been 'burned over' a few times soon learned to 'test the spirits' and recognize what was not scriptural, edifying or unifying. But if there were counterfeit experiences, that was only because the real thing was so wonderful.

---

1. A typical version of this testimony from the early years into the 1960s was 'Praise God! I'm saved, sanctified, filled with the Holy Ghost, a member of the great Church of God and on my way to heaven I am determined to hold out to the end'.

2. Perhaps more than any other group in North America today, Pentecostals have developed a special sensitivity for charlatans and the merely exotic. Many traditional or classical Pentecostals were distrustful of Jimmy Swaggart, embarrassed by Oral Roberts and in open disagreement with many of the beliefs and practices of the Bakkers long before any of their scandals broke in the news. All Christian groups have scandals—usually not very original: i.e. money, sex, power—but Pentecostals are especially open to criticism because of their 'high' claims and expectations.

3. G.B. Cashwell, *AF* 1.6 (1907), p. 3.

The Threefold Pentecostal Experience

It will now be profitable to consider the 'Pentecostal experience' of the believer in its correlation with the view of God, the means employed, the evidences sought and the results desired. Recalling Runyon's analysis of experience in terms of its source, telos, accompanying transformation and attendant feelings, it will be noted that this discussion builds on his insights with some modifications. God is the source and, in a real sense, the *telos* of these experiences. God forms persons in and through these experiences in the missionary fellowship for eternal fellowship with himself in the consummated kingdom. The penultimate goal of this formation is readiness or fitness for missionary service.

Early Pentecostalism organized its understanding of the Christian life around the three 'blessings' or 'experiences' of justification, sanctification, and Spirit baptism. Each 'experience' is a penultimate realization of an aspect of the coming kingdom and is correlated with an attribute of God. The experiences recapitulate the progressive unfolding of God's economy of salvation. The manifestation of the gifts of the Spirit confirm that the first-century power is still being given, God is still the source; and, most importantly, the power of the end is now at work moving all things to their completion in Christ. What did it mean, then, to be justified, sanctified and filled with the Holy Spirit in light of the imminent return of Christ?

Justification. To experience justification was simultaneously to testify to forgiveness, new birth, regeneration, adoption and being in a new world. To be 'saved' in a Pentecostal setting meant an entry into the training program of a missionary fellowship in which, with sins forgiven, one could then continue to walk in the light, make things right with persons whom one may have offended (restitution), and forgive those who had sinned against one. God was a righteous God and righteousness was a word to describe all the requirements of a right relationship or a walk in the light with him. (How can two walk together, except they be agreed?)[1] If one were truly justified, one would not walk in darkness and sin anymore. Now, through the power of the Spirit, one could resist the devil, deny the flesh and walk separated from the world. One should 'walk the talk' and 'talk the

---

1.   1 Jn 1.6; Amos 3.3.

walk'. To do less was to be a hypocrite at best and at worst to backslide. All 'experiences' were amissible, and all were capable of increase as one grew in wisdom and knowledge and strength.

In justification one acknowledged the will of God in all the Scriptures as the direction for all of life. As Jesus came to do the will of the Father, to fulfill all righteousness, so each believer was to walk in righteousness, to become the righteousness of God in Christ, so that they would shine as lights in a dark and dying world. It was urgent that the light shine, especially since, in the last days, the darkness would increase and good and evil would grow up together.

Rules of righteousness, holiness practices adopted from the nineteenth-century Holiness movement, served to make a difference between the church and the world, the saint and the sinner. As the light of Scripture shined on the path by means of the Word and Spirit, one was to walk in it. Failure to do so meant going back. The choice was to go on to the end or to go back. This view of the Christian life as journey is captured in the gospel song, 'I Feel Like Traveling On':

1. My heavenly home is bright and fair,
    I feel like traveling on,
    Nor pain, nor death can enter there,
    I feel like traveling on.

2. It's glitt'ring tow'rs the sun outshine,
    I feel like traveling on
    That heavenly mansion shall be mine,
    I feel like traveling on.

3. Let others seek a home below,
    I feel like traveling on,
    Which flames devour or waves o'er flow,
    I feel like traveling on.

4. Be mine a happier lot to own,
    I feel like traveling on,
    A heavenly mansion near the Throne
    I feel like traveling on.

5. The Lord has been so good to me,
    I feel like traveling on,
    Until that blessed home I see,
    I feel like traveling on.

CHORUS
Yes, I feel like traveling on, I feel like
    traveling on;
My heavenly home is bright and fair,
    I feel like traveling on.[1]

Many other songs spoke of moving on and implored the Savior to 'Lead me all the way across the stormy sea of life'.[2] The worshipers would often declare in song that they 'did not want to get adjusted to this world',[3] because 'Holiness unto the Lord'[4] was their watchword. To be righteous was to heed the voice of God with urgency while the 'Latter Rain Is Falling'.[5] One was called to live as 'If the End of the World Were Today'.[6]

Something of the early Pentecostal ethos and social location is captured in the following gospel song, 'What a Shame on People who Do that Way':

1.   Some folks go to meeting because they love God,
      And follow the path which the pilgrims all trod;
      'Tis a peace, 'tis a peace for the people who do that way

2.   Some folks go to meeting and in it delight,
      They love to praise Jesus from morning till night;
      'Tis a peace, 'tis a peace for the people who do it that way.

3.   Some folks go to meeting and grumble and shout,
      And in a short time Christian folks turn them out,
      'Tis a shame, 'tis a shame, for people who do that way.

4.   Some preachers hold meetings and wear their long coats,
      But all they are good for is getting our goats;
      Turn away, turn away, from preachers who do that way.

5.   Some folks go to meeting and take the front pew,
      And after the meeting still smoke, swear, and chew;
      'Tis a shame, 'tis a shame, for the people who do that way.

---

1.   E. Haynes and M.S. Lemons, *Church of God Songs: Tears of Joy* (Cleveland, TN: Church of God Publishing House, 1920), p. 26.
2.   *Church Hymnal*, p. 22. See also 'Jesus, Hold My Hand', p. 52.
3.   *Church Hymnal*, p. 218, 'I Don't Want to Get Adjusted'.
4.   *Church Hymnal*, 'Holiness unto the Lord' by Mrs C.H. Morris appears in Pentecostal hymnals from the earliest days to the present.
5.   Haynes and Lemons, *Church of God Songs: Tears of Joy*, p. 8.
6.   Haynes and Lemons, *Church of God Songs: Tears of Joy*, p. 97.

6. Some folks go to meeting, all wearing fine clothes,
    But at the true gospel, they turn up their nose;
    Turn away, turn away from the people who do that way.[1]

It was this strong sense of the church as a covenanted, disciplined body of believers (like the Anabaptists of the left wing of the Protestant Reformation) that gave them identity and a sense of belonging; although obviously it could make anyone coming into that ethos feel very uncomfortable! This band of faithful followers construed the wicked as weary and restless and themselves, though very active, as having a divinely given rest of soul:

'There Remaineth a Rest'

1. There remaineth a rest for the good and the blest,
    For the faithful, the tried and the true;
    And its for us today, who will walk in the way,
    Jesus tells us just what to do.

2. Let us fear lest we fall, there is rest for us all,
    Lest we falter beside the way;
    It is grace for the hour, O, it's wonderful power,
    When the Comforter comes to stay.

3. You may find it too late, when you call at the gate,
    If you trifle the time away;
    He is calling you now, will you humbly bow,
    He will save you from sin's dark way.

4. There is danger I say, should you turn Him away,
    He so sweetly is calling now;
    Will you turn Him away 'till the great judgment day?
    Why not come and before Him bow?

    REFRAIN
    There is rest, sweetest rest, for the good and the blest,
    And a home in the sky someday;
    Rich rewards for us there, in those mansions so fair,
    If we follow Him all the way.[2]

The paradox of rest and work is caught in even sharper contrast in a selection from the 1908 Songs of Pentecostal Power entitled 'We'll Work till Jesus Comes':

1. Haynes and Lemons, *Church of God Songs: Tears of Joy*, p. 98.
2. Haynes and Lemons, *Church of God Songs: Tears of Joy*, p. 4.

1.   O Land of rest, for Thee I sigh, When will the
       moment come;
     When I shall lay my armor by, and dwell in
       peace at home?

2.   No tranquil joys on earth I know, no peaceful
       sheltering dome;
     This world's a wilderness of woe, this world
       is not my home.

3.   To Jesus Christ I fled for rest; He bade me
       cease to roam,
     And lean for succor on His breast, till He
       conducts me home.

4.   I sought at once my Savior's side, No more my
       steps shall roam;
     With Him I'll brave death's chilling tide,
       And reach my heav'nly home.

     CHORUS
     We'll work till Jesus comes,
     We'll work till Jesus comes
     We'll work till Jesus comes,
     And we'll be gathered home.[1]

In this song Pentecostal piety portrays the world as a place of
weariness and woe. But this same world is a harvest field which is
destined to be completely renewed in the millennium. The world at
present, however, is a system of interlocking spiritual-institutional
realities which are driven by the lust of flesh, the lust of eyes and the
pride of life.[2] When one is born again, one no longer follows the
'world's crowd' but follows Jesus in righteousness.

In this present age of moral chaos, to be a disciple was to follow in
the way of righteousness and to live by a certain rule or discipline of
life. This was more than the mere application of biblical principles to
various situations and decisions. It was a discerning, personal following of Jesus in the Spirit. There were conditions to be met if one
continued in the way faithfully, and the chief of these was humility.

1.   R.E. Winsett, *Songs of Pentecostal Power* (Dayton, TN: R.E. Winsett,
1908), p. 179.
2.   1 Jn 2.15-17.

'Humble Thyself to Walk'

1. If thou wouldst have the dear Savior from heaven,
   Walk by thy side from the morn 'till the even,
   There is a rule that each day you must follow,
   Humble thyself to walk with God.

2. Just as the Lord in the world's early ages,
   Walked and communed with the prophets and sages,
   He will come now if you meet the conditions,
   Humble thyself to walk with God.

3. Just as a stream finds a bed that is lowly,
   So Jesus walks with the pure and holy,
   Cast out thy pride, and in heart felt contrition,
   Humble thyself to walk with God.

REFRAIN
Humble thyself and the Lord will draw near thee,
Humble thyself and His presence shall cheer thee;
He will not walk with the proud or the scornful,
Humble thyself to walk with God.[1]

The justified were to walk humbly in the light, and that requires the Spirit as surely as a flashlight requires batteries. The concern for walking in the Spirit, in the presence of Jesus, meant that sin was very personal. This is one of the important contributions of the movement even today: a sense of sin not only as transgression but as a personal affront to the Holy Spirit and a hindering of the historical process which is, by the Spirit's superintendency, moving toward the end in the kingdom of God. Sin is transgression, but it is even more fundamentally a rejection of the conviction or convincing of the Spirit concerning sin, righteousness and judgment. One cannot be a convincing witness if one is not daily living out of the convictions taught by the Spirit concerning these realities. The Spirit may be grieved, resisted, insulted, quenched, lied to and, most seriously, blasphemed.[2] But in order to walk in the light one had to walk in the Spirit who would lead into all truth, show things to come, make known the things of Christ and so forth.[3]

Walking in the Spirit requires not only illuminaton—that was foundational to everything—but also calling, appointment, direction,

1. W.J. Rogers, 'Humble Thyself to Walk', in Winsett, *Songs*.
2. Eph. 4.36; Acts 7.51; Heb. 10.29; 1 Thess. 5.19; Mt. 12.31; Lk. 12.10.
3. Jn 14–17.

wisdom and timing of the Spirit. Scriptural behavior required the continual, particular actions of the sovereign Holy Spirit who was also Lord and leader of the saints. This was expressed in the testimonies as a narrative of providence and the Christian life as a conversation involving God, believers and the world. Pentecostal piety, like Wesleyan spirituality was very much in accord with the Johannine order: walking in the light, fellowship, and thus ongoing cleansing from all unrighteousness![1]

The ordering and directing of life by the Spirit and the walk according to that order and direction was righteousness. This walk began in a regenerative act which gives the believer a new source for life; now he or she could walk according to the Spirit and not the flesh. As a testimony to and a first act of righteousness the Pentecostal believer would 'follow Christ in baptism' thus declaring publicly that one was now available to 'fulfill all righteousness'.[2] This was a corporate celebration and carries a special blessing and increase of joy. It was almost always by immersion on profession of faith, and, during the first ten years of the movement, universally in the name of the Father, Son and Holy Spirit. To be baptized indicated not only conversion but also a willingness to follow all that the Lord commanded. The daily penultimate goal was to walk in the light.

Sanctification. The narrative of justification usually involved confessing the resistances and hold-outs in the believer's life and the desire to fulfill the will of God. Doing the will of God, walking in the light, resisting the devil, and denying the self were all good. But sanctification involved actively seeking all the will of God for one's life, loving the Lord with the whole heart and joyfully bearing burdens without grumbling and complaining. Initial sanctification occurred with justification and the new birth, but entire sanctification was to be expected, desired and sought. Again, as in the case of justification and new birth, listening to Scripture, testimonies and songs prepared the way. 'Is your All on the Altar?', 'Cleanse Me' and Phoebe Palmer's 'The Cleansing Wave' were all sung as was, of course, Charles Wesley's unsurpassable 'Love Divine'. The effect of this process of exposure to holiness preaching, teaching, singing and testifying is captured in the narrative song by F.M. Graham:

1.   1 Jn 1.7.
2.   Mt. 3.13-17.

'We Will Sing and Preach Holiness'

1.   When I first heard of holiness I thought it must be right;
      It seemed to fit the Bible, And be the Christian's light.
      I heard the people singing and testifying too;
      They seemed to love their Savior, As Christians ought to do.

3.   I little thought of joining, I said I could not stand,
      To be among that people, That's called the 'holy band'.
      The world looked down upon them, And said they were so rash,
      They often spoke against them, And said they were but trash.

4.   But as I went to hear them, And saw the way they did,
      I saw they had a treasure, From worldly people hid.
      They seemed to be so happy, And filled with Christian love;
      When people talked about them, They only looked above.

5.   My heart began to hunger, And thirst and burn within:
      I wanted full salvation, A freedom from all sin.
      I went to God for holiness, And called upon His name;
      He cleansed my heart completely, And filled it with the same.

6.   And now I'm one who bears that name, That happy holy band;
      I've crossed the river Jordan, And in the Canaan land,
      The atmosphere is pleasant, And fruit of every kind,
      When you reach heaven's portals, I'll not be far behind.[1]

If righteousness was a right relationship and direction for life, holiness was the standard for living and the essence of the Christian life. Desire for sin was to be crucified, deeds of the flesh mortified and sinful stains and tendencies cleansed. If justification signaled a radical break with the world, then sanctification was a radical dealing with the flesh, the old nature or the carnal self. The self was denied in justification and was to be so daily thereafter. But in sanctification the self was to come into a new integration of perfect love perpetuated in continual spiritual respiration. Entire sanctification, the complete inner cleansing, would be evidenced in an abiding joy, thanksgiving and prayerfulness. The Holiness practices were no longer righteous limits to be obeyed whether one felt like it or not. Now they were merely the first steps, the basic training to exercise one in righteousness unto holiness of heart and life. In love the commandments were no longer burdensome or grievous.

But what of a second definite experience of sanctifying grace? Even

---

1.   F.M. Graham in Winsett, *Songs*, p. 213.

at Azusa there were those who experienced no interval between sanctification and Spirit baptism, but received both simultaneously. Yet it was important to the leaders at Azusa, W.J. Seymour in particular, to characterize Spirit baptism as the outpouring of the Spirit 'upon the sanctified life'.[1] Justification and sanctification were two separate works of grace. They were the works of grace which had been restored to the church through the Lutheran and Wesleyan reformations respectively. Spirit baptism was upon the sanctified life. The Spirit witnessed with the human spirit that the work was accomplished.

In justification one was to walk in all the light, in the will of the Father. In sanctification the believer was to walk in the perfect love of Jesus. That love filled the heart and without it nothing else profited.[2] Since Jesus prayed for the sanctification of his disciples and those who should come after them, believers should pray for their sanctification. As he sanctified himself in total self-offering unto death, so the believer should crucify the flesh with its passions and be completely at rest in the Father's hands.[3] The means of sanctification were the Spirit, the washing of the Word and, supremely, the blood of Jesus. The Spirit directed the believer to the inner resistances to the will of God. There needed to be a harmony of will and nature in the believer analogous to that harmony that is holiness in God. Indeed, the coming into that harmony and peace in love was the very essence of sanctification. It was a delight in the will and presence of God, and a wholehearted desire to be pleasing to the Lord in all things. When one was sanctified the body of believers rejoiced upon hearing the testimony and then were there to assist the growth in sanctification which would come, now unimpeded by the resistance of the flesh.

Faith overcame the world, crucifixion killed 'the flesh'. But what about the devil and his opposition to the mission that was the very heart of the church's life?

1.   The *Apostolic Faith* faith statement, found in almost every issue, held that Spirit baptism was to be upon the sanctified life.

2.   1 Cor. 13.

3.   R.H. Gause, in the most significant Pentecostal soteriology to date, deals with the problem of fragmented, episodic and often seemingly arrested stages or salvation experiences. He makes extensive use of Jn 17 to show the interrelationship of sanctification, joy, unity and mission. See R.H. Gause, *Living in the Spirit: The Way of Salvation* (Cleveland, TN: Pathway Press, 1980).

Spirit Baptism. It was a third experience, the baptism in the Holy Spirit, which equipped the believer to do spiritual battle in tearing down strongholds of the enemy and reaching the lost. How was the power of the Spirit related to the previously mentioned purity of heart and life? In 1908 *The Apostolic Faith* answered a series of questions on various aspects of Christian living, and many of the first ones had to do with sanctification, Spirit baptism and the question of evidence.

Questions Answered

Should a person seek sanctification before the baptism with the Holy Ghost?
Yes, sanctification makes us holy, but the baptism with the Holy Spirit empowers us for service after we are sanctified, and seals us unto the day of redemption. Sanctification destroys the body of sin, the old man Adam. Rom. 6.6, 7... when a man has been saved from actual sins, then he consecrates himself to God to be sanctified, and so his body of sin is destroyed or crucified...

What is the real evidence that a man or woman has received the baptism with the Holy Ghost?
Divine love, which is charity. Charity is the Spirit of Jesus. They will have the fruits of the Spirit. Gal. 5.22. 'The fruit of the Spirit is love, joy, peace, longsuffering, gentleness, goodness, meekness, faith, temperance; against such there is no law. And they that are Christ's have crucified the flesh with the affections and lusts.' This is the real Bible evidence in their daily walk and conversation; and the outward manifestations; speaking in tongues and signs following: casting out devils, laying hands on the sick and the sick being healed, and the love of God for souls increasing in their hearts...

Is it necessary to have hands laid on in order to receive the Holy Ghost?
No; you can receive Him in your closet. The gift of the Holy Ghost comes by faith in the word of God. You may receive the Holy Ghost right now, that is if you are sanctified... The baptism of the Spirit is a gift of power on the sanctified life, and when people receive it, sooner or later they will speak in tongues as the Spirit gives utterance. A person may not speak in tongues for a week after the baptism, but as soon as he gets to praying or praising God in the liberty of the Spirit, the tongues will follow. Tongues are not salvation. It is a gift that God throws in with the Holy Spirit. People do not have to travail and agonize for the baptism, for when all work ceases then God comes. We cease from our own works, which is a very type of the millennium.

Does a soul need the baptism with the Holy Ghost in order to live a pure and holy life?

No. Sanctification makes us holy, Heb. 2.11... The Holy Ghost never died for our sins. It was Jesus who died for our sins, and it is His Blood that atones for our sins... 1 John 1.9, 7... It is the Blood that cleanses and makes holy, and through the Blood we receive the baptism of the Holy Spirit. The Holy Ghost always falls in answer to the Blood.

Is the speaking in tongues the standard of fellowship with the Pentecost people?

No; our fellowship does not come through gifts and outward demonstrations but through the Blood by the Spirit of Christ... If a man is saved and living according to the word of God, he is our brother, even if he has not got the baptism with the Holy Spirit with tongues.[1]

Two related questions were asked concerning the possibility of the restoration of a 'lost Pentecost' and how to keep 'the anointing of the Spirit after receiving the Pentecost'. The editor replied with regard to the first that a person could 'repent and do the first works, and consecrate to receive sanctification, and wait for the baptism' again.[2] The presumption was that the Pentecostal experience was lost because of 'falling into temptation and being overcome by Satan'. To the question concerning maintenance of Pentecostal anointing he replied that it could be kept by 'living in the word of God with perfect obedience'. No antinomianism there! Some had apparently wondered about the place of Bible study after 'receiving the Holy Ghost'. The editor gave the following caution to the questioner:

Yes (we need to study); if not one becomes fanatical or many times will be led by deceptive spirits and begin to have revelations and dreams contrary to the word, and begin to prophesy and think ourselves some great one, bigger than some other Christians. But by reading the Bible prayerfully, waiting before God, we become just little humble children, and we never feel that we have got more than the least of God's children.[3]

These questions and answers, reminiscent of John Wesley's conferences with his ministers over a century earlier, indicate that very early in the revival there was an ongoing corporate reflection upon the living reality of God in their midst. Scripture, testimonies, songs, prayer vigils, poetry, spiritual gifts, godly lives—all served to

1. *AF* 1.11 (October–January, 1908), p. 2.
2. *AF* 1.10 (September, 1907), p. 2.
3. *AF* 1.10 (September, 1907), p. 2.

form persons who shared a common story. In all this the pre-eminent authority was Scripture.[1] The Spirit unfolds the Scriptures from 'Genesis to Revelation and all you do is to follow on'. According to the Scriptures, 'freelovism' and anything associated with sexual impropriety is condemned as being from the 'pit of hell. It is a dragon to devour those who get out of the Word...but He has given His children to know these spirits.' Since there is no mention in Scripture of writing in unknown languages, then it was not encouraged in the Azusa meetings. Everything was to be measured 'by the Word that all fanaticism may be kept out of the work'.[2]

A statement of faith was developed early in the revival at Azusa and published in several issues of *The Apostolic Faith*. It consists of brief phrases, Scripture quotations, affirmations as to the restoration of apostolic faith and the 'old time religion' practices of camp meetings, revivals, missions, street and prison work and Christian unity everywhere. This combination of beliefs, declarations and practices was a definitive list of distinctives made by those who saw themselves as a small but significant band of pilgrims.[3]

The Way of the Kingdom

In justification, sanctification and Spirit baptism the believers were enabled to walk in the light, in perfect love, and in power and demonstration of the Holy Spirit, respectively. This was the way of the kingdom. It was a journey into and with a righteous, holy, powerful God who was transforming them and the world by the power of the gospel in preparation and anticipation of the final apocalypse. The unfolding of the biblical drama, church history and individual history, all of this was the unfolding of God's historical revelation. The Scripture was the normative prescription and description of these events but the lives of believers were significant as living epistles and lights shining in the evening light, which signaled the twilight of the old age and the dawning of the new. And through it all the overriding and determining factor was the final revelation of God: the goal of all history, all nations and all people. To believe in this righteous, holy, powerful God whose kingdom was righteousness, peace and joy in the Holy Spirit was to be transformed unto that end

1. *AF* 1.10 (September, 1907), p. 2.
2. *AF* 1.10 (September, 1907), p. 2.
3. See the earliest statement of faith in *AF* 1.1 (1906), p. 2.

through Christ in the Spirit. The indeterminate but imminent coming of Jesus then, in the first century, and today, among Pentecostals in pneumatic continuity with these early pioneers, was the decisive belief and daily milieu for all the worship and witness practices.

> 'Jesus is coming soon', is the message that the Holy Ghost is speaking today through nearly everyone that receives the baptism with the Holy Ghost. Many times they get the interpretation of the message spoken in an unknown language and many times others have understood the language spoken. Many receive visions of Jesus and he says, 'I am coming soon.' Two saints recently in Minneapolis fell under the power, were caught up to heaven, and they saw the New Jerusalem, the table spread, and many of the saints there, both seeing the same visions at the same time. They said Jesus was coming very soon and for us to work as we had little time.[1]

The Pentecostal narrative beliefs under the influence of this apocalyptic vision of imminent fulfillment called forth distinctive practices, which were themselves signs, confirmations and celebrations of the power and legitimacy of the beliefs. And, at times, they became the basis for the refining, correcting and supplementing of the beliefs. The worship and witness were the means of expressing and inculcating the narrative beliefs. All the practices of the nineteenth-century Holiness movement, evangelical revivalism and early Methodism in the United States and Great Britain ('personal testimony, speaking in tongues, emotional and motoric outbursts, prostrations, spontaneous prayer, altar calls, prayer room, prophecies, hand shaking, and broader corporate involvement in worship and ministry'[2]) appeared in Pentecostalism, as well as many of the more traditional liturgical practices. The difference was the gestalt, that particular mix of eschatological intensification evidenced in the urgency, expectancy and manifestations of the Spirit which gave rise to a missionary fellowship whose 'this is that' (Acts 2.16) affirmation of the Latter Rain turned members of the Holiness movement into members of a global Pentecostal missionary force.

---

1.   *AF* 1.11 (October–January), 1908, p. 2.
2.   Ranaghan, 'Rites', p. 654.

Pentecostal Practices: Worship and Witness in the Light of the End

The Last-Days' Restoration of the Full Gospel

Speaking in tongues and healing had been occurring throughout the nineteenth century. Indeed, Pentecostals were later to show a limited but significant continuity of tongues and other gifts erupting throughout history from Pentecost to the present. In addition there was already a widespread belief in the premillennial coming of the Lord. But speaking in tongues and healing as signs of the eschatological inbreaking of the kingdom of God, signalling the imminent return of Christ, was not so prevalent, and certainly interpreting the 'fivefold gospel' as a last days' restoration for the proclamation of the gospel of the kingdom in all the earth was unheard of before the emergence of the twentieth-century Pentecostal renewal.

This is not to say that eschatology played no role in the theology of the nineteenth-century Holiness movement itself. From the time of John Wesley's sermon 'On the Wedding Garment'[1] there had always been a concern for preparation and readiness among those teaching Wesleyan sanctification. The gift of healing was the notable nineteenth-century manifestation which both looked back to Jesus' ministry and forward to Jesus' millennial reign when there would be no more sickness. Yet, by and large, the whole range of gifts of the Spirit was seen as rare or occurring only here and there, without eschatological significance or import for the understanding of the Christian life, nature of the Church, and missionary witness.

The same could be said for the more general notion of 'power' for service. The purity and power components of the nineteenth-century sanctification teaching had been like two sides of a coin. They were addressed to the need for personal piety and power for holy living, and the latter included spreading scriptural holiness throughout the land by means of evangelism and various programs of social reform. These practices of personal dedication and social witness were carried out to express and propagate the Holiness emphases, and they were the application of Holiness beliefs. With the eschatological intensification within the so-called more radical wing of the Holiness movement; however, these practices were seen as readiness for and anticipations of the end.

---

1.   Wesley, 'On the Wedding Garment' (see p. 54 n. 1).

But what necessitated distinguishing sanctification from Spirit baptism? What gave this new impetus and direction to the movement? Yes, the eschatological categories had shifted from post- to pre-millennialism. Yes, there was a shift from an emphasis on sanctification to baptism of the Spirit, from purity-power to power for service and holy living. Tongues could have been understood as evidence of sanctification seen as Spirit baptism or vice-versa. There was already a recognition of the difference between purity and power.

The central theological reason for this distinction rested on an awareness of the difference between the mission of Jesus Christ and the mission of the Holy Spirit. The Holy Spirit was now not only the Spirit of Christ, but also the sovereign Lord. Believer's lives were to conform to Christ, but their witness was to be like the Spirit's. This parallelled Jesus' own witness which was itself by the power of the Spirit. But this also meant that believers had to deal with, wait upon, and seek the Spirit for leading, understanding and empowering. This represented a shift from what was essentially and functionally a binatarianism to a more trinitarian practice with the accompanying danger of a new unitarianism of the Spirit.

Ironically, but with a kind of revivalistic 'Jesus-centric' logic, the unitarianism which did develop was one of the second instead of the third person of the Trinity. Perhaps this 'Jesus name' or 'Jesus only' split within early Pentecostalism was a way of registering a subliminal sense of the danger of tritheism and acknowledging the strong 'Jesus-centric' piety of early Pentecostalism and previous revivalism. It was perhaps also a 'logical' conclusion from the movement's fivefold full gospel concentration on Jesus as Savior, healer, sanctifier, Spirit-baptizer, and coming king, in which the Spirit was understood as merely instrumental.

Whatever the outcome of the historical investigation of the paradigm shift which resulted in Pentecostalism's separation from the Holiness movement, and whatever the verdict as to the theological reasons or concerns ingredient in that shift, it is clear from an analysis of the ensuing practices that the eschatological presence of God in, among and through these Pentecostals resulted in a heretofore unseen recovery of the universal call to witness in the power and demonstration of the Spirit in order to carry out the universal mission of the church in the last days. The missionary, charismatic nature of the church, and therefore of the Christian life, was now a central normative issue and concern.

Supernatural evidences, leadings and manifestations characterized the new movement. The hard claim was that every believer in particular and the church universal was called to be a Christ-like witness in the power and demonstration of the Holy Spirit with an eschatological sense of urgency and passion. Pentecostals were not more emotional than believers in the previous century's revivals and awakenings. They were struggling to find a new theological integration which would do greater justice to the new experiences, practices and biblical insights that were emerging.

Pentecostal practices were those actions undertaken on the basis of the beliefs, expressive and formative of the affections, and impacted by the inbreaking of the kingdom of God in spiritual power and manifestations. It was important to 'walk the talk' and 'talk the walk'. One cannot understand Pentecostal spirituality apart from exposure to the congregational and individual practices of worship and witness under the influence of the end times. Beliefs about the Bible, the Second Coming, the Holy Spirit, the Christian life and worship itself are expressed in and shaped by these practices. If, as was stated in Chapter 1, the Pentecostal theological task is understood as a discerning reflection on lived reality, then it becomes apparent that for Pentecostals, like liberationists (though, of course, also different from them), reflection on a distinctive praxis, an apocalyptically informed one, is essential to that task.

Rather than merely listing some of the practices, my procedure will be to group a select number of them using four categories which are descriptive of the spirituality and are themselves reflective of the particular eschatological experience of the Pentecostals. These four descriptive-analytical categories are:

    a.   Fusion–Fission Tensions.
    b.   Oral-Narrative Formation.
    c.   Spirit–Body Correspondence.
    d.   Crisis–Development Dialectic.[1]

---

1.   S.J. Land, 'Pentecostal Spirituality: Living in the Spirit', in L. Dupré and D. Saliers, *Christian Spirituality: Post-Reformation and Modern* (New York: Crossroad, 1989), pp. 484-90.

The fusion–fission category is placed first because it most directly and decisively represents the already–not yet tension in Pentecostal apocalypticism. This tension is also reflected in the other three categories and is, therefore, fundamental to any explanation of Pentecostal practices. Fusion refers to those polarities or pairs of concepts which are of equal importance and, in the apocalyptic fire of the spirituality, are fused phenomenologically. Fission, on the other hand, refers to those elements or dynamics which are separate, of unequal value to the believer and are sometimes mutually exclusive. The former (fusion) expresses an integration while the latter (fission) expresses a segregation or important distinction.

Fusion: The Inbreaking and Transformation of the Kingdom
Space and time are fused in the prophetic reckoning created and sustained by the Spirit of the end. Here and now, there and then are telescoped and traversed by the Spirit so that there is a personal impact of the already–not yet tension in the affective response, and observed behavior. Pentecostals who are moved deeply and powerfully by the Spirit will laugh and cry, dance and wait in stillness. In the Spirit they 'already' participate in the marriage supper but also live in the 'not yet' of a lost world. As has been discussed earlier, the Spirit acts as a kind of 'time machine' via the Word, enabling the believer to travel backward and forward in salvation history and to imaginatively participate in the events that have been and are yet to be. The power who raised Christ from the dead is moving all things toward the parousia. The Spirit poured out at Pentecost is filling every believer in such a way that everyday time is *kairos* for those upon whom the end of the ages has come.[1] But every fulfillment, every 'already', has an overplus of not yet or promise. The world and believers are fallen but being redeemed. The body is dying but is now the temple of the Holy Spirit, a part of the body of Christ.

In the 'already–not yet' time of overlapping aeons believers may speak in tongues and proclaim in the vernacular the mighty acts of God. Doxology is for now and then and reflects the fusion of the worship and witness of the church. Pentecostals in the Third World

---

1.   The setting of Acts 2 is the 'last days' and early Christians characterized themselves as those upon whom the ends of the ages had come (1 Cor. 10.11). This was also the historical perspective of early Pentecostals.

will often move the worship service into the streets after a full morning of worship. During the afternoon they will sing, testify and pray for persons in the street in a fusion of worship and witness, (*leitourgia* and *martyria*). The power of the kingdom to come is at work through the Holy Spirit to make all places and times serve the glory of God.

This intensification of joy means also at the same time an intensification of sorrow or longing (see Chapter 3). The longing is the affective recogniton of the 'not yet' for those who are lost and for the world as a whole. And so there is a pessimism of nature (groaning and sighing in the Spirit) and an optimism of grace (rejoicing in the Spirit). Pentecostal missionary practice seems more like post-millennial optimism ('We will bring in the kingdom by proclaiming the gospel'). But Pentecostal worship evidences a premillennial pessimism concerning the capabiuty of any human agency effecting the kingdom. Optimism, pessimism or both? It appears that, for them, God will not save the world on the basis of their works, but he will not save it apart from them either. The kingdom is present and will be consummated. To believe that is to live out of the power of the Spirit who directs and empowers the worship-witness praxis of the church. It is the Spirit himself who is in, and the source, of this joy and sorrow. The Spirit groans and sighs with all creation and within the believer. He creates and sustains this longing. Even though, obviously, the Spirit knows the end and indeed is the sufficient, efficient means of its accomplishment, there is still, in the Spirit, a divine longing. It is impossible to be filled with such a Spirit and to remain passive. It is cause neither for despair nor naive optimism. It is a sober joy, a tearful rejoicing and a realistic hope.

Fusion also describes the relationship of the individual to the community. The body of Christ is a tabernacle made up of living stones for a habitation of God through the Spirit.[1] As a communion in the Holy Spirit members respond to one another and the world out of the fundamental and prior response to and in the Holy Spirit. The congregation responds as a whole to the moving of the sovereign Spirit. Corporate, interactive worship is deeply felt and easily observable in Pentecostal settings. The gifts of the Spirit are distributed by the sovereign Spirit as he wills for the good of the

---

1.   1 Pet. 2.5.

whole, and it is the fact that all are responding to the same indwelling, infilling Spirit that makes corporate discernment and receptivity possible. The manifestation of gifts always bears the stamp of the present talents, personalitites and culture of the believer but that is fused with the unmistakable 'not yet' eschatological character of the Holy Spirit and his gifts. The Spirit is already poured out and gifting the body, but the believers are not yet as receptive and expressive as they shall be in the consummation of the age. The impact of the Fall upon the understanding, will and emotions is still felt even and especially among those who are filled with the love of God, sanctified and fit for the Master's use.

Pentecostals believe that the Bible is the Word of God written. Most subscribe to some form of verbal inspiration, infallibility and, for almost all North Americans, would espouse inerrancy if asked. The official statements, usually copied from evangelicals, do not accurately reflect the reality of the Scripture as Spirit-Word. The Spirit who inspired and preserved the Scriptures illuminates, teaches, guides, convicts and transforms through that Word today. The Word is alive, quick and powerful, because of the Holy Spirit's ministry. The relation of the Spirit to Scripture is based on that of the Spirit to Christ. Even as the Spirit formed Christ in Mary, so the Spirit uses Scripture to form Christ in believers and vice-versa. Anointed preaching, teaching and witnessing evidence this wholeness, this fusion of Spirit and Word, Spirit and Christ.

The Spirit is the Spirit of Christ who speaks scripturally but also has more to say than Scripture. The Spirit-Word directs the everyday life and witness of believers and the church as they are led into all truth. Spirit and Word are fused, are married, and can only be separated or divorced at great peril and price to the church and believer. The Word comes in words and in the power and demonstration of the Spirit. If it is not communicated out of the fullness of the Spirit, then the communication is not fully scriptural. If it is not scriptural, then, no matter how apparently charismatic it is, it is not spiritual, of the Holy Spirit. Of course this discernment calls for a body of people who are formed in the Spirit by the whole counsel of God.[1] Each person as bearer of the Spirit is hearer of the Word and

---

1. The Church of God Declaration of Faith, similar to so many others in early Pentecostalism, stood for 'the whole Bible rightly divided' as their rule of government, fellowship and discipline.

vice-versa. And all bearers of the Word are those who hear what the Spirit says to the church. If a Pentecostal congregation is not responsive to a preacher, it usually means that he or she is either not anointed or not preaching the Word. Whenever the fusion is violated the congregation will register it by withholding the 'Amen'.[1]

The ministry practices, especially of the early Pentecostals, indicated a fusion of clergy and 'laity', males and females, races and classes. Clergy and laity are functional distinctions in a gathering in which all have some gift to offer; no one gift is more valued or essential than another. All are needed or they would not have been provided by the Holy Spirit. The Spirit is poured upon male and female, therefore each is called upon to worship, witness, and to manifest the gifts and graces of God. Women would preach, lay hands on the sick, plant churches, prophesy, speak in tongues and help in all phases of the total ministry. All, in the light of the end, are to submit to one another and assist one another toward that goal. They are to wash one another's feet in cleansing preparation for that end and in view of their servanthood to one another.[2]

With regard to salvation and the daily walk of holiness, faith and works, 'talk and walk', love and obedience, gospel and law are fused. Love obeys. Those freed by the gospel, from the perspective of the gospel, allow the law to keep them dependent on grace and guided into righteousness. The kingdom that is coming is to be a kingdom of righteousness, therefore believers must now practice that righteousness in restitution for wrongs committed against others. Faith alone justifies through grace. But the faith which justifies is never alone; it is always, in the Spirit, the faith which works through love. To be in the faith is to be faithful. To be unfaithful is to be an adulterer who has fallen out of love with God.

Pentecostals believe that Christians can and have defected or 'backslid'. They practice disfellowshipping and restoration in relation to such persons. They call upon those crucified with Christ to crucify the 'affections and lusts'. The objective is fused with the subjective. They do not see this as works-righteousness. They see faith as

1. This is not to deny gullibility, ignorance of the Word, congregational immaturity, charlatans with wrong motives, those mistaking exuberance for genuine anointing, etc. It is to affirm the usual practice informed by years of experience in 'testing the spirits'.

2. Thomas, *Footwashing in John 13*.

working righteousness but not inevitably or necessarily. Persons can resist the leading of the Spirit, the light of the Word and fall back. Christ's message to the churches in Asia in the book of Revelation has been used by Pentcostals since the 1906 Azusa Revival to show the importance of hearing what the Spirit says to the churches. For just as individuals can fall away so can churches be deceived into thinking all is well and living on past reputation.[1]

As a result of this emphasis Pentecostals often practiced a very strict discipline which recognized very few indifferent matters, (the so-called *adiaphora*). Holiness prohibitions against dancing, attendance at movie theatres (worldly amusement), wearing jewelry (worldly luxury and adornment, or vainglorious displays) and so on became tests of fellowship rather than matters for further discussion and cultivation. In an effort to keep the church pure and ready, many persons were offended or taught an 'all or nothing, now' approach to church discipline. When the apocalyptic fervor was high, of course, most people were glad to submit to these lists of rules or holiness practices. However, as the fervor subsided and incomes rose, more became affordable; and, as a result, many third- and fourth-generation believers went to other more lenient churches. For most of the early believers, however, these practices were inherited from the Holiness movement and were seen as being consistent with a full commitment to the God who was looking for a people who were holy and blameless before him in love.[2] These practices also served to give a social identity and sense of distinction between the church and the world. This was further reinforced as a result of a lot of initial persecution, including violence against persons and destruction of property. Epithets such as 'holy roller' served to drive people closer together and cause them to seek even more scriptural justification for those things practiced among them in dedication to God. The plain, simple life of sacrifice, consecration and witness was consistent with the vision of the kingdom that must shine brightly from within to a watching world.

The fruit of the Spirit and the gifts of the Spirit were fused as were the salvation experiences of regeneration, sanctification and Spirit baptism. It was not just a matter of adding Spirit baptism to sanctification in order have a separate movement. Nor did it seem right to

1. Rev. 1–3, esp. 3.1.
2. 1. Thess. 5.23.

dissociate the two. Spirit baptism as God's power poured out upon the sanctified life was a reaffirmation of the earlier Holiness insistence on purity and power as two sides of the same coin. Though logically and experientially separable, they could occur simultaneously, but they should not be dissociated theologically. Being and doing, fruit and gifts of the Spirit, character and personality were to be seen as an integrated whole. God was preparing a Bride who was consecrated and caring, watching and working. The fusion of these elements of the Christian life was consistent with the eschatological fulfillment. One did not have to await the redemption of the body in resurrection to know the fullness of salvation as regeneration, sanctification and Spirit baptism. The fruit and the gifts together comprised a complete or whole witness to the power of the gospel. The Spirit integrated the inward and outward. These signs or evidences were necessary not only for personal assurance but also for pastoral care and the public witness and influence of the church.

In the fusion or union with Christ one was fused or joined to the Father and the Spirit. Indeed the Spirit was the agent of such fusion. Such a union with a righteous, holy, powerful God necessitated and would result in appropriate transformation and development. In this regard justification asked for sanctification which in turn asked for Spirit filling for worldwide evangelism and mission. The justice, love and power of God became in the believers a deep, motivating passion for the kingdom.

Fission: Participating in the Kingdom within a Fallen World
If fusion tends to favor the 'already' side of the tension, then fission tends toward the 'not yet'. The polarities here are unique, sharply separated and, in some instances, mutually exclusive. God and Satan, light and darkness, saint and sinner, church and world are all examples of such mutually exclusive elements. The polarity is seen most clearly in the practice of exorcism, in which the demonized person was separated from the demon by the force of the Spirit driving out the evil spirit. Then the person could hear the gospel and be fused or joined to Christ.

The 'world' was seen as an interlocking system—socio-political, economic and spiritual—that was passing away. Persons were either of the world or of the Word. To be of the world was to be motivated by the lust of the eye, lust of the flesh and pride of life.[1] Worldliness and godliness were mutually exclusive. To become a Christian is to receive the Spirit of God and to reject the spirit of the world. Men and women were called upon to come out of the world, to be delivered from all binding vices, to leave worldly luxuries, intoxicating beverages, harmful habits (such as smoking) and to cease frequenting worldly amusements where there were lewd displays contrary to the Spirit of holiness.

Pentecostals instrumented separation from this world through conformity to the next. In doing so they radically relativized this world and worldly involvements. The world rejected them, and they rejected the world. They were in the world as witnesses, not as part of the system. Early on pacifism was quite common and the point was often made that they were citizens of the kingdom of God first and last.[2] Because they did not retire to a separate geographical location as did the Amish, for example, their differences in conversation, dress, worship, witness, and so on were all the more important to their sense of identity and belonging. Their intense sense of the otherness of God and his coming kingdom seemed to drive them to find ways in which to bear witness to that in their daily life.

When someone came from the world into a Pentecostal fellowship there was often a great deal of spiritual energy released in the ensuing fission. Dramatic conversions and deliverances were the rule. It was eventful because of the sharp distinction and the cost that had to be counted. But if there were tears and travail as one was born into the new 'world' on the way to consummation, there was also great joy. The tears and joy served to bind the new believer to the body and to reinforce the body's resolve. They experienced their own conversion again, were urged on in sanctification, and felt a fresh surge of the power of the age to come. Witnessing drew the line between the church and world and invited the world to cross the line.

There is another type of fission. This time, instead of signaling mutually exclusive polarities, the purpose is to indicate things which are distinguished in that the first item is valued more than the second and takes precedence over it. Examples are revelation and reason, head and heart, Scripture and 'creeds'.

1. 1 Jn 2.16.
2. J. Beaman, *Pentecostal Pacifism* (Hillsboro, KS: Center for Mennonite Brethren Studies, 1989).

Pentecostals would found Bible schools and institutes to train persons for ministry. These schools, as they developed throughout the century, were places where reason would serve revelation. Reason could not produce revelation, and without revelation reason did not discover what was truly important. The 'truths' of secular learning had to be relativized to the larger truth and interpreted within it, that is, within the larger cosmic reality of the kingdom of God. How could one truly know the significance of the past and present or this or that discovery, much less put it to its proper use, without an understanding of the purpose and goal of all existence? Indeed, learning could be dangerous. Plenty of educated persons rejected the things of the Spirit. Many of them attended so-called Christian schools where they were taught to distrust God and the Bible and the church.

The heart was the center of person; it was the seat of mind, will, and affections. The whole person had to be moved by the Spirit and Word of God. If the head was addressed apart from the heart being aflame with the love of God only pride could result.[1] 'Out of the heart the mouth speaks.'[2] The social location, increasing pluralism and concomitant relativization of all values influenced the Pentecostal response to education. But the foremost concern was to honor what was most important—what 'thus saith the Lord'.

The Spirit-Word of Scripture took priority over church and creeds. Creeds were like fixed fortifications in a battle that required mobility, adaptability and flexibility. Bartleman, who was present at Azusa, quoted Philip Schaff approvingly:

> The divisions of Christendom will be overruled at last for a deeper and richer harmony, of which Christ is the key-note. In Him and by Him all problems of theology and of history will be solved. In the best case a human creed is only an approximate and relatively correct expression of revealed truth, and may be improved by the progressive knowledge of the church, while the Bible remains perfect and infallible. Any higher view of the authority of creeds is unprotestant and essentially Romanizing.[3]

1. *DPCM*: L.F. Wilson, 'Bible Institutes, Colleges and Universities', pp. 57-65; J.M. Baldtree, 'Christian Day Schools', pp. 167-69; C.M. Robeck, Jr, 'Seminaries and Graduate Schools', pp. 772-76; J.M. Baldres, 'Sunday Schools', pp. 835-37.

2. Lk. 6.45.

3. F. Bartleman, *Azusa Street* (South Plainfield, NV: Bridge Publishing, 1980), p. 167.

Bartleman wanted a unity in Christ not in creeds, because therein all God's people could be one 'irrespective of race, color, social standing, or creed'.[1] Quoting a prominent preacher who was addressing some Pentecostals as an 'outsider' he warned that 'the beautiful Pentecostal work, so full of promise, where God has designed to come in and fill souls and wonderfully baptize them in the Holy Ghost, is broken and peeled and ruined for lack of love'.[2] Further he cites John Wesley's discussion of 'opinions' and 'bigotry' and his reminder that when the believers were first filled with the Holy Ghost, they were of 'one mind, as well as one heart'.[3]

Creeds, according to the early Pentecostals, were designed to keep people out, to divide the body and to say what God could and could not do. They seemed to shut down the sovereignty of the Spirit and to frustrate the desire of Pentecostals to have a church unified in the Spirit for last-days' mission. It was necessary judiciously to apply scriptural insights to daily decisions and situations. But creeds tended to be exalted to the place of Scripture and that just would not do. The Spirit was over the church. The Spirit was prior to Scripture. So, the order of authority was Spirit, Scripture, church. Without the Spirit there would have been no Word, incarnate or written; without the Word, no church. In practice this meant that preaching and prophesying (or its equivalent, tongues plus interpretation) were all to be tested by the Scriptures in the community of Spirit-filled and gifted believers. In this way the church could continue to grow in understanding and be corrected if it got off the track.

Ironically, this anti-creedalism became something of a creed itself with the result that some Pentecostals believed that they had the pure Word while others had only creeds and organizations of human origin. They were trying to preserve the sovereignty and priority of the Spirit and in the process often became very inflexible and intolerant. But the intent was to be open and to seek a missionary unity of the Spirit for the urgent task of evangelization. Eventually, however, the Pentecostals, in response to internal dissensions and external accusations, were forced to develop their own creeds, with

1. Bartleman, *Azusa Street*, p. 167.
2. Bartleman, *Azusa Street*, p. 167.
3. Bartleman, *Azusa Street*, pp. 168, 169.

code names like 'Statement of Fundamental Truths' or 'Declaration of Faith'.[1]

Pentecostals had experienced something which the creeds had led them neither to expect nor to seek, something, rather someone (the Holy Spirit), who gave them new courage, assurance and power. Thus it was better to place one's trust in the Holy Spirit who unites than in creeds which divide. They knew they had beliefs, most of them in common with other Christians, but without the dynamic of the Holy Spirit upon and through their lives, the creeds were seen as empty shells and barriers for the missionary unity of the church. R.G. Spurling, early leader of the Christian Union (later to become the Church of God in Cleveland, Tennessee), said that the church fell into 'creedalism' when it lost the link of love in the golden chain of redemption. Changing the metaphor, he asserted that love of God and neighbor were the two golden rails upon which the church like a train should run.[2]

Contrary to much popular misconceptions Pentecostals, though suspicious of restrictive creeds, were meticulously concerned, as their internal debates and divisions prove. W.J. Seymour warned Pentecostals of the danger of 'Impure Doctrine':

> We find many of Christ's people tangled up in these days committing spiritual... as well as physical fornication and adultery. They say, 'Let us all come together; if we are not one in doctrine, we can be one in Spirit.' But, dear ones, we cannot all be one except through the Word of God. He says, 'But this thou hast that thou hatest the deeds of the Nicolaitans, which I also hate.' I suppose that the apostolic church at Ephesus allowed people that were not teaching straight doctrine, not solid in the word of God, to remain in fellowship with them; and Jesus saw that a little leaven could leaven the whole, and His finger was right upon that impure doctrine. It had to be removed out of the church or He would remain the light and break the church up. When we find things wrong, contrary to Scripture, I care not how dear it is, it must be removed. We cannot bring Agag, which represented satan himself, the carnal nature or old man; but Samuel said Agag must die, and he drew his sword and slew him. Christ's precious word, which is the sword of Samuel, puts all carnality and sin to death... There are many people in these last days that are not

1.   The Assemblies of God 'Statement of Fundamental Truths' and the Church of God 'Declaration of Faith' (Cleveland, TN).

2.   R.G. Spurling, *The Lost Link* (Turtletown, TN: Farner Church of God, 1920).

going to live a Bible Salvation, they are going to take chances. But may God help everyone, if their right hand or right eye offend them to cast it from them. It is better to enter into life maimed, than for soul and body to cast into hell fire.

The Lord says, 'He that hath an ear, let him hear what the Spirit saith unto the churches; to him that overcometh will I give to eat of the tree of life which is in the midst of the paradise of God.' O beloved, if we expect to reign with the Lord and Savior Jesus Christ, we must overcome the world, the flesh and the devil. There will be many that will be saved but will not be full overcomers to reign on this earth with our Lord. He will give us power to overcome if we are willing. Bless his holy Name.[1]

In the eschatological context in which the discussion took place, impure doctrine led to impure lives; and the end of that would be either ruin or loss of reward. Some believers would go through the Great Tribulation because of unconfessed, presumptuous and/or carnal indulgences. There would be a loss of reward. Thus, whether or not one was from a Wesleyan background emphasizing a second definite work of grace (sanctification), one needed power to 'overcome the world, the flesh and the devil'. The primary pastoral concern was not over this or that creed but that someone should be solid in the Word, teaching straight doctrine—straight out of the Word!

In time, however, such pastoral concern hardened. Rules for holy living developed, while under the influence and power of the apocalyptic vision, which prohibited even those questionable things not specifically proscribed by Scripture, but thought to be in violation of scriptural teachings. These are practices which might cause a sister or brother to stumble. These rules (such as dealing with a member who smoked) would be discussed and pastoral admonitions would be offered, usually with advice concerning being merciful and longsuffering toward the carnal, immature or weak.[2] Over time, however, these restrictions became hard and fast laws for immediate enforcement. They became tests of fellowship and requirements for entry into full membership, a kind of holiness catechism which had to be believed and obeyed if one was to be a full participant in the covenanted band of believers. A little leaven could leaven the whole

---

1. *AF* 1.11 (October–January, 1908), p. 3.
2. R.H. Gause, 'The Historical Development of the Doctrines of Holiness in the Church of God' (unpublished paper, delivered to Holiness Study Project, Mt Paran Church of God, Atlanta, Georgia, 1973).

lump. Purity of heart required purity of doctrine and life. Without the pursuit of holiness one could not see the Lord.

Also evident in this sort of teaching is the relationship between the Spirit, Christ and the Word of Scripture. Just as Jesus had specific knowledge of the faults, compromises, faithfulness and steadfastness of the churches of Asia, so he also spoke to the specific situation of contemporary churches and applied the scriptural teaching by means of the Holy Spirit who searched the hearts and lives of all.

Pastoral concern could also lead to disagreement over doctrine. William Durham developed the non-Wesleyan 'finished work' view of sanctification to account for those persons, who, though they had no definite crisis experience of sanctification, did 'have the baptism'. Yet it was also pastoral concern which led Wesleyan Pentecostals to reject Durham's new teaching and Seymour to lock Durham out of the Azusa mission! For the Wesleyan Pentecostals power was to be upon and for the sanctified life; thus to turn sanctification into something practically identical to regeneration followed by mere growth was to lose the specificity, dynamic and eventfulness of the Wesleyan teaching. Growth without crises was not only uninspiring, it was dangerous, for it undercut the hope of real and definite transformations.

This division would confirm to many that creeds represented division in the body which could be healed only through arriving at a new consensus in love. Since sanctification was seen as perfect love casting out all fear and binding the body together, the early Pentecostals saw this very painful dispute as striking at two of their most vital tenets: missionary unity and readiness for the coming of the Lord. Yet pastoral concern for sound doctrine seemed to make creeds unavoidable. As Seymour noted,

> The only way to keep foul and false hellish spirits out of the church of Christ is to have sound doctrine. 'Fortify the walls'.[1]

But if Seymour and others offered the 'sound doctrine' argument in one hand, they also usually had in the other hand a more pragmatic test for the movement's legitimacy as a whole.

> The thing that makes us know that this 'latter rain' that is flooding the world with the glory of God is of the Lord, is because we know that the devil is not in such business... This work is not to build up some great

1. *AF* 2.13 (May, 1908), p. 2.

machine—not to be some great something but to get souls saved and living in unity with Christ.[1]

The church is not essentially a machine or organization created by humans; it is an organism. There is a fusion of clergy and laity, male and female, fruit and gifts, but a fission of church and world, and doctrine serves to define those limits. Without those limits there is no clear identity and health. Pentecostals developed different polities, but eventually all—whether congregational, presbyterian or episcopal—were qualified by the dynamic leveling of the Pentecostal presence who turned everyone into a priest, prophet, saint and witness. Offices of the church—ministry gifts such as pastor, apostle, teacher, prophet, and so forth—were to be recognized by the body and could only be effective if the body confirmed the gift. The attraction to evidences and results signaled a shift from the qualitative to the quantitative. But after getting burned by charlatans and the many weird persons that such a movement usually attracts and makes a place for, Pentecostals quickly (as early as the Azusa revival) developed tests of discernment involving sound doctrine and the fruit of the Spirit; these will be discussed in Chapter 3.

Oral-Narrative Formation: The Speech of the Kingdom
In all it was important to observe the fission or distinction between the Holy Spirit and the human spirit. Inducing spiritual experiences was and still is abhorrent to Pentecostals. *The Apostolic Faith* exhorted,

> Honor the Holy Ghost. Someone may say, 'If you can speak in tongues, let me hear you.' Don't ever try to do that. The Holy Ghost will never speak in that way. It is not you that speak but the Holy Ghost and He will speak when He chooses. Don't ever try to speak with tongues or say that the power belongs to you. It is by My Spirit, saith the Lord. When saying or speaking in tongues, your mind does not take any part in it. He wants you to pray for the interpretation, so that you can speak with the Spirit and with the understanding also (1. Cor. 14.16).[2]

Though Seymour and others were obviously aware that they were speaking, yet it was vitally important to overemphasize the Holy Spirit as sovereign source. If this were true of speaking in tongues it was true of all other gifts; indeed it was true of the whole Christian life.

1. *AF* 2.13 (May, 1908), p. 2.
2. *AF* 2.13 (May, 1908), p. 2.

'Not I, but Christ. Not my spirit, but the Holy Spirit.' That would be a fair characterization of the concerns and affirmations of the early Pentecostals. Speaking in tongues was the point at which the Holy Spirit and the human spirit, the church and the kingdom existed in the most personal yet corporate dynamic tension of the 'already–not yet'. It is what is most evident to outsiders and it is a practice which paradigmatically and dramatically underscores the oral-narrative character of Pentecostalism.

Speaking in tongues was sign, gift and evidence. When interpreted, it was a sign equivalent to prophecy, to the unbeliever who would often be convicted upon hearing it. It was a sign to the whole church of the restoration of the 'early rain' of apostolic power and gifts being restored in a 'latter rain' for missionary activity. It was evidence of Spirit baptism.

Over the years, in response to charges of demonism or derange-ment, Pentecostals hardened their claims for tongues as initial evi-dence. At first, as noted previously, there was a recognition of Spirit baptism apart from tongues, with the gift of tongues usually following at a later time. Early Pentecostals further qualified the initial evidence teaching by emphasizing the importance of the fruit of the Spirit as the sure, lasting proof of Spirit baptism.

Speaking in tongues was personal and corporate expression. As personal edification it was available to each believer as an eschatolo-gical prayer language, an immediate response to the coming kingdom in which God will be all in all and all speech will be out of hearts aflame with the presence of the Spirit. Tongues underscored the ineffability of God who was the source of wonder and delight. It was also a means to express the inexpressible in the eschatological lan-guage of the human heart and heaven.

If love was the fount of and gateway into the fruit of the Spirit, then speaking in tongues came to exercise a similar function in relation to the gifts of the Spirit. Here is fusion or union of this world and the next, divine and human in a communion so intense that initiation and response become a kind of dance with the Holy Spirit leading. There was an obvious Spirit–body correspondence in which that which is most characteristically human and constitutive of human community (i.e. language) required a new speech incapable of being co-opted by the routinizing of church bureaucracies or worldly regimes. Tongues, interpretation, wisdom, knowledge, prophecy, teaching, testimony, praise and so on, all are intensively personal, intensely corporate and eschatologically oriented. The shape of Pentecostal worship and witness would be incomprehensible without them.

Thus in testimonies the apocalyptic *telos* was the force pulling the testifier along as she or he told of the providential events, the miraculous happenings, the eventful existence of the journey toward the kingdom of righteousness, holiness and power which was even then at work. Everyone listened, identified and responded in hopeful longing which served to sanctify and form them as a body of witnesses. Stories merged with *the* story. What must have seemed a cacophany of sound and a pandemonium of celebration was, to the Pentecostals, a concert of prayer, a stereophonic praise temple and a proleptic dance of the kingdom. Where the Spirit was, there was liberty.

Speaking in tongues, visions, dreams and so forth under the constraints of 1 Corinthians 12–14,

> liberate[s] the people of God from dehumanizing cultural, economic, and social forces. They create room for an oral theological debate... unfreeze liturgical, theological and socio-political formulae and replace imported ideologies... with the political literacy of the whole people of God, practiced and learned within the framework of an oral liturgy for which the whole congregation is responsible; this is an authority based on speech, narrative and communication which 'enters into conflict with authority which is based on status, education, money and judicial power'.[1]

The dance of joy and the celebration of speech were evidence that victims were freed to become participants in salvation history.[2] Music was and is very important in that celebration; it expresses, directs and deepens that joy. The rhythmic and repetitive nature of much of the singing reflected this joyful celebration or feast of Pentecost in the light of the end, or, to come from the other direction, the marriage supper of the Lamb anticipated in every Lord's Supper. Hymns of

---

1. W.J. Hollenweger, 'Pentecostal and Charismatic', in Jones, Wainwright and Yarnold (eds.), *The Study of Spirituality*, p. 553.

2. Dan Albrecht characterizes Pentecostalism as a revitalization movement in 'An Investigation of the Sociocultural Characteristics and Dynamics of Wallace's Revitalization Movements: A Composite Analysis of the Works of Four Social Scientists' (unpublished paper, Graduate Theological Union and the University of California at Berkeley, 1989). See L.P. Gerlach and V.H. Hine, *People, Power, Change: Movements of Social Transformation* (New York: The Bobbs-Merrill Co., 1970).

revivalism, of the Holiness movement and of the Wesleyan renewal were sung along with new gospel songs which were usually a testimony, exhortation or chronicle of the journey toward 'home'. The oral-narrative liturgy and witness of Pentecostals was a rehearsal of and for the kingdom of God. They rehearsed for the coming of the Lord, the final event of the historical drama; and the songs, testimonies and so on were a means of grace used to sanctify, encourage, mobilize and direct them on their journey.

Spirit–Body Correspondence: The Acts of the Kingdom
When the congregation gathered for worship they moved as one body-mind-spirit in response to the Holy Spirit. The interactive patterns of African spirituality and nineteenth-century revivalism were taken over, indeed were already in place wherever the revival had spread. It was and is a liturgy of, by and for the people. The correspondence between Spirit and body is evident in a great variety of psychomotor celebration. The Pentecostal believers exist in the Spirit between creation and consummation—on the way to the end where there will be a spirit body in perfect correspondence with the Holy Spirit and freed of all the effects of the Fall.[1] The body is dead because of sin, but it is the cleansed temple of the Holy Spirit. The cleansing of the blood makes possible the indwelling of the Spirit which constitutes Christian existence. To be in Christ is to have the witness of the Spirit. But the conscious, ongoing, abiding of the Spirit requires a clearing of the internal channels of receptivity and a renewal from the tendency to sin, to resist and thus to grieve the Spirit. This is sanctification through mortification and vivification, putting off the 'old person of sin' and 'putting on the new in Christ'.[2] Atonement provided redemption, through the body of Christ for his body the church. It was a bodily event that looked forward to a universal resurrection of glory for those joined to Christ. The body is the Lord's and is to be offered a living sacrifice here and now.

Pentecostals had a total 'body life' of worship. The whole body responded and each person presented his or her body in receptivity and yieldedness to the Lord. Hands would be raised in praise and longing for his coming as the clouds of heavenly glory descended upon them. Hands would reach out to touch Jesus and by his Spirit

1.   1 Cor. 15 characterizes the resurrection body as a spirit-body.
2.   Eph. 4.22.

receive healing and help. Hands would clap for joy at the mighty and wonderful deeds and presence of God. Hands would clasp and clench as believers reverenced and 'held on' to God for a blessing. The right hand of fellowship would be extended to all those coming into full membership in the church. Bodies would sway in the heavenly breezes blowing from the throne of God. Hands would be laid upon those seeking healing, needing encouragement, or being set forth by the body for some particular ministry.

The gift of healing was not limited to a healing evangelist. Most healings occurred within the corporate ministry of the church. The healing evangelists simply represented this ministry gift and it was operated through them to touch unbelievers as a sign gift. Hands of the elders would reach to anoint with oil so that the healing balm of Calvary could be applied in the Holy Spirit to the wounded and weary ones. Salvation and healing were for the body—the whole person—and were a provision of the atonement.[1] They expected everyone to be healed but if they were not, they simply kept praying and expecting the coming of the Lord.

Funerals were times of grief and celebration. Thus the regular worship times of laughter and tears, eschatological joy and longing for the lost, were preparation for the loss of death. Words would be spoken at the funerals concerning the faithfulness of the Lord and often gifts of the Spirit would operate to assure them. God could raise the dead—and there were many reports of this—but if God did not raise them now, he would soon.

The body was for the Lord, therefore periods of fasting were to draw nigh to God with one's whole being. This bodily dedication was necessary, because spirituality involved the whole person and all of his or her life. Fasting was not a punishment; it was a feeding on the Lord and drinking of the Spirit.

Spirit–body correspondence was evidenced also in the ordinances: in the washing of baptism, the eating and drinking of the Lord's Supper and, for some, the washing of the saints' feet. Baptism was in recognition of the conversion of the individual and that all righteousness might be fulfilled.[2] Great joy and celebration would attend baptisms which were usually, though not of necessity, in a lake, river or ocean. The Spirit of God would come close and everyone

1.   'The Healing Waters', in Winsett, *Songs*, p. 135.
2.   Mt. 3.15.

would praise God that another person had come to join them on the missionary journey toward the kingdom. Baptism was not a converting sacrament of initiation, but it was a means of grace in that it represented walking in the light, public witness, remembrance and following of Christ in public solidarity with the church. Babies were dedicated to the Lord, but would not be lost if they died before baptism.[1] Baptism was individual but corporate. It was the acceptance of the call to become a holy witness in the power of the Holy Spirit. It was a death and resurrection ritual of remembrance and hope. For many it was repeated if they had been baptized before conversion or had backslidden. If ·other churches were offended because of rebaptism the Pentecostal answer was that of the early Anabaptists: the first baptism was no baptism at all. Baptism did not save; in fact nothing one could do or had done would save. Only the gospel was the power of God unto salvation to everyone who believed.

If baptism was the sign of starting out in service to the Lord or the way to the kingdom, then the Lord's Supper was the sign of ongoing nurture and fellowship. The real presence of God was never an issue. Through the Spirit God the Father and the Son met them in the Lord's Supper. Since it was neither a converting ordinance (though that could happen) nor absolutely necessary for daily health, it was not celebrated as often as in most mainline churches—certainly not every Sunday, with a few exceptions.[2] Christ was made effectively present by virtue of the Holy Spirit. To eat or drink with unconfessed sin was to court danger, sickness or even death. Pentecostals took the warnings to the Corinthians to heart, thus making communion a solemn time of soul-searching and consecration.[3] But on the other hand it was a joyous anticipation, if one prepared for it properly. Questions for self-examination, hortatory direction and joyous anticipation were offered as seen in the following gospel song:

1.   Most immerse but the Pentecostal Holiness Church gives their members a choice of modes and ages (infant, child, youth or adult).
2.   The Elim Pentecostal Churches of Great Britain celebrate the Lord's Supper each week.
3.   1 Cor. 11.

'The Glorious Marriage Supper of the Lamb'

1. When 'mid sounds of earthly voices, none your accents ever hear,
    Will your tones be thrilling or redemption's psalm?
    Will your soul in blood-washed garments fair and spotless then appear,
    At the glorious marriage supper of the Lamb?

2. Will you be among the members who are undefiled,
    Called from earthly conflict into heaven's calm?
    Will you by His Son's atonement unto God be reconciled,
    Ere the glorious marriage supper of the Lamb?

3. Now put on the wedding raiment and be ready for the call,
    With your sin-wounds cured by Calvary's healing balm;
    Bow before the blessed Jesus and proclaim Him Lord of all,
    At the glorious marriage supper of the Lamb.

    REFRAIN
    O the glorious marriage supper of the Lamb,
    O the glorious marriage supper of the Lamb;
    Robed in garment's snowy-white, will you meet the saints of light,
    At the glorious marriage supper of the Lamb?[1]

Persons could be converted, healed, sanctified and filled with the Spirit in conjunction with the Lord's Supper because it was a part of the ongoing missionary worship and witness of the body. But it was definitely not 'the mass' or the *sine qua non* of Christian existence. The Lord's Supper was important because Jesus was present keeping the Passover and promising the parousia in the Holy Spirit.

Those groups which washed feet did so in obedience to John 13 and saw this as a time of cleansing and service to one another. In this way the leveling effect of Calvary was realized and the daily cleansing from sin unto servanthood was acknowledged, prayed for and received. Believers were encouraged to confess to one another, especially if they had an ought against someone. All members of the church participated, as could all believers, in the observance of the washing of the saints' feet. This was usually done in conjunction with the Lord's Supper and thus the two together constituted a blessing of cleansing, service and nurture in obedience to the Lord's commands.

To caricature this as a mere remembrance or doing of one's duty, as the word 'ordinance' implies, would be to miss the richness of the actual practice. Pentecostals, they believed, were commanded to do these things just as they were commanded to rejoice and receive the

1.   Winsett, *Songs*, p. 110.

Spirit each day. These were times of great blessing and deepening. At Azusa the Lord's Supper was memorial, anticipation and healing, as Seymour testified:

> We find as we partake of this ordinance, it brings healing to our bodies if we discern the Lord's body by faith... It also teaches us salvation and sanctification through the Blood. Our souls are built up, for we eat His flesh and drink His Blood.[1]

The word 'sacrament' was seen as a non-biblical word of Roman Catholic derivation which was associated with mechanical ritual. Never mind that the word 'ordinance' was non-biblical also; it was closer to the idea of obeying the specific command of Jesus. To eat, drink, baptize and wash feet was to do it unto the Lord; and he was present in, with, under and through these acts. Testimonies would be given during the ordinances to chronicle the narrative journey from the past, through the present and toward the future kingdom.

Crisis–Development Dialectic: The Process of the Kingdom
The narrative journey of Pentecostals in the light of the apocalyptic vision could be characterized as a crisis–development dialectic. Whereas some Christians marked the journey with sacraments which were a kind of crisis, for Pentecostals crisis points were times when God did something decisive which made possible a personal or corporate development that, before that time, was not possible. For example, when an individual was healed (a near universal Pentecostal testimony), their life was radically changed. Now they were living in a world of surprises and divine visitations, as well as daily divine support. No longer could they embrace a strict dispensationalism which bracketed gifts in the first century. Now they were living in the end times.

Regeneration, sanctification, Spirit baptism and various gifts of the Spirit were crises within and with a view toward an apocalyptic development which was a revelatory unfolding of God's continual acts of redemption in history. Salvation history was not primarily a matter of ideas, illumination and belief. It was fundamentally deliverance, turning, listening, watching, walking, waiting on the Lord who had acted, was acting and would act. God's activity was the basis or ground for the believer's acts. Individuals were not alienated from

1. Seymour, 'The Ordinances Taught by our Lord', *AF* 1.10 (September 1907), p. 2.

their works by a doctrine of salvation by grace alone which made works seem positively useless if not bad. One worked because God was at work. Works expressed the activity of God in and through and among the people whom he was empowering.

Salvation history was an ongoing history of revelation. The Bible was a closed canon but revelation continued because God was not yet all in all. Nothing revealed would be unbiblical, but it was beyond the Bible because salvation history had progressed beyond the first century. All that the Spirit spoke was scriptural, but not all that he spoke was in the Bible. It was not the role of the Spirit only to repeat Scripture. Guidance and gifts would be operated by the sovereign Spirit in edifying the church and witnessing in the world.

History was not a series of disconnected episodes but neither was it the smooth unfolding of life as the fruit from a seed in the changing seasons. One would be saved out of darkness into light and then walk in that light. As a person walked in the light, more light would be given. One would make restitution and bring forth fruit meet for repentance; that is, one would leave off sinning and make wrongs right wherever possible. In sanctification there would be a crisis of wholehearted love which concentrated on a complete yieldedness and availability for whatever assignment the Lord of the church might make by the sovereign action of the Holy Spirit. Then, in God's own time, one could be filled with the Holy Spirit and thus equipped for witness in word and deed, power and demonstration of the Holy Spirit.

These three crises committed one to a life of righteousness, purity and witness in the light, love and power of God. As God had revealed himself as Father-creator, Son-redeemer, and Spirit-sustainer in the biblical development of salvation history, so the believer's life recapitulated the biblical order or the comings of God into human experience. The church itself, though falling away at the time of Constantine, was restored successively through the crises of Luther (justification), Wesley (sanctification) and Pentecostalism (Spirit filling). This whole process would one day be radically altered by the second coming of Christ which would end history but also make possible a new, undreamed of process of adoration and joy.

The crisis–development dialectic was thus characteristic of a view of the biblical drama, the church's history and the individual believer's journey. A critique of this will be offered in Chapter 4, but for now at least it can be seen that the Pentecostals were advocating neither a smooth continuity with tradition nor a complete discontinuity. Perhaps it could best be characterized as a continuity in discontinuity. Churches and individuals had been and could be wrong. Presuppositions and traditional views could be radically altered by the intervention of God. What was being called for was a reforming and renewing praxis.

Pentecostal Praxis: Action-Reflection in the Spirit

Thus far the significance of the Pentecostal understanding of the presence of God has been assessed and followed by a description of Pentecostal narrative beliefs. The Pentecostal practices, all under the influence of the apocalyptic vision which gave them urgency and focus, have been categorized and briefly described. The presence of the Spirit of the end sets in motion a people with a story to tell. Each chapter of that story reflects the end to which they are called and toward which they press inviting everyone to join them.

The 'already–not yet' tension must be maintained because, if resolved either way, the mission will be hindered if not forfeited. There can be no escape into the 'not yet'. It will come to them in God's time, at any time. On the other hand, there can be no 'already' setting up of the kingdom here and now, an accommodative, triumphal venture not requiring the radical inbreaking of God. Persons, churches and world, are presently under the impact and influence of the Spirit who works in all, pressing and driving toward the end. The presence of the Spirit signals a continuing crisis in the development of the world and its history over against the salvation history of the world.

In this eschatological praxis of the Spirit as he informs, forms and transforms all things, the Pentecostal believer was called to be like Christ and like the Spirit; or, to put it more accurately, to be like the Spirit in order to be like Christ. Like the Spirit, the believers were to bear witness to Christ and not to themselves. The fruit of the Spirit was the Spirit's work to manifest Christ in the character of the believers. The gifts of the Spirit were to manifest the power of God in the service of the gospel ministry of evangelism and edification. Like Christ the believers were to depend on the Holy Spirit and not on autonomous human reason or the arm of flesh. Only the Spirit could enable the church to overcome the enemy. Only the Spirit could maintain the unity of the body in the peace of Christ. Only by the

Spirit could one see the light, walk in the light and thus walk as Christ walked.

Thus Pentecostal praxis was not just the practice of gifts or exuberant worship. It was not merely the stating of a few distinctive beliefs about Spirit baptism or tongues. Rather, it was a corporate action-reflection in the Spirit that sought to bear witness to Christ by the proclamation of the gospel in power and demonstration of the Holy Spirit. At first they were sure that tongues would be for the evangelization of all nations without having to learn the foreign languages—a kind of short cut before the end. That idea soon was proven wrong. But it was certainly possible; anything was possible with God. Anything was possible except that which violated Scripture and was not Christlike.

The praxis of the Spirit, action-learning within his action and teaching, was a missionary praxis which revealed the kingdom of God.[1] The Spirit was and is the supreme missionary strategist. The praxis was evidenced in worship and witness through practices, inherited from the two previous centuries of revival and reform, which bore the distinctive stamp of apocalyptic vision. This stamp or seal of the Spirit could also be seen in the responsiveness, joy, tarrying, longing and immediate urgent missionary witness. Living in this praxis of the Spirit, the transcendent presence of God, meant living in paradox: in but not of the world, already saved but not yet resurrected, already healed but dying, already filled, but longing for the day when God would be all in all, having very limited abilities but the unlimited power and gifts of God, organizing and making faith statements but decrying creeds and organizations, living in expectant readiness in the face of the imminent return of Christ but not knowing when it might be.

For those who spoke with the 'tongues of men and angels' the only way to survive, thrive and go forward was in the love of God. They banded together, 'fortified the walls' and proceeded to cultivate disciples in a missionary fellowship with an apocalyptic vision. The beliefs and practices taken as a living whole and informed by the presence of the Spirit of the end were distinctive. The powerful, sensed presence of the Spirit led to a clear testimony focused on Christ as Savior, Sanctifier, Healer, Baptizer in the Spirit and coming King. But these distinctive beliefs and practices as a whole were rooted in

---

1.   Pomerville, *The Third Force*.

distinctive Pentecostal affections which essentially characterized the believers. The affections were normed, shaped and altered by these beliefs. The practices grew out of and fed the affections. But without these affections there would have been no continuing Pentecostal identity and presence in the twentieth century. It was because of, and in order to nurture, these affections that they were a people at rest yet always at work, watching and 'Waiting on the Lord'.

1. Waiting on the Lord for the promise given;
    Waiting on the Lord to send from heaven;
    Waiting on the Lord by our faith receiving;
    Waiting in the Upper Room.

2. Waiting on the Lord, giving all to Jesus
    Waiting on the Lord, till from sin He frees us;
    Waiting on the Lord for the heavenly breezes;
    Waiting in the Upper Room.

3. Waiting on the Lord, longing to mount higher;
    Waiting on the Lord, having great desire;
    Waiting on the Lord for the heavenly fire;
    Waiting in the upper room.

    CHORUS
    The power! The power!
    Gives victory over sin and purity within;
    The power! The power!
    The power they had at Pentecost.[1]

---

1. Winsett, *Songs*, p. 172.

Chapter 3

PENTECOSTAL SPIRITUALITY AS MISSIONARY FELLOWSHIP:
AN AFFECTIVE INTEGRATION

Pentecostal Identity: Liberation for the Kingdom

'Praying through' from underneath

Pentecostals do not emphasize the intensity of feelings, though they are often called upon to defend or explain their strong show of emotion. The Enlightenment view of the opposition of reason and emotion, as well as the fundamentalist emphasis on their 'balance', combine to produce a cultural suspicion, if not outright derogation, of 'Holy Rollers'. Emotions are associated with bodily feelings and motions which are deemed inappropriate for the privatized faith of the middle and upper classes. Therefore when a person oppressed by society and sin 'prays through' that oppression to a new identity in the kingdom of God and there is attendant upon this event intense emotion, it has sometimes been slandered as 'orgiastic' religion by news reporters and other opinion makers. Poor African Americans and uneducated Caucasians alike are seen as crude and disorderly—even though persons of culture may at times enjoy listening to their singing or observing their exuberant celebrations. As Vance Packard, eminent North American sociologist, has observed: it is a long way from Pentecostalism to Episcopalianism in the United States.[1] Thus there is the matter of social class as well as the Enlightenment cultural perspective on religion to take into account; these factors merge in a class-cultural bias against movements of the poor in general and Pentecostalism in particular.

But in a postmodern era perhaps the dichotomy of reason and emotion, which has characterized much of American historiography, can be transcended, and new, more wholistic, integrative categories devised. Pentecostals, perhaps more than any other group, came to

1.   V. Packard, *The Status Seekers* (New York: D. McKay Co., 1959).

recognize the dangers of mere emotionalism very early in the movement. The strong emotions and the recognition of the dangers were both part of the legacy of nineteenth-century revivalism. But when persons, who had seen themselves (as well as having been perceived by others) as determined by the socio-political, economic, educational, class and racial forms, broke through by the power of the Spirit into a new existence of freedom and belonging, there were usually tears of joy and shouts of victory in the camp of the prayerful. They were truly liberated and not merely informed. God, who had liberated them, would soon liberate the whole world at the Second Coming of Christ. One was to go about doing good and witnessing in the power of the Spirit in light of this soon coming kingdom. But who was one supposed to be? What should characterize a Pentecostal believer? Surely not a series of emotional episodes. No, there was a certain vision of what it was to be as well as to give a witness to Jesus Christ; and contained within this vision was an implicit correlation of the character of God and that of the believer, between the Holiness language of love and the Pentecostal language of power.

Becoming a Pentecostal Witness

This chapter analyzes the distinctive Pentecostal experience in terms of religious affections. These affections are shown to characterize Pentecostals and, further, it is demonstrated that they bear the mark or impact of the apocalyptic vision and power of the movement. The transcendent presence of God moves and transforms believers affectively as he conforms them to himself and, therefore, fits them for the coming kingdom.

It will be recalled from Chapter 1 that spirituality involves the integration of beliefs, practices and affections. Christian spirituality as embodied by Pentecostals calls for discerning reflection in the light of the vision of the kingdom of God. This reflection is the heart of the theological task for Pentecostals. Chapter 1 also traced something of the Holiness-transformationist roots of the movement with an explanation of the emergent 'fivefold gospel' of the kingdom. Chapter 2 discussed the power of the apocalyptic presence of the Holy Spirit and his effect upon each experienced and enacted aspect of Pentecostal life. Pentecostal narrative beliefs told a story of the restoration of the 'fivefold gospel' to the church and the cultivation of the persons who received and believed that gospel as a way of life. Songs, testimonies, gifts and a variety of other worship and witness practices were categorized and analyzed to show the effect of the 'already–not yet' tension. The language of love and the language of power were seeking a translation or fusion that would bring soteriology and eschatology, church and kingdom, Christ and Spirit into a new synthesis. The 'five-fold gospel' was Christocentric because of the witness, power and presence of the Holy Spirit. This gave the movement a shape, direction and theology which represented an eschatological intensification and pneumatological emphasis within the Holiness movement.

While the identification of sanctification and Spirit baptism gave way to an appreciation of the experimental and theological distinction of the two, their interrelationship within the apocalyptic horizon of expectation and preparation remained crucially important in defining the new movement. Both the character and vocation of a Pentecostal were bound up in the doctrines of sanctification and Spirit baptism, respectively. This character and vocation are captured in the following exhortations to the saints at Azusa.

> Tongues are one of the signs that go with every baptized person, but it is not the real evidence of the baptism in the every day life. Your life must measure up with the fruits of the Spirit. If you get angry, or speak evil, or backbite, I care not how many tongues you may have, you have not the baptism with the Holy Spirit. You have lost your salvation. You need the Blood in your soul...
>
> Many may start in this salvation, and yet if they do not watch and keep under the Blood, they will lose the Spirit of Jesus, which is divine love, and have only gifts which will be as sounding brass and a tinkling cymbal, and sooner or later these will be taken away. If you want to live in the Spirit, live in the fruits of the Spirit every day... [1]

Sounding very much like the apostle Paul speaking to the Corinthians, Seymour admonished,

> O beloved, our reigning time has not come yet. We are to be with the Babe from the manger to the throne. Our reigning time will come when Jesus comes in great power from the throne. Until then we are to be beaten, to be spit upon, and mocked. We are to be like His son. [2]

The character or fruit of the Spirit that should, according to Seymour, characterize those early persecuted witnesses are analyzed

---

1. *AF* 1.10 (September, 1907), p. 2.
2. *AF* 1.10 (September, 1907), p. 2.

in this chapter as Pentecostal affections. The chapter will (1) show that underlying the affections there was an implicit God–salvation correlation, (2) briefly discuss the general definition of Christian affections, (3) describe the apocalyptic affections of Pentecostals, (4) note the important role of discernment and discipline for the identification, cultivation and preservation of true affections, (5) discuss the Pentecostal understanding of prayer as it shapes and expresses the affections, (6) show that the ruling affection is the passion for the kingdom and, finally, (7) demonstrate throughout that the missionary fellowship through its worship and witness calls forth, forms, reinforces and directs the constituent affections of Pentecostalism.

Pentecostal Affections: Embodying and Longing for the Kingdom

An Implicit Correlation: The 'Theo-Logic' of the 'Three Blessings'
Participation in the Pentecostal narratives and practices enabled an affective transformation which was implicitly correlated with certain divine attributes, the apocalyptic vision and individual testimony. The following chart displays this correlation.

God–Salvation–Kingdom Correlation

God	Righteous	Loving Holy	Powerful
Christ	Savior	Sanctifier	Spirit Baptizer
Salvation	Justification-Regeneration	Sanctification	Spirit Baptism
Kingdom in Spirit	Righteousness	Peace	Joy

The testimonies, tracts and songs express a longing to be like Christ, to live a 'godly life'. The three attributes of righteousness, love and power are correlated implicitly with the view of Christ as Savior, sanctifier and baptizer in the Spirit and the Christian testimony to justification, sanctification and Spirit baptism.

The concern for righteousness is expressed in relation to conversion and continuing in the Way. The early statement of faith of the Apostolic Faith Mission at Azusa stood for

> the restoration of the faith once delivered to the saints...
> Teaching a Repentance—Mark 1.14, 15.
> Godly Sorrow for Sin, Example—Matt. 9.13. 2 Cor. 7.9, 11. Acts 3.19.
>   Acts 17.30, 31.
> Of Confession for Sin, Example—Luke 15.21 and Luke 18.13.

Forsaking Sinful Ways—Isa. 55.7. Jonah 3.8. Prov. 28.13.
Restitution—Ezek. 33.15. Luke 19.8.
And faith in Jesus Christ
First Work—Justification is that act of God's free grace by which we
         receive remission of sins. Acts 10.42, 43. Rom. 3.25...
The Blood of Jesus will never blot out any sin between man and man
         [which] they can make right; but if we can't make wrongs right
         the Blood graciously covers (Matt. 5.23, 24).[1]

From this statement it seems that God's gracious justification or pardon through repentance and faith in Jesus Christ in no way removes the necessity of restitution and reconciliation among persons whenever possible (if they are within range and still living). The believer was sorry for his or her sins against God and thus had a 'godly sorrow'. But the confession and repentance of sin was not only a belief in the righteousness of God in Christ but also a declaration to walk in the light, to walk righteously in the world. Indeed, to 'teach God's people to observe all things whatsoever He has commanded... practicing every command and living by every word that proceedeth out of the mouth of God'[2] is what it means to believe in 'a full gospel'.

Therefore, the 'full gospel' was not limited to the fivefold formulation. The 'full gospel' was the 'whole Bible rightly divided', the whole counsel of God. Old and New Testament Scriptures, as noted earlier, were used in establishing the way of righteousness. The 'Lord of hosts is exalted in justice and the Holy God shows himself holy in righteousness' (Isa. 5.16). Walter Brueggemann's conclusion regarding this Isaiah passage is applicable to the early Pentecostal belief: 'A social practice of righteousness impinges upon the character of God... Restoration of the covenant between Yahweh and Israel depends on a proper social practice'.[3]

Pentecostals believed that the practice of some churches had led to antinomianism or to a dead faith without works. Indeed, some churches by their formal, mechanical approach had made the righteous guilty and thus had removed the righteousness of the righteous.[4] In contrast, the Pentecostal community mirrored the development of faith in the

---

1. *AF* 1.10 (September, 1907), p. 2.
2. *AF* 1.10 (September, 1907), p. 2.
3. W. Brueggeman, *Hope Within History* (Atlanta: John Knox, 1987), p. 35.
4. Brueggeman, *Hope*, p. 35.

book of Isaiah as it 'gathered around the text' and matured 'in its embrace and practice of God's righteousness'.[1]

But this development of faith was more like a reformation and a new beginning. It was a restoration to what they believed was a more biblical pattern that came shatteringly in moves of harsh discontinuity. It was a new development requiring 'harsh displacement, a breaking of old configurations of power and self-serving value'.[2] This discontinuity or displacement was accompanied by intense inner struggle and longing; and this was true whether one was a new convert or a member from another church coming into new light. To come this way was to begin again at the beginning; it was to commit to follow Christ wherever He might lead. It was to agree to walk in all the light God might give as it shined upon one's path. Justification was pardon but never justification for unrighteousness. Salvation was to become like God. It began with turning toward and walking in the light and it continued just as it had begun.

After the light of justification and the requirement of a righteous God more light was given concerning the holiness of God and the sanctification of the believer. This was understood in terms familiar to those out of or influenced by the nineteenth-century Holiness movement. Again the *Apostolic Faith* at Azusa affirmed the

> Second work—sanctification is the second work of grace and the last work of grace. Sanctification is that act of God's free grace by which He makes us holy. John 17.15, 17.— 'Sanctify them through Thy Truth; Thy Word is Truth'. I Thess. 4.3. I Thess. 5.23; Heb. 2.11; Heb. 12.14.
>
> Sanctification is cleansing to make holy. The Disciples were sanctified before the Day of Pentecost. By a careful study of Scripture you will find it is so now. 'Ye are clean through the word which I have spoken unto you' (John 15.3; 13.10); and Jesus breathed on them the Holy Ghost (John 20.21, 22). You know that they could not have received the Spirit if they were not clean. Jesus cleaned and got all doubt out of his church before He went back to glory.[3]

Later in the same issue of *The Apostolic Faith* the following exhortation to purity was given:

> Blessed are the pure in heart. We do not get this purity till we are willing to let Him have His way to the fullest extent of the word. We are clay in

1. Brueggeman, *Hope*, p. 33.
2. Brueggeman, *Hope*, p. 36.
3. *AF* 1.3 (1906), p. 2.

the Potter's hands. We must have the self well [*will*] removed in order to receive Him. As long as we have something to say, 'I don't like this or that', we cannot receive the Holy Ghost'.[1]

Sanctification involved a complete yieldedness and availability to God. Holiness was God's essential nature and therefore it could be asserted that

the object and end of all the precious Scripture is that a *definite work* may be wrought out in our hearts by the Holy Ghost. God's design through the ages and through all His work with the children of men, has been to implant *His own nature-love*, in a fallen race...

Dear ones, have we got that burning passion for souls of the lost? When we are persecuted and tried for the word of God, can we say in our hearts, Lord, forgive them, for they know not what they do?... It is sweet to have the promise of Jesus and the character of Jesus wrought out in our lives and hearts by the power of the blood and the Holy Ghost, and to have that same love and that same meekness and humility manifested in our lives for *His character is love*...

Dear loved ones, we must have that pure love that *comes down from heaven*, love that is willing to suffer loss, love that is not puffed up, not easily provoked, but gentle, meek, and humble. We are accounted as sheep for the slaughter daily. We are crucified to self, the world, the flesh, and everything, that we may bear in our body the dying of the Lord Jesus, that our joy may be full even as He is full.[2] [emphasis mine]

Sanctification, which begins in new birth, is actualized in a subsequent definite work. It is a definite work because it is a definite, dynamic reality. Salvation is a partaking of and a participation in the divine life. The character of holiness is love in the believer. It is a perfect love filling the cleansed, emptied vessel and without which the believer's gifts, sacrifices and righteous deeds will profit nothing. The measure of love given in new birth, along with the graces therein implanted come to full fruitfulness in sanctification. This entire sanctification is a 'burning passion for souls' that enables one to forgive one's persecutors. The power of the blood in sanctification is a necessary and logical prerequisite for the power of the Holy Ghost in Spirit baptism. Purity precedes power in the logic of early Pentecostal faith development because one must be a witness in character and deeds. The righteousness of God was to the faithfulness of the believer as the

1. *AF* 1.3 (1906), p. 2.
2. 'Bible Salvation', 'Sanctification and Power', 'The Character of Love', *AF* 1.3 (1906), p. 4.

holiness of God was to the love of the saints. The way of righteousness and the burning passion of love asked for the power to make the witness an effective demonstration of the power of God.

The baptism with the Holy Ghost was the aspect of salvation corresponding to the attribute of divine power. It was the 'gift of power upon the sanctified life'.[1] The baptism will fade away if one does not walk in the light of righteousness as it shines upon one's pathway. The Holy Spirit would not continue to empower one walking in darkness and the Spirit could not continue to fill those who did not abide in the perfect love of God. Those who were baptized with the Spirit 'must die daily that Christ may abide in you. If we begin to get puffed up, God will set us aside, but if we give Him all the glory, He will use us to scatter this light'.[2] All the experiences of grace were amissible and required an ongoing moment-by-moment abiding. Nothing could remove believers from the hand of Christ, but they must abide in him in loving obedience by the grace and power provided. The power of the Holy Spirit was given for a specific purpose:

> when we get the baptism with the Holy Spirit, we have something to tell, and it is that the blood of Jesus Christ cleanseth from all sin. The baptism with the Holy Ghost gives us power to testify to a risen, resurrected Savior. *Our affections are in Jesus Christ, the Lamb of God that takes away the sin of the world.* How I worship Him today! How I praise Him for the all-cleansing blood![3] [emphasis mine]

Praise and proclamation, the presence of Jesus and the Spirit, and the affections in Christ and the power of the Spirit are all fused in a call to Christian character and vocation.

Throughout the literature of the early revival there is this explicit correlation of the righteousness, holiness and power of God and the righteousness, love and power of the believer. The logic was not that of a formal order of salvation so much as an experiential, dispensational-like development of the believer in righteousness, love and power.

The superlatives of the descriptions of the gospel and the Christian life speak of the implicit correlation of theology, prayer and salvation:

1.   *AF* 1.3 (1906), p. 2.
2.   *AF* 1.3 (1906), p. 2.
3.   'River of Living Water', *AF* 1.3 (1906), p. 2.

walk in all the light (God is righteous, God is all light, and there is no darkness in him); the full gospel (the fullness of God in Christ); entire sanctification (God is holy, God is love); be filled with the Spirit (God is all-powerful). To relate rightly to God—that is, to know and to follow God—required a progressive transformative development. Participation in the Pentecostal worship and witness over time produced an 'affective transformation in which lives were formed and shaped' by their experience of God.[1]

These Pentecostal testimonies and the correlative view of God were teleologically related to the kingdom of God understood as righteousness, peace and joy in the Holy Spirit. The righteousness of justification was maintained by walking in the light by grace through faith. The peace of perfect love (which 'casts out fear', 1 Jn 4.18) was maintained by walking in love with no inner resistance or 'hold-outs'. The joy of the fullness of the Spirit was strength and encouragement to believers as they walked in the Spirit and not after the flesh. To believe in the kingdom of heaven, both here and now and there and then, was to long for a kingdom of light and righteousness, holiness and love, power and demonstration of the Spirit who would fill all things. The Spirit would lead into righteousness. The Spirit would search the heart and, by the Word, point out what was not like Christ and therefore carnal. The Spirit would fill and lead in powerful witness. The Spirit would express himself through gifts and the fruit that was the divine character being formed in the believer by virtue of participation in the divine life. The Father, Son and Spirit, by the Spirit, came to take up their abode in the believer.

If the gifts and fruit were the external witness, then the witness of the Spirit was the internal assurance and evidence for justification, sanctification and Spirit filling. And speaking in tongues, the eschatological language of heaven, was at once both internal and external witness, evidence and assurance. It was a tangible, existential demonstration of that communion, conversation and intercourse which was what being a Christian was all about. It was a dismantling of the unrighteous Babel of the world in praise, a longing cry of the oppressed for the beloved, and a shout of the eschatological fulfillment already breaking in but not yet fully interpreted.

In these ways the early Pentecostals, implicitly at least, correlated

1. H. Knight, 'The Relationship of Narrative to the Christian Affections' (unpublished paper, Emory University, 1987).

their vision of the kingdom, the Christian life and God. Their beliefs and practices, through the worship, fellowship and witness of the church, were expressive and determinative of certain Pentecostal affections. Before describing these affections it will be well to discuss the general characteristics of 'affections' and to show how Christian affections are distinguished from natural ones or mere 'feelings'.

The Christian Affections: A General Description
Any consideration of affections is complicated by the broad range of meanings and valences of feeling attached to any one of them. Consider the following example.

Sue Smith loves her cat, her husband and her green, two-door automobile. She has had her cat for ten years, her husband for five years, and her green Subaru sedan for one year. Sue takes Samantha, her cat, with her everywhere she goes, and if it is cold outside or the cat is not feeling well Sue tries to stay home and care for it. Sam, her husband comes and goes freely, with or without Sue and Samantha. He has his own small car. Although Sue has told Sam that she trades all her cars after the first twenty thousand miles, he knows that for now she loves this car and does not let anyone, including him, drive it. Her car is a private, personal space for Sue and her cat.

Sue, like most people, has several 'loves'. Each love represents something meaningful and enjoyable in her life and what they represent is shaped by the significance she assigns to them, the amount of time invested, how each 'object' of her love has responded to her, what she expects from each, along with the pain and pleasures. Sue also uses the word 'love' in relation to chocolate ice cream and trips to the zoo. Often these 'loves' will conflict and they have different valences. For example, when Samantha dies, if Sue leaves Sam what does this say about her 'love' for the cat versus that for her husband?

Sue's life and 'loves' reveal the confusing way that emotions, feelings and affection language is often used. The usual response to Sue would be to tell her that she is behaving unreasonably. Her emotions are out of control or balance. This post-Enlightenment dichotomizing or playing off of reason against emotion is characteristic of most of modern Western culture.

Public life is usually dictated by reason with the private life reserved for the idiosyncratic and irrational 'feelings'. This view of reason and emotion is also evident in the evaluation of religious

traditions. Everyone knows that Pentecostals are emotional and
Episcopalians are reasonable. From animal passions to sweet reason-
ableness the spectrum of religious ethos is displayed with control,
balance, moderation and quietness among the usual, prevailing criteria
for diagnosis and prescription.

If the object of the affection is not a cat, spouse or car but God,
then the situation is further complicated in that God is usually
construed as the supreme concern or the one demanding overall
loyalty. If there are different gods and different construals or ultimate
concerns, then the affection will be different. Earlier, spirituality was
·defined as the integration of beliefs, practices and affections. This
spirituality is a way of life involving knowledge, actions and affects.
These affects or affections are both evoked and expressed by the
actions and beliefs.

Christians confess that God is love. This love is made known
through what God has said and done, is saying and doing and will say
and do. 'God so loved the world that He gave His only begotten Son'
(Jn 3.16). This says something about the object of God's love, the
world, as well as the source, God. The nature of the gift given says
something simultaneously about the source, the object and the gift. It
is not possible to understand this affection, this love, apart from this
gift. Indeed it is not possible to receive the gift without love. Scripture
further specifies that Christians are to love one another as Christ loved
the disciples and others during his earthly ministry.[1] This love is shed
abroad in human hearts by the Holy Spirit who moves Christians in a
compassionate following of Christ.[2] If the heart is understood to be
the integrative center of the mind, will and emotions then it is clear
that affections are more than mere feelings and Christian affections
are meant to characterize a person's life.

For John Wesley and Jonathan Edwards true religion or authentic
Christianity was centered in the religious affections. Wesley abridged
Edward's *Treatise on the Religious Affections* for inclusion in his
Christian library for Methodist ministers and leaders. For Wesley, the
love of God and neighbor was the heart of true religion without which
one was not a Christian.[3] His doctrine of entire sanctification was a
way of underscoring the affective transformation wrought in Christ

---

1. Jn 15.12.
2. Rom. 5.5; Mt. 15.32.
3. Knight, 'Relationship', p. 6.

by the Holy Spirit through the means of grace. This fullness of love issued forth in a life of perpetual (even eternal) growth in the grace and knowledge of God as well as the mature manifestation and integration of the fruit of the Holy Spirit. Robert Roberts, Don Saliers and Hal Knight are contemporary Christian scholars who have emphasized, in varying ways, the constant theme of the importance, if not centrality, of religious affections in understanding the Christian life.[1] There is here no mere balancing of head and heart, of thought and feeling; rather there is an integration, an affective understanding which is essential to Christian existence. This faith 'is constituted by a new disposition of the heart which orders all the powers of emotion, perception, will and understanding. The affected heart and the intellect are not opposed in true faith; nor are they finally two kinds of capacities which are joined by an act of the will.'[2] Jonathan Edwards formulates this affective understanding in the following manner:

> As, on the one hand, there must be light in the understanding, as well as an affected fervent heart, where there is heat without light, there can be nothing divine or heavenly in that heart; so on the other hand, where there is a kind of light without heat, a head stored with notions and speculations, with a cold and unaffected heart, there can be nothing divine in that light, that knowledge is no true spiritual knowledge of divine things.[3]

There is an epistemological as well as a theological point to be made here, and underlying both is the relationship of Jesus and the Spirit. Jesus is presented to the person through the scriptural testimony by the Holy Spirit. It is the Spirit who moves upon the person to receive Christ. To receive the witness of the Spirit is to receive Christ. But this, then, must also mean that one receives the Spirit. The light and the heat, the truth and love are inseparable because the work of the

---

1.   See D.E. Saliers, *The Soul in Paraphrase* (New York: Seabury Press, 1980); *idem, Worship and Spirituality* (Philadelphia: Westminster Press, 1984); R.C. Roberts, *Spirituality and Human Emotion* (Grand Rapids: Eerdmans, 1982); *idem, The Strengths of a Christian* (Philadelphia: Westminster Press, 1984), and H.H. Knight, III, *The Presence of God in the Christian Life* (Metuchen, NJ: Scarecrow Press, 1992).

2.   Saliers, *Soul*, p. 10.

3.   J. Edwards, *Treatise Concerning Religious Affections* (ed. J. Smith; New Haven: Yale University Press, 1959), p. 120.

Spirit and Christ are one work of salvation. To know the truth is to love; to know the truth is to do the truth. Thus to hate, to withhold love is to lie.[1] The fanatics of the rationalist or enthusiast types are both addressed and given a deeper understanding of Christian existence from these scriptural and theological perspectives. H. Richard Niebuhr, in a penetrating insight expressed a desire to

> follow in Edwards' footsteps more, and undertake an exploration of the land of emotions with a certain hypothesis amounting to conviction...the hypothesis that contrary to prevalent opinion about the emotions—they put us into touch with what is reliable, firm, real, enduring in ways that are inaccessible to conceptual or spectator reason.[2]

The conclusion must be that, whatever else it may be,

> the Christian faith is a pattern of deep emotions. It is gratitude to God for creation and redemption, awe and holy fear of the divine majesty, repentance and sorrow over sins, joy in God's steadfast love and mercy, and love to God and neighbor. To confess faith in God is to live a life characterized by these emotions.[3]

These 'deep emotions' are the fruit of the Holy Spirit which are formed in some one who believes the gospel of Jesus Christ and construes the world accordingly. Traits like gratitude, compassion and confidence 'are what make a person a Christian; they are the definition of Christian spirituality'.[4]

In the light of the foregoing discussion the following summary statement may be made: Christian affections are objective, relational and dispositional. To say that Christian affections are objective means that affections take an object. In this case the object is also the subject: God is the source and object of Christian affections. The God who proves righteous, commands righteousness. The God who is love and has 'so loved', evokes love. The God who has acted powerfully to deliver, gives power and strength.[5] What God has said and done, is saying and doing, will say and do is the source and *telos* of the affections.

---

1. 1 Jn 1.6; Rev. 22.15.
2. H.R. Niebuhr, 'Coale Lectures' (Andover Library, Cambridge, MA: Manuscript), cited in P.M. Cooey, *Jonathan Edwards on Nature and Destiny* (Lewiston, NY: Edwin Mellen, 1985), p. 1.
3. Saliers, *Soul*, p. 11.
4. Roberts, *Strengths*, p. 22.
5. Eph. 6.10.

God's righteousness, love and power are the source of correlative affections in the believer. The narratives describing these attributes of God evoke, limit and direct the affections of the believer. God as righteous, loving and powerful is also the *telos* of Christian existence and thus of the affections. To believe God is to receive the kingdom of righteousness, peace and joy in the Holy Spirit and to await its coming consummation.

To believe in God and therefore to receive the kingdom is to acknowledge that Christian affections are relational. Christian beliefs and practices shape and express these affections. Christian affections require for their proper genesis and ongoing expression a relationship with God, the church and the world. This is most obvious in a consideration of that affection which is also the chief theological virtue, love. But as we shall see shortly, it is no less true for other affections. Christian affections cannot be summoned at will. Nor are they a pick and choose kind of emotional smorgasbord for connoisseurs of affective development. They depend on the initiating, sustaining and directing of the Sovereign Lord of the church.

John Wesley, who spoke of perfect love as wholehearted devotion to God, acknowledged that the Christian life was from first to last a work of the Spirit on a moment-by-moment basis. Wesley asserted, 'We feel the power of Christ every moment resting upon us, whereby alone we are what we are...and without which, notwithstanding all our present holiness, we should be devils the next moment'.[1] For Wesley such a relational understanding of faith entailed regarding spiritual pride as more deeply sinful than any 'voluntary transgression of a known law of God'.[2] The relationship of faith, obedience and love was the meaning of faith for Wesley and for those traditions which flow from eighteenth-century Methodism. Wesley saw this integration in James, Paul and especially in the epistles of John.[3] To be 'saved', to be a Christian, was to be rightly related to God and therefore one's neighbor.

If affections are objective and relational, they are and must also be dispositional. Again, for example, God who is love has commanded love for himself and others; and this love which the apostle Paul says

---

1.   J.L. Peters, *Christian Perfection and American Methodism* (Grand Rapids: Zondervan, 1985), pp. 187-88.

2.   Peters, *Christian Perfection*, pp. 187-88.

3.   John Wesley's *Notes on the New Testament*.

'abides' is to characterize Christians. Without it no matter what or how much they believe, no matter how much they give to the poor, no matter how many gifts of the Spirit they manifest or how great a sacrifice they make, it will profit them nothing.[1]

Love in particular and Christian affections in general are not passing feelings or sensate episodes. Affections are abiding dispositions which dispose the person toward God and the neighbor in ways appropriate to their source and goal in God. Feelings are important but they come and go, are mixed and of varying degrees of intensity. Moods too are variable, but affections characterize a person. One might, with adrenalin flowing, heart pumping and mood considerably elevated, breathe a silent thanks after a near miss on the highway. But this does not mean that one is a grateful person, much less a thankful Christian. How often have Christians been reminded that it is one thing to hear, with assent and tears, a message exhorting to compassion on Sunday and another to practice it on Tuesday? The point is that to have compassion is to be a compassionate person.

Further, to be a compassionate person is to construe the world differently. As one considers the plight of the homeless person sitting outside the market where one shops, one is convicted by the life teachings and Spirit of Jesus to act in a personally and socially responsible manner. It is no mere feeling. It is a dispositional, motivational relationship in which the believer, the homeless person and Christ are implicated by the Spirit in a life of responsible action. Affections are construals of and concerns for the world. As such they are also 'reasons' for action. When asked why one acted in a certain way toward the homeless person, the reason would be that one was compassionate. It would be irrational—contradictory of the logic of the Logos—to turn away in unconcerned apathy. The biblical depiction of the identity of God and the world on the way to the kingdom form, shape and direct the expression of the affections.

The Apocalyptic Affections: 'On the Way Home'
The differences between Lutherans and Roman Catholics are not only of a theological nature; they are also affective differences. The world is construed differently and the Christian affections are mixed in a different way for Lutherans than for Roman Catholics. One can drink

1.   1 Cor. 13.

whole milk from different dairies and detect differences in the taste because of the different climates, feed, species of the cows and processing methods. The 'sincere milk of the Word' tastes differently for reasons that are at least analogous.[1] An Anabaptist minister and an Eastern Orthodox priest may be able ultimately to affirm the other as Christian, but at the Lord's Supper they know that they are different.

Pentecostals are not just more exuberant than some other Christians. All the significant Christian affections are there but the profile is different. The apocalyptic vision and transcendent presence of the power of the age to come alters the affective chemistry in significant ways. The sense of urgency concerning the missionary task and readiness for the soon coming of the Holy Lamb of God alters the affections not only in quantitative intensity but also in terms of the qualitative mix or characteristic gestalt.

Recalling what was said in Chapter 2 concerning the characterization of apocalyptic in terms of break, hope and cosmic drama, it is understandable why those accustomed to power through prediction and control, whether in society or in the church, are uncomfortable at least with this spirituality. The sense of the inbreaking of the kingdom of God in Jesus Christ and in personal existence affirms the primacy of grace over against the inexorable, internally conditioned or socially dominated historical process.[2] Such a radical hope protects faith from a more subtle and prevalent threat than radical doubt or error: the trivialization and/or cooptation of faith in modern society. Particular events, specific instances of the gifts of the Spirit operating in a worship setting or in the market place of witness, these particular occurrences are seen as part of a larger cosmic drama in which one is a participant and not a victim. The sovereign Spirit of God is moving and working in all things for the good of those who love God. Everyone is playing a part and the final outcome will affect everyone.

One's response to God and one's neighbor expresses what one truly believes concerning the end. To walk in righteousness is to believe in and be led toward the kingdom of righteousness. To walk in wholehearted love is to believe in and be led toward a kingdom of perfect love and peace. To walk in the power of the Holy Spirit is to walk in joyous confidence and courage in the face of all opposition toward a kingdom in which God will be all in all. One is affected by and

1.   1 Pet. 2.2.
2.   Mills, 'New Heaven? New Earth?', pp. 98-100.

toward the kingdom of God that is already at work in and among believers through the Holy Spirit. The 'not yet' of the kingdom is known in 'foretaste' and 'down payment' but nevertheless remains future, new and something utterly gratuitous—as gratuitous as creation, the incarnation or one's own new birth. Neither perseverance nor parousia are inevitable.[1] Each is gratuitous. For the Pentecostal the power of the Spirit strengthens, sustains and directs all the affections through all the trials and temptations of life toward the goal of the kingdom of God.

It will be neither possible nor advisable to discuss all the Pentecostal affections, and one must also resist the temptation to pick one or more as the 'essence' of the spirituality. Robert Roberts gives a clear warning concerning

> [the] distortion that Christian spirituality is likely to suffer when a thinker alights on some single 'essence' of spirituality such as simplicity or openness to the future or authenticity or social justice. Such concepts probably capture something about Christian spirituality, but it is unlikely that any such essence hunting will preserve the richness of the biblical concept.[2]

And so, this explication will eschew both exhaustive analysis and reductionist essentialization; instead, it will focus on three important affections which are correlated with the view of God, the kingdom and salvation discussed earlier in this chapter. The three selected are also related to the traditional theological virtues of faith, love and hope, respectively. The three affections, with certain attendant synonyms or closely related affections, are as follows:

1. Gratitude (praise, thanksgiving)
2. Compassion (love, longing)
3. Courage (confidence, hope)

Obviously all Christians are or should be characterized by these affections. Therefore, the effort here is to depict each of these in its distinctive Pentecostal ethos. The following chart shows something of the structure and interrelationships of the Pentecostal affections.

---

1. Heb. 6.1-12.
2. Roberts, *Strengths*, p. 23.

Pentecostal Affections

	Gratitude (thanks, praise)	*Compassion* (love, longing)	*Courage* (confidence, hope)
Source in God's:	Righteousness	Love (Holiness)	Power
Testified to as:	'Saved'- Regenerated	Sanctified	Baptized in Spirit
Opposed by: *Which are*	World	Flesh	Devil
overcome by:	Faith (1 Jn 5.4)	Crucifixion (Gal. 5.24, Rom. 8.13)	Resistance (Jas 4.7)
Walk: *Evoked and*	In Light	In Love	In Power of Spirit
Expressed in:	Worship	Prayer.	Witness
Christ as:	Savior	Sanctifier	Spirit Baptizer

Gratitude. Since all blessings flow from the gracious action of God, gratitude is the initial and continually relevant Christian affection which, through remembrance and thanksgiving, preserves the believer from the mutually conditioning sins of forgetfulness and presumption. Along with all Christians, Pentecostals give thanks for what God did throughout biblical history to create, call, deliver and preserve a people for divine fellowship. But Pentecostals lay particular stress on the fact that God not only has acted generally in history, but has done so in their history. Everything good, they acknowledge, flows from Calvary into their lives through the continuing gracious actions of God who seeks and saves the lost. The ongoing action of God is decisive and crucial; it is experienced as a series of events or crises within, and with a view toward, a certain development toward the kingdom. To be 'saved' is to be forgiven, regenerated, adopted, cleansed, indwelt by the Spirit and incorporated into the people of God in the world. Salvation is fundamentally a transformation in conformity with the character and purpose of God. God is righteous and saves in order that believers may walk in the light or walk in the works that were ordained before the foundation of the world.[1] The righteousness of God is revealed and made effective in what God has done; the righteousness of believers is given as a gift with and through

1.   Eph. 2.10.

the faith that works through love.[1] Righteousness is imputed in order to be imparted, and it is clear that justification is to be 'no excuse for sin'.[2] One is saved when one repents and receives Christ the Savior through faith by grace. One is declared righteous and simultaneously, by grace, declares for the righteousness of God. Righteousness is everything required for and in a relationship with a just and holy God. At the heart of this relationship is the law of love.

Children, youth and adults can receive Christ. Infants are usually dedicated to the Lord and recognized as part of the covenant community. But at the 'age of accountability' when they know right from wrong and consciously experience the conviction and wooing of the Lord they are to receive Christ and be born again.[3] Only infants and the mentally handicapped are exempted from this receiving of Christ through faith and repentance. One is responsible only for the light one has! Christ's atonement avails for them and for all like them.

Gratitude, then, is evoked through remembering what God has done in Christ to atone for sins, what God has done to call one out of the world of lost souls, what God is doing to keep and perfect, and what God will do to bring in the kingdom. It is a hedge against forgetfulness. The holiness of God coupled with the divine gracious care fills the believer with thanksgiving, fear and awe. One shows gratitude through verbal and physical acts of thanksgiving. It is striking how often one will hear 'Thank you, Lord' or 'Praise the Lord' in a Pentecostal service. In fact these are perhaps the most frequently recurring phrases. Indeed, the testimonies, songs, prayers, offerings, manifestations of gifts, ordinances, and so on—all the elements of Pentecostal worship are instrumented for the evoking and shaping of thanksgiving and praise. God is said to dwell in the praises of his people, and through the various means of grace (songs, testimonies, preaching, teaching, prayer, ordinances, and so on) he shapes women and men into grateful persons.

But gratitude is expressed not only by what is said but also by what is done. As a hedge against presumption, it is shown by walking in all the light God gives, as the Spirit shines this light of the Lord upon the

1. Gal. 5.6.
2. *AF* 1.6 (February–March, 1907), p. 2.
3. Pentecostal Holiness ministers baptize infants but still admonish the parents to nurture the child and, at the appropriate age, call for repentance and expect a regeneration by profession of faith.

path of the pilgrim. This is not righteousness of works. As *The Apostolic Faith* asserted,

> This is not a 'do, do' religion, but it is the religion of the Lord Jesus Christ. Man has got to be born again. You cannot get it through moral culture, refinement, or giving up, but you must be born into it. It is through God's beloved Son who washes you, cleanses you, and makes you a fit subject for heaven.[1]

The believer remembered in song that 'Love lifted me...out of the angry waves...when nothing else could help'.[2] Believers were 'in a new world' since the Lord saved them.[3] In gratitude to God they must, when Scripture illuminated by the Spirit shined on their path, 'go forward or else backslide'.[4] As they received 'more' of the Holy Ghost, they would be expected, if it were authentic, to express more love, humility and praise.[5]

God thus has a purpose and plan for each life and each church. Gratitude means attending to the light of Scripture and the everyday voice of the Spirit, so that the general shape and specific directives of the Lord of the church may be realized in Christian service and witness. The life of faith is a life of faithfulness which is borne of grace and has its constant end in gratitude.

The grace of God and the gratitude of the believer are personal. The Holy Spirit is God's gracious presence, God's active favor, and God's effectual working in the believer. The Spirit personally orders the grateful heart so as to conform the individual to Jesus Christ. Although, 'Thank you, Father' and 'Thank you, Holy Spirit' are commonly heard in Pentecostal worship, it is 'Thank you, Jesus' that most frequently expresses gratitude. All blessings flow from the Father in the Spirit through Jesus.

To be grateful is also to remember where you have come from. *The Apostolic Faith* in January of 1907 exhorted its readers to recall when they were 'poor and ugly' in their own sight, because that was when God 'exalted and used' them. But when they 'got to be some great Nebuchadnezzar', then God will turn them out 'to eat grass like an ox.

---

1. *AF* 1.6 (February–March, 1907), p. 1.
2. Winsett, *Songs*, p. 258.
3. V.B. Ellis, 'I'm in a New World', *Church Hymnal*, pp. 94, 95.
4. *AF* 1.6 (February–March, 1907), p. 1.
5. *AF* 1.6 (February–March, 1907), p. 1.

Keep little and God will use you.'[1] Humility is the companion of
gratitude.

One is grateful to be a part of the holy people of God and to be out
of the world that is blind and bound. Friendship with the world will
dull and eventually destroy thankfulness and praise to God because
one of the chief marks of a 'worldly' person is that he or she is
unthankful.

The ways of God are not the ways of the world. Their methods are
different. The 'world' rejected Jesus, and has persecuted his disciples
throughout history. Pentecostals are one of the most persecuted and
martyred bodies of twentieth-century Christians. In some Central
American countries for example, they have been killed by the 'right'
and the 'left'. This does not mean they have tacitly endorsed the status
quo. It means they have taken a third way and disavowed the ways of
the world.

One of the deep sources of ongoing thanksgiving and gratitude is
the sense of belonging to the church of the living God and no longer
being a part of the world which is passing away. Even when
Pentecostals cannot tell the time and place when the Lord saved them,
they still have a definite sense of being called out of the world and into
the church on the way to a kingdom of righteousness. Every time
someone is born again and waits with the church, the believers
remember, rejoice and look forward to the final homecoming. The
source is the righteousness of God, the way is a walk in the light, and
the goal is a new heaven and new earth wherein dwells righteousness.
This 'faithful faith' is the victory that overcomes the world.

Gratitude is a powerful reason and motivation for witness. The
sharp delineation between church and world heightens the pain of
separation which the church in general and the believer in particular
feels. Though believers hate evil and are not friends of the world,
they nevertheless remember that God so loved them while they were
in the world. Indeed they are now in and not of in order to love the
world as God does. The world is an enemy to be loved. They are, to
use Niebuhr's terminology without buying into all his conclusions,
against the world in order to be for its transformation—which has
already begun in them. Christ is against, and the transformer of,
culture.[2]

1.   *AF* 1.5, (January, 1907), p. 1.
2.   H.R. Niebuhr, *Christ and Culture* (New York: Harper & Row, 1951).

In most Pentecostal services prayer requests will be offered for the lost—neighbors, relatives, fellow workers and so on. Neighbors are lost and deluded, but God is graciously at work convicting, blessing, judging and drawing them to Jesus Christ. Anger because of the binding of Satan, sorrow for the lost condition of these persons and joy over their deliverance, and a celebration of life and mission of the church are all in evidence. When someone is saved, and there are millions of such testimonies during this century, there is great rejoicing.

In summary, gratitude is grounded in and shaped by the gracious righteousness and merciful faithfulness of a holy, compassionate God. To be saved, pardoned, justified or born again is to be taken out of the unrighteous 'world' and placed in the body of Christ so that one may, with all the believers, become the righteousness of God in him toward the world. One gives thanks by walking in the light, being a light (in terms of Christian character) and doing deeds of righteousness so that others will believe and glorify God. Gratitude as thanksgiving and praise is characteristic of Pentecostal worship and is a passionate reason for the shape and content of the worship and witness of Pentecostals. To construe God as gracious, the world as lost and oneself as delivered or rescued is to be gratefully disposed toward God, in worship and for witness.

Compassion. If gratitude is the foundation of the Pentecostal affective structure, the interior of the building is a compassionate, longing love. Pentecostals, emerging as they did from the nineteenth-century Holiness movement, have a concern for holiness as perfect love or wholehearted devotion to God. Though they have been noted for their fierce doctrinal disputes, it is nevertheless widely recognized that Pentecostal congregations have a deep love for God, for one another and for the lost. Objectively, they would acknowledge that God is love; therefore, believers must love as God does and must be, to that extent, holy. This is what it means to have the mind of Christ.[1] If righteousness is fundamentally but not exclusively associated with the covenant faithfulness of God the Father to the creation, then love as compassion is primarily associated with Jesus.

For Pentecostals, as for John Wesley, their sins nailed Jesus to the

1.   Roberts, *Strengths*, p. 26.

cross and could, if returned to, even now represent a crucifying afresh of the Son of God.[1] Just as God in righteousness by grace creates a new people who belong to him and to one another, so God in holy love will create a new heart which is aflame with holy zeal and longing for the kingdom. If one is stirred to righteous indignation at the sight of the unrighteous violations of the world, then to this is joined a compassionate longing for the salvation of the lost and the coming of Christ. In the fullness of the kingdom everything will be holiness unto the Lord and without holiness no one will see the Lord.[2] This holiness is not that which is given in the article of death or at the resurrection and glorification of believers. It is, rather, a cleansing of the heart,[3] a washing of the robes and a cleansing 'from all filthiness of flesh and spirit perfecting holiness in the fear of God'.[4] Though the world had been abandoned, yet it remained in the form of evil thoughts, tempers, desires and ways.

As Wesley would have said, though sin remained, it no longer reigned. The believer wanted to do the right thing and to walk in the light. Pentecostals want to witness in the power of the Spirit. But the desire for holiness or sanctification is at heart a desire for God himself, to be like Christ in love. To have this love requires self-denial; indeed self-will is often construed as the heart of the problem. The sinful desires and tempers have to be mortified, put off and expelled by the love of God. The blood of Christ, the Word and the Spirit are collectively the agents of cleansing. What keeps one from being moved toward the lost and suffering mass of humanity? Inner resistances, the cares of this life, carnal desires, all these are hindrances to the notion of compassion and the infilling of the Spirit.

The desired purity of heart is given when believers 'are willing to let Him have His way to the fullest extent of the word'. Then they will be 'clay in the Potter's hands...and "self" will be removed'.[5] Indeed this emptying is necessary if one is to be filled with his Spirit; when the filling occurs, then the first thing that can be told is that 'the blood

1.   Heb. 6.10. Most Pentecostals are, broadly speaking, Arminians.
2.   Heb. 12.14. See also 'Holiness Unto the Lord', in A.J. Showalter, *The Best Gospel Songs and their Composers* (Dalton, GA: A.J. Showalter, 1904).
3.   'The Cleansing Wave', in Winsett, *Songs*.
4.   2 Cor. 7.1.
5.   *AF* 1.3 (1906), p. 2.

of Jesus Christ cleanses from all sin'.[1] The believer has his or her affections in Jesus Christ, the Lamb of God that takes away the sin of the world.[2] One must stay in the cross and die daily if power is to rest upon one's life and witness.[3] Sanctification was the center or heart of 'Bible Salvation' for the believers at Azusa and millions subsequently. It was 'God's design through the ages and through all His work with the children of men…to implant His own nature—love, in a fallen race'. It was 'sweet to feel the tender thrills of that love, going through every part' of one's being.[4]

Jesus is the center and model of compassionate love. To be compassionate is to be moved toward others as he was. The Spirit moves upon those who are emptied out and yielded to manifest the character of love which is described in the following short exhortation from Azusa:

The Character of Love

It is sweet to have the promise of Jesus and the character of Jesus wrought out in our lives and hearts by the power of the Blood and the Holy Ghost, and to have that same love and that same meekness and humility manifested in our lives, for His character is love. Jesus was a man of love. The people flocked to Him to hear His words. Women lugged their babies in the hot sun and spent days listening to the words of Jesus. Men got into boats and went across the sea to see Jesus and hear His precious words. While there were many that followed for the loaves and fishes, many followed Him for healing. Yes, He was a man of love. He was the express image of the Father, God manifest in the flesh.

Dear loved ones, we must have that pure love that comes down from heaven, love that is willing to suffer loss, love that is not puffed up, not easily provoked, but gentle, meek and humble. We are accounted as sheep for the slaughter day by day. We are crucified to self, the world, the flesh and everything, that we may bear about in our body the dying of the Lord Jesus, that our joy may be full even as He is full.[5]

If they were going to fill the world with the doctrine of Christ before his soon coming, early Pentecostals realized that they must be emptied of all that would hinder their availability and character as

1. *AF* 1.3 (1906), p. 2.
2. *AF* 1.3 (1906), p. 2.
3. *AF* 1.2 (1906), p. 4.
4. *AF* 1.3 (1906), p. 4.
5. *AF* 1.3 (1906), p. 4.

witnesses. As faith is the victory over the world which secured the
believer in righteousness for walking in the light, so crucifixion is the
biblical strategy against the flesh with its hindering passions and
desires. The passion of Christ for one's sins becomes, when struggling
against those same sins, compassion. The compassion for those bound
in sin, enslaved in the passions, is possible only in Christ.

Like all the Christian affections, compassion is sustained by abiding
in Christ. Without the compassion of Christ one cannot face, confess
and mortify one's own sinful passions. As love grows, so does hatred
of these passions and a desire to reach the sheep scattered with no
shepherd.[1] To construe one's heart as having the same sorts of evil
passions, selfish motives and senseless resistance to grace as those in
the world is to move toward the world with humility. When there is
no known hold-out or resistance but only a consciousness of love it is
a wounded love which, even when it grows, recognizes how totally
dependent upon the faithfulness, longsuffering and love of God one is.
Fallibility, neurotic fears and repressed resistances remain. Only in
constant openness to the compassionate love of God, in searching of
the Spirit, and in faithful fellowship of the saints is it possible to avoid
self-deception or immobilizing despair.

Compassion moves one to respond according to the pattern of
Christ. Compassion is the reason and the motive for that response in
and by the Spirit. Compassion longs for all to know the love of God
and for the kingdom to come. Compassion is borne of inner peace
with God based on and flowing from the peace made at Calvary. It is
the healing of the heart that makes one like God and therefore for
others.[2] Compassion is suffering love wounded by the suffering of
others who do not know or have rejected Christ.

When Pentecostals 'pray through' about their resistances or hold-
outs, and 'kill' the untoward affections, God's love fills their hearts.
This is usually attended by tears and laughter, by sorrow and joy, by
delight in and longing for the Beloved. These feelings are common
among Pentecostals. In this way one acknowledges affectively the
death, crucifixion of self with Christ, and the resurrection. This is a
deepening of those changes which were brought about in the new
birth.

1. Mt. 9.36.
2. As God is 'for us' (Rom. 8.31).

The progression or logic of the soteriology is reflected in the affections. Justification and new birth ask for sanctification which asks for Spirit baptism. So then the gratitude and thanksgiving associated with initial salvation, when the love of God is shed abroad in the heart by the Holy Spirit, ask for or tend toward the fullness of love which is called entire sanctification. The crucifying and putting off of the deeds and carnal affections is not so as to merit entire sanctification; they are necessary in order to be filled with or to be decisively determined or moved by love. Initial sanctification, associated with the real change accompanying new birth reaches its goal in entire sanctification. The fullness of freedom associated with new birth moves forward the fullness of love in entire sanctification as one walks in the light of the Scripture. The sin tendency as resistance, hold-outs, self-will and so forth is to be acknowledged, confessed, hated, mortified and put away even as one reads the Word, yields to the searching of the Spirit, and does all the good he or she can. The old is replaced with the new.

It is good to be moved by gratitude toward the lost, hurting and oppressed. In this way one shows that one is grateful. On remembering those in need one remembers whence one has come. But compassion is a deeper binding to the crucified one and to the lost. Compassion moves with urgency, pity, longing for the lost. Compassion moves the believer toward the world and draws the world into the sphere of redemption. Gratitude looks up to God continually; compassion looks out to the lost longingly. If gratitude is the hedge against presumption, forgetfulness and mere duty, then compassion is the safeguard against hardness of heart, complacency and sentimentality. Compassion sings, 'Rescue the perishing...care for the dying'.[1] The holiness of God in Christ by the Holy Spirit cleanses and consumes with holy zeal. To become compassionate is to carry daily in one's body the dying of the Lord.[2] Pentecostals characteristically travail in prayer for the lost, afflicted and oppressed.

Pentecostal songs would be used to call believers to prayer, typically during an 'altar service', and to guide these prayers toward consecration and cleansing. Compassion could and did move the regenerate, and all were called upon to be witnesses. Nevertheless carnality would hinder their witness, imperil their salvation and be a stumbling block to others. If compassion toward others was to come

1. 'Rescue the Perishing', *Church Hymnal*, p. 145.
2. 2 Cor. 4.7-10.

to full expression then love for God must be as complete as possible. The capacity for this love would increase but the hindrances must be removed and selfishness rooted out.

A few representative songs will illustrate this desire to be sanctified, fully yielded and available for the Master's use. The first are selections from an Assemblies of God collection entitled *Melodies of Praise*.[1] In the selection 'Jesus I Come' the congregation sings,

> Out of unrest and arrogant pride,
> Jesus I come, Jesus I come;
> Into Thy blessed will to abide,
> Jesus, I come to thee;
> Out of myself to dwell in Thy love,
> Out of despair into raptures above
> Upward for aye on wings like a dove,
> Jesus, I come to Thee.[2]

The connection between consecration and Spirit filling is made explicit as believers are urged to

> Be filled with the Spirit.
> Yield completely to the One Who cleans'd
> And made you whole;
> Be filled with the Spirit.

1.   These hymns are chosen because the Assemblies of God are supposedly the 'baptistic' or two-blessing wing of the movement (saved, filled with the Spirit). Though the theologies of the 'baptistic' and 'Wesleyan' Pentecostals may differ over what does or does not, can or cannot happen in sanctification, yet the concern for holiness, purity and consecration is still evident in the following hymns. This is true throughout the movement, and was even more obvious in and characteristic of the early Pentecostals. Though rejecting an 'eradicationist' view of sanctification, the Assemblies of God, nevertheless, did adopt a statement on 'entire sanctification' in their earliest Statement of Fundamental Truths. This was no doubt an attempt to hold the various Wesleyan Pentecostals who had not yet embraced Durham's finished work doctrine. James Bowers has chronicled an account of how the three-blessing paradigm began to weaken and then almost fade away in the North American constituency of the Church of God. See his 'Sanctification in the Church of God: A Shift From the Three Blessing Paradigm' (Southern Baptist Theological Seminary, 1985).

2.   Cited in Ranaghan, 'Rites', p. 736 as a 'Conversion' song but is also illustrative of consecration and cleansing.

> You need the precious love of God
> To fill and flood your heart;
> Until there is no room
> For carnal self to have a part.[1]

In 'Bring your Vessels not a Few' those who are seeking for the infilling and blessing of the Lord in their heart and life are instructed,

> Bring your empty earthen vessels,
> Clean thru' Jesus' precious blood,
> Come, ye needy, one and all;
> And in human consecration wait
> Before the throne of God,
> Till the Holy Ghost shall fall.[2]

As they seek the 'Pentecostal Blessing' they pray that God will cleanse their 'hearts from sinful leaven'.[3] In 'Waiting on the Lord' for the promise of the Father, they acknowledge that the power of Pentecost 'gives victory over sin and purity within'.[4] The Pentecostal soul longs for 'Higher Ground' and to go 'Deeper, Deeper' in the love of Jesus every day.[5]

> Deeper, deeper in the love of Jesus
> Daily let me go;
> Higher, higher in the school of wisdom
> More of grace to know.
>
> CHORUS
> O deeper yet, I pray.
> And higher every day,
> And wiser blessed Lord,
> In Thy precious holy Word.
>
> Deeper, deeper! Blessed Holy Spirit,
> Take me deeper still,
> Till my life is wholly lost in Jesus
> And His perfect will.

---

1. Ranaghan, 'Rites', pp. 738, 734.
2. Ranaghan, 'Rites', p. 739.
3. Ranaghan, 'Rites', p. 741.
4. Ranaghan, 'Rites', p. 746.
5. Sanctification is not the static, terminal stage which, when reached, spells the end of this longing. It is the abiding in wholehearted, longing expectation. It is characterized by the joy of union and wounded longing.

Deeper, deeper! Tho' it cost hard trials,
Deeper let me go!
Rooted in the holy love of Jesus,
Let me fruitful grow.

Deeper, higher ev'ry day in Jesus,
Till all conflict past,
Finds me conqu'ror, and in His own image
Perfected at last.

Deeper, deeper in the faith of Jesus,
Holy faith and true;
In His power and soul,exulting wisdom
Let me peace pursue.[1]

This gospel song is important for several reasons. It shows that the holy life is a daily pursuit requiring divine wisdom from the Word of God. It indicates that the depth dimension is reached when the Holy Spirit, who searches the deep things of God, takes the believer deeper into Christ—lost in him and his perfect will. This will perhaps cost 'hard trials' but it is necessary to be rooted deeply if one is to be fruitful. Apparently love is the ground or fundament from which all the fruit of the Spirit springs; to go deeper in love is to go deeper in faith (the faith of Jesus) and to pursue peace. This is reminiscent of the passage often quoted among Pentecostals, 'Pursue peace with all, and holiness without which no one shall see the Lord' (Heb. 12.14).

As early as 1908 the Pentecostals were singing 'Is Your All on the Altar?', 'None of Self and All of Thee', 'His Way with Thee', 'The Cleansing Wave' and 'Higher Ground'.[2] There are tensions between a thoroughgoing Wesleyan and other formulations of sanctification in these songs. But through them there is a richness and a struggle to articulate a deep, abiding longing for God and a fullness of love which is not fully appreciated by merely reading the early and somewhat meager Pentecostal statements of faith.

This all-consuming love for God was finally a longing for the coming of the Lord. Pentecostals' love was a 'Longing for the Dawning' of the day of the Lord when all conflict would be past.[3] The object of this affection was most often Christ himself and the great

1.   Winsett, *Songs*, p. 219.
2.   Winsett, *Songs*, pp. 212, 174, 261, 180, 120.
3.   Winsett, *Songs*, p. 164.

'Meeting in the Air' with all the saints of old.[1] As they sang 'Oh, I Want to See Him' they beseeched the Savior, 'O Lord, How Long?'[2] In the meantime the agenda was captured in such songs as, 'I'll Go Where You Want Me to Go', 'Sitting at the Feet of Jesus', and 'We'll Work till Jesus Comes'.[3]

Such longing kept one separate from the world but moved one toward the lost. The peace of sanctification did not lead to complacency because sanctification as love must necessarily become compassion in a world that is lost and suffering. In such a world the ministry of healing expressed and evoked compassion and longing.

At Azusa Seymour linked sanctification of soul and body and asserted that both, along with all other blessings of salvation, were provided in the atonement. Seymour was a literalist when it came to healing. God would sanctify 'bodies from inherited disease... Every drop of blood we received from our mother is impure. Sickness is born in a child just as original sin is born in the child. He was manifested to destroy the works of the devil. Every sickness is of the devil.'[4]

Though not all Pentecostals since then would share this metaphysics, most would continue to affirm and practice a joint ministry to soul and body. As the sick come forward for prayer the congregation often sings 'The Healing Waters', which focuses not on physical healing, but forgiveness, bliss, 'precious perfect love, and rest!'[5] There are thousands of testimonies all over the world to healings.

Some see healing as one of the major emphases, if not the characterizing aspect, of the movement. But be that as it may, it is true that when one was healed, there was joy *and* sorrow. The joy was obviously because of the miraculous help given to the afflicted and the assurance given to all the witnesses. But everyone was reminded of his or her mortality. *All* were never healed; *some* were. And the ones who were not were always in substantial enough numbers to create a longing in the fellowship for the great day of final salvation and universal healing. The healing evangelists may have had their theories as to why this or that person was not healed, but the masses of

1. Winsett, *Songs*, p. 257.
2. E. Haynes and M.S. Lemons, *Church of God Songs No.3* (Cleveland, TN: Church of God Publishing House, n.d.).
3. Winsett, *Songs*, pp. 210, 203, 179.
4. *AF* 1.1 (1906), p. 2.
5. Winsett, *Songs*, p. 135.

believers knew it was a mystery.[1] They, along with compassionate pastors, cared for and comforted the afflicted who joined with them in rejoicing with the healed. The doubts and struggles created by the formulas of faith, then and now, would only yield to the compassion of the body of believers who, as a whole and individually, knew that all would eventually die. Compassion for the sick and suffering was always most intense among those who had the least medical care available or who could least afford it. This compassion was rooted in fundamental notions of creation of the body, resurrection of the body, a millennial kingdom of a new heaven and earth and, most of all, the ministry of Jesus.

The love of God shed abroad in the believer's hearts at regeneration grew in the 'hungry' till it filled them with longing for God and compassion for the lost. The songs, testimonies, sermons, altar services, healing services, rescue missions, soup kitchens, orphanages and missions both evoked and expressed love, longing and compassion. Gratitude turned one toward the world in thankfulness and a desire to tell others the good news. Compassion moved one toward the lost, afflicted and perishing in obedience to the pattern of Christ's ministry. The world was overcome in the faith that was at once a personal victory and a corporate commitment. The flesh was crucified, and through consecration and cleansing, compassion could move one back into the world from which one had come.

But the evil spirits would not be moved by gratitude or compassion. The rejection, hostility and persecution of the world could soon wear down compassion. The wounded and weary realized there were real dangers to be faced and real evils to be overcome. The grace of regeneration had given power to resist the evil inclinations from within and allurements from without. The grace of entire sanctification gave the inner freedom which delighted in the will of God and longed for the salvation of the world. But walking in the light or righteousness and walking in love was not the same as walking in the power of the Spirit. Believers needed courage and fortifying to sustain their battle against powers and principalities. They needed the full panoply of gifts and graces to proclaim the gospel in word, power and demonstration of the Spirit. This power—this authorized power of God— would bring courage to witness and, if necessary, to suffer and die.

1. *AF* 1.11 (October–January, 1908), p. 3: 'We ought to claim perfect health in the atonement of Jesus'.

With this courage they would, could and did go all over the world witnessing to the lost and warning the church to get ready for the kingdom of righteousness, peace and joy that would soon dawn upon the world.

The move toward a new integration of the affective life, one that seeks to incorporate new power, courage and confidence into a life of active gratitude and compassion can be seen in the following testimony which is quoted at length from *The Apostolic Faith* paper in 1908. Miss Antoinette Moomean of Eustice, Nebraska narrates her journey from the mission field of China to the Azusa Street Revival. This testimony conveys the ethos, affective tone and something of the instrumented means used to effect affective transformation. It is clear from this account that baptism in the Spirit meant a strengthening of all that had gone before in her Christian development and a discovery of 'the secret of the endurance of the martyrs'. It is an interesting weaving together of doctrine, affect, gifts, practices and self-disclosure. There were and are hundreds of thousands of testimonies like this one. It provides a good transition from the preceding discussion of gratitude and compassion to the succeeding and final affection to be considered, courage.

> On leaving China, October, 1906, I was asked to investigate the Apostolic Faith Movement in Los Angeles, where they claim to have manifested the same gifts of the Holy Ghost as of old (I Cor.12.8-10). I heard such contradictory reports that I kept away for some time, but praise God, He had His hand upon me for this wonderful gift, and I had no rest until I went and heard and saw for myself.
>
> It only took a short time after the beginning of the first meeting, to know it was of God. And when the altar call came, I went forward.
>
> Before this I had asked God to turn His great searchlight upon my heart and was astonished to find so much worldliness, spiritual pride, vanity, insincerity, lack of love, selfishness, and other things. When I had left for the foreign field seven years before this, I thought I had died to everything; but when the Spirit began to deal with me in preparing me for the fullness of the Spirit, I found I was very much alive, in fact had scarcely begun to die to self. Although the Lord had given me wonderful victories in my life and what I thought was the baptism of the Spirit, yet when God began to search me as never before, I had to confess that I had never even been sanctified.
>
> I had been taught the suppression theory and now and again the 'old man' would pop up in greater or less degree; sometimes harsh words did not escape, but I would feel the boiling up inside. But God showed me

that His word meant just what it said, that provision was made in the atonement—not only for our sins but our sin, the old Adamic nature (Rom. 6.6, 18, 22). How I did rejoice at the last, the longing of my heart to be rid of that which had kept me from being entirely free from sin, was to be satisfied. I had sought my baptism of the Spirit three times, when the Lord told me that I must be sanctified before the Spirit could take full possession of my body. Just so were the disciples sanctified before Christ left them (John 17.17, 19), that they might be ready for the baptism of the Spirit.

After some of the saints had prayed for me, one of them asked me if I had the witness of the Spirit to my sanctification according to Heb. 10.14, 15. For some years back when I had been taught of the Spirit to keep 'short accounts' with the Lord, and there was nothing left to do in the way of restitution; and having laid all on the altar, I knew I had met the condition, and that God had fulfilled His promise; although there was no other feeling than the assurance that God had done the work because of His Word. I then began to praise God audibly, and in a few minutes I was flooded with billows of glory, and the Spirit sang through me praises unto God. Besides this witness of the Spirit, was the witness of the fruits; for under whatever provocation, there is no uprising, for there is nothing to rise up. Glory to Jesus.

When sanctified, I was filled with such glory that I felt sure it must be the baptism, which did not come for three weeks. In the meantime, the power was upon me almost continually, sometimes lying under the power for hours, while I consecrated myself to God as never before.

At last after a real dying out, as I never dreamed could be possible on earth, in the upper room at Azusa Mission, the promise of the Father was made real to me, and I was charged with the power of God and my soul flooded with glory. The Spirit sang praises unto God. Glory to Jesus. He gave me the Bible experience, speaking through me in other tongues.

The Lord showed me that the cross was going to mean to me what it had never meant before. One morning the Spirit dealt with me, singing through me—

> Must Jesus bear the cross alone,
> And all the world go free:
> No, there's a cross for every one,
> And there is one for me.

The last line He just seemed to burn into my soul by repeating it over and over again. Sometimes the Spirit would sing a line and then sob out a line. Although I wept and was in anguish of soul, it was all in the Spirit.

The life of Jesus passed before me, and He asked me if I was willing to follow Jesus in living absolutely for Him in ministering unto others. I thought I had known something of what this meant in China; but now to preach the everlasting Gospel in the power and demonstration of the Spirit and to truly go out on the faith line and to minister day and night, sometimes unto the hungry multitudes in the face of fierce opposition, meant far more than ever before. But He enabled me to say, 'By Thy grace I will bear this cross'.

The Garden scene came up before me next, as the Spirit again sang, 'Must Jesus bear the cross alone?' And He seemed to say, 'Your friends will forsake you, your own family will misunderstand you, you will be called a fanatic, crazy; are you willing to bear this cross?' Again I answered, 'By Thy grace, I will'.

The crucifixion scene then came before me and it seemed as if my heart would break with sorrow, and I could only wait in silence. Then I said, 'Lord, if it was to be beheaded, I could; but—' I could go no further. Later in the day, the Lord spoke to me again as I was under the power. It seemed as if I would perish in soul anguish. I was unconscious of the workers all about me. It seemed as if Jesus Himself stood beside, looking down upon me. I could only say, 'Jesus, Jesus, Jesus, I will, I will, I will'. His promise came to me as distinctly as if audibly [and] said, 'My grace is sufficient for you'. And in a flash, He gave me to understand the secret of the endurance of the martyrs who were burned at the stake with the glory of heaven upon their faces, and seemingly free from pain. And He enabled me to say, 'Yes, Lord, your grace is sufficient'.

Then the Spirit began to sing in a joyful strain, repeating over and over again the last line until I could almost see the crown:

> The consecrated cross I'll bear,
> Till Christ has set me free;
> And then go home a crown to wear,
> For there's a crown for me.

To sum it up, the baptism of the Spirit means to me what I never dreamed it could this side of Heaven: victory, glory in my soul, perfect peace, rest, liberty, nearness to Christ, deadness to this old world, and power in witnessing. Glory to His name forever and forever![1]

Courage. The faithfulness of the grateful and the zeal of the compassionate are deepened and strengthened by the courage associated with Spirit baptism. In regeneration one belongs to the new people of God and gives thanks; in sanctification one receives a new heart of compassionate love for God and others; and in Spirit baptism one receives an 'authorized strength' to be a courageous witness in word and demonstration of the Spirit.[2] The faith of the new people of

1. *AF* 1.11 (October–January, 1908), p. 3.
2. The words *exousia* and *dunamis* (transliterations) mean authority and force, respectively; both words are frequently translated as 'power'.

God overcomes the world as the redeemed follow the leading of the
Spirit-Lord. The discipline of crucifixion or mortification neutralizes
the inner hindrances to the fullness of love and compassion that is the
essence of sanctification. The infilling of the Spirit enables the believer
and the church to resist the devil and to assault spiritual strongholds
with spiritual weapons.[1]

We have already seen how righteousness and sanctification, along
with their corresponding affections of gratitude and compassion, are
thoroughly apocalyptic in orientation. The deepening of love in
sanctification is the result of and issues in a further intensification of a
yearning for the consummation of the kingdom of righteousness
where everything will be ordered according to the covenant purposes
of God. Perfect love longs for all God's children to be home with the
Lord, so that the Pentecostal vision of heaven is at once theocentric
and anthropocentric.[2] The deeper peace with God associated with the
mortification of the carnal desires and fullness of love is an anticipation which looks forward to the perfect peace (*shalom*) and well-being
associated with the new heaven and earth.

The power given in Spirit baptism strengthens all the other fruits of
the Spirit and gives courage and boldness borne of confidence in God.
This brings great joy in believing because the believer can, in addition
to standing and suffering for the gospel, also take the offensive and
engage the forces of unrighteousness, hatred and oppression in prayer,
service and witness. The confidence of this courage looks at what God
has done and already is doing. This confidence in God, because of the
fulfilled promises and ongoing guidance, builds a hope which looks
forward to the day when God will be 'all in all'.[3] Just as the Spirit fills
the reconciled, sanctified believer who then praises and proclaims
God, so also one day everything and everyone will praise God.

These three affections can also be seen as safeguards against certain
dangers. A grateful, thankful walking in the light guards against

---

1. Eph. 6.10-20, Jas 4.7.

2. In Heaven: A History the authors divide the views of ultimate destiny into
two major camps: the theocentric or more individualistic, contemplative, and the
anthropocentric, more social vision of a great reunion. Pentecostals hold something
of both views in terms of ultimate destiny and in light of their penultimate
eschatological worship. See C. McDonnell and B. Lang, *Heaven: A History* (New
Haven: Yale University Press, 1988).

3. 1 Cor. 15.28.

presumption or mere mechanical duty. Grace is the foundation for everything given and promised; and every day is experienced as a gift of forgiveness, cleansing and enablement. Gratitude disposes toward obedience, while a wanton, lascivious disregard for scriptural limits and directives is guarded against when the heart is truly thankful. Compassionate, wholehearted love in and through Christ guards the soul against sentimentality, apathy and hardness of heart. The believer at peace through the cross is a peacemaker through compassion. The courage that is given to the grateful, compassionate seekers after righteousness is a hedge against despair. Believers are called to take up their cross and follow, and not merely to be victims. However, they are to follow courageously. It is important to wait upon the sovereign Spirit, because to go forth without the Spirit's leading is to go without his power. Techniques may be used to induce 'sensations of power' but real power belongs to the Spirit alone. Power, like holiness and love and grace, is the believer's possession only in a derivative and relational sense.

The Spirit is 'the Faithful Guide'[1] and 'Bishop of the Church'.[2] It is His office and work 'to preside over the entire work of God on earth—' (Jn 10.3). Jesus has sent the Holy Spirit to be the chief bishop and 'not men'— (Jn 14.16; 15.26; 16.7-14). It is the Holy Spirit who infuses with divine power and invests with heavenly authority and, therefore, no 'religious assembly is legal without his presence and his transaction'. He is the 'Teacher of teachers'. So many of God's people are without divine power and 'experiential salvation' today because they do not accept him as their teacher, leader and comforter. It is the power of the Spirit that gives bishops and elders their authority today. His 'credentials' must be put in their hearts if they are to be co-workers with and partakers of him. The enduing of power is their single most important qualification for office. Without this the leaders cannot witness to the uttermost parts of the earth with the people. The Spirit 'takes the members into the church and, if they commence sinning', the Holy Spirit as 'the chairman and bishop, the presiding elder, turns them out'. There can be no power in the church and hence in the members unless the Holy Spirit is heeded. No one can take the place of the Spirit.

1. Haynes and Lemons, *Songs No. 3*, p. 111.
2. *AF* 1.9 (June–September, 1907), p. 3.

Many people today think we need new churches... brick structures, modern improvements, new choirs, trained singers right from the conservatories, paying from seven to fifteen hundred dollars a year for singing, fine pews, fine chandeliers, everything that could attract the human heart to win souls to the meeting house is used in this twentieth century. We find that they have reached the climax, but all of that has failed to bring divine power and salvation to precious souls. Sinners have gone to the meeting house, heard a nice, fine, eloquent oration on Jesus, or on some particular church, or on some noted man. The people have been made glad to go because they have seen great wealth, they have seen people in the latest styles, in different costumes, and loaded down with jewelry, decorated from head to foot with diamonds, gold and silver. The music in the church has been sweet, and it is found that a good many of the church people seem to be full of love, but there has always been a lack of power. We wonder why sinners are not being converted, and why it is that the church is always making improvements and failing to do the work that Christ called her to do. It is because men have taken the place of Christ and the Holy Spirit.[1]

The Spirit is the Lord who leads the church into battle and devises the tactics that will be effective in bringing glory to God and sinners unto the kingdom. Pentecostals tend to see themselves as an army of the Lord. Each one is a 'Soldier in the Army of the King', and the church moves like a mighty army on 'the Tribulation Way' as it is 'Marching to Our Home on High'.[2] In courage and hope the church is 'waiting on the Lord', while serving in the 'Armies of Zion'.[3] Each soldier is confident that 'When the Roll is Called Up Yonder' she or he will be there.

Confidence and hope are respectively the already–not yet polarities of courage. The believers' confidence is built as new persons are born into the kingdom and they witness healings, exorcisms and other answers to prayers. Corporate worship is 'joy unspeakable and full of glory'.[4] As confidence in the leading and presence of the Spirit builds, so does the vision of hope as believers sing, 'O What Joy It Will Be'.[5]

Many Pentecostal believers are arrested and many have been imprisoned, tortured and killed. But it is common for them to sing,

1. *AF* 1.9 (June–September, 1907), p. 3.
2. J.D. Vaughan, *The Silver Trumpet* (Lawrenceburg, TN: James D. Vaughan, 1908), pp. 43, 59.
3. Winsett, *Songs*, p. 2; Showalter, *The Best Gospel Songs*, p. 158.
4. 1 Pet. 1.8.
5. Haynes and Lemmons, p. 165.

preach and witness in the prisons, even founding prison churches. From the Pentecostals imprisoned in Los Angeles at Azusa to the more recent Soviet Pentecostal prisoners, to Chinese, African, South and Central American believers, all have undergone persecution and frequently have paid with their lives. Pedro Pablo Costillo, the current overseer of the Church of God in Nicaragua was imprisoned under the Sandanista regime. He preached to and baptized prisoners in each and every section of the prison in which he was placed. Upon his release he elected to stay in the country and lead his people in 'evangelistic and social ministry' to the needs of the Nicaraguans.[1]

It takes courage to eschew the 'right' and the 'left' and find a 'third' way of peace. In the most oppressive environments the joyful praise of the Pentecostals can be heard. While it is true they provide a 'haven for the masses', it is nevertheless also true that their courage is by no means a passive resignation. What was said at Azusa could still be said throughout the Third World today—they are 'ready not only to go to prison but to give our lives for Jesus'.[2] 'Arrested for Jesus'.

As at the beginning of the movement the poor, the young and the formally untrained go out to local and foreign fields to serve. A short article in *The Apostolic Faith* paper of October, 1906 captures this populist uprising of the Spirit.

Back to Pentecost

What mean these salaried preachers over the land that will not preach unless they get so much salary? People have wandered from the old landmarks... Get back. You have no time to lose. We must all be up and doing something for perishing souls around us. Do you want to be blest? Do you want the approbation of God? Be a servant to humanity. The loaves and fishes did not multiply in the hands of our blessed Redeemer till he began to give out to the hungry.

God does not need a great theological preacher that can give nothing but theological chips and shavings to people. He can pick up a worm and thrash a mountain. He takes the weak things to confound the mighty. He is picking up pebble stones from the street and polishing them for His work. He is using even the children to preach His Gospel. A young sister, fourteen years old, was saved, sanctified, and baptized with the Holy Ghost and went out, taking a band of workers with her, and led a

1.   Interview with the family of Pedro Pablo Costillo (Managua, Nicaragua, October, 1989).

2.   *AF* 1.1 (September, 1906), p. 4.

revival in which one hundred and ninety souls were saved. Salaried ministers that are rejecting the Gospel will have to go out of business. He is sending out those who will go without money and without price. Glory to God for this Apostolic day.[1]

The faithful everywhere reported and still report 'signs following' which hold the faith and hope, confidence and courage of the witnesses.[2] Individuals would have dreams and visions and be called to foreign fields. In 1906 Lucy Leatherman of New York City reported to *The Apostolic Faith* that she had been called to Beirut. God asked her if she would be willing to 'go with him to the wild Arab of the desert' and she said 'yes'.[3] Yet, those who trust in dreams or manifestations or tongues of the Spirit were cautioned to maintain a guard because these could not be the ground of their confidence. The Spirit is not a permanent possession of theirs or their church.

Those who receive the baptism with the Holy Ghost and speak in tongues and then backslide from this state may retain the speaking in tongues for a while after divine love is gone, but gradually this gift will melt away. A very little harshness or a critical suspicious statement about a brother will grieve the tender, sensitive Spirit. A careful and constant guard must be made, lest the flesh arise and destroy the fragrance and sweetness of this Spirit walk. Preachers often go too far and try to emphasize in fleshly vehemence a good point made by the Spirit. All such conduct will receive a gentle rebuke of the Spirit and, if heartily repented of, will soon be overcome, and result in greater confirmation of God's power in one's life.[4]

The courage to be a witness in the world in opposition to the demonic spirits was borne of the power of the Spirit who, by his constant, searching presence, strengthened the affections, manifested the needed gifts and drove the enemy out of the possessed and back from the believer. The grace of forgiveness and mercy gave the believer the courage to face the world and their own sins in responsibility and humility. The grace of sanctification gave confidence and joy as believers gained victory in the inner struggles with the flesh. The

1.　'Back to Pentecost', *AF* 1.2 (October, 1906), p. 3.

2.　*AF* 1.3 (November, 1906), p. 4.

3.　*AF* 1.3 (November, 1906), p. 4. For example, Margaret Gaines, a Church of God Missionary, left Alabama in the 1950s to live among the Arabs in Palestine as a teacher, pastor, church planter.

4.　*AF* 1.4 (December, 1906), p. 4.

grace of Spirit filling continually gave courage and strength to oppose and to discern the enemy of the saints.[1]

Gratitude, compassion and courage grow from the righteousness, love and power of God and are construals of the world in the light of the kingdom of righteousness, peace and joy in the Holy Spirit. Believers are to be continually grateful to God, compassionate through Christ and courageous in the Holy Spirit. But since they are still in though not of the world, still in flesh though not of the flesh, and still opposed on every hand by a crafty and cunning adversary, the possibility of deception is very real. Cultural, carnal and demonic elements can only be distinguished by the Holy Spirit.

A Disciplined Discernment: Word and Spirit
The. early Pentecostals were accused of being demonic, deranged, deluded and/or divisive. Those making the charges usually did so on the basis of Pentecostal claims to spiritual gifts that clearly, to them at least, were limited to the first century. Others criticized the strong emotion, mixing of races, and prophesying of women and men.[2] *The Apostolic Evangel* published in Royston, Georgia in 1907 responded by advancing 'Some Infallible Evidences that the Modern Pentecost Is of God'. The article listed four evidences which could assist in discerning the spirit of Pentecostalism; in addition, the article gave two brief exhortations to the Pentecostals themselves. The evidences were: (1) the intense hunger for *righteousness* in those who were filled; (2) the deep *crucifixion* of self, which is what the devil puffs up and uses; (3) the continual *praises* to God; and (4) the increase of the 'unspeakable *love* of God and one another that accompanies Spirit baptism' (emphasis mine).[3] The admonitions to Pentecostals had to do with judging others and power. The *Evangel* suggested that when they got their Pentecost they would be 'just as true to God and His Word as even on outward as well as inward things, but you will be forever done measuring the height of people's experience by the cut of their clothes'. In addition, Pentecost will, supposedly, cure them of their stress on 'noise as power...God will not give His glory to noise;

1. 'Demons Cast Out', *AF* 1.6 (February–March, 1907), p. 3.
2. H. Ward, 'The Early Anti-Pentecostal Argument', in Synan, *Aspects*, pp. 99-122.
3. J.H. King (ed.), *The Apostolic Evangel* 1.4, p. 1. Cf. King's very influential, *From Passover to Pentecost* (Memphis, TN: H.W. Dixon Printing Co., 1914).

although He reserves the right to make all the noise He pleases'.[1] If the admonitions deal more with matters of style and taste, the firm evidences are more substantial tests of authenticity.

Coming out of a perfectionist, revivalist background, Pentecostalism, from the first, had to oppose fanaticism while striving to 'let the Spirit have His way'. Those gathered at the Azusa Mission in 1906 developed guidelines for recognizing fanatics:

> Fanatics are marked by harshness towards those who do not fall in line with them, an [and] Jesus is not held up. Sooner or later the fruits of the flesh appear in a lack of holy living.
>
> We note these things because some honest souls have feared that this Pentecostal movement was fanaticism. So we mark some of the features of the meetings which are the opposite of fanaticism. Divine love to all, especially to the church, the body of Christ, of which every justified soul is a member. Humility: this is a humble work in a humble place and we are glad that it is. We humble ourselves under the mighty hand of God and constantly search the scriptures to know His whole will and plan. Holy lives: these people are living holy lives, separate from the world, the flesh and the devil, and rescuing other souls to a life of purity and holiness. There is a Holy Ghost shine on the faces of the workers. Is this the work of the devil?[2]

A few insights can be gleaned from the foregoing quote. In keeping with 1 John 3, Pentecostals looked at the source and results of supposed spiritual manifestations and persons. If Jesus was 'not held up' then the manifestation was fanatical. Harshness was clear proof that the chief characteristic of Jesus, divine love, was missing. Next to love in importance was humility and humble, submissive searching of the Scriptures for 'his whole will and plan'. Holy lives of witnesses who have a 'Holy Ghost shine' of glory and joy are also highly valued. So in addition to the very important inner witness of the Spirit, believers could check their and others' lives for the confession to Christ which sought to edify the church in love, further the mission and manifest the fruit and gifts of the Spirit and not the flesh.

Those who were 'walking in the light' would recognize darkness. So it was important to walk in all the light one had.[3] Those who had crucified the flesh and were guarding their heart and desires in wholehearted love to God and compassion to the lost would be most

1. King, *Apostolic*, p. 1.
2. 'Marks of Fanaticism', *AF* 1.2 (October, 1906), p. 2.
3. *AF* 1.3 (1906), p. 2.

sensitive to carnality arising from within or masquerading from without. They were not to trust themselves but trust the cross of Christ. In this way through searching the Scriptures and their hearts everything could be kept under the blood. *The Apostolic Faith* exhorted the faithful to remember that

> When men and women are saved and sanctified, they need the Blood just as much as they ever did. We should not trust ourselves in half a second; we need the Blood every moment.[1]

Yielding to the Spirit for a daily filling so that his presence and leading is decisive for the manner and direction of life enabled one to recognize more readily another spirit and detour off the 'highway of holiness'. The gift of discerning of spirits was operated in the church body whenever there was a need. It was not equated with prudence, although experience and maturity were highly regarded. Exorcisms were performed whenever the body determined by the Spirit that a demonized person was present. They were exorcized in the name of Jesus and there are to this day thousands of testimonies of persons thus delivered and taken into the fellowship.[2]

The norm which was and is referred to over and over again in Protestantism was the written Word of God, the Holy Scriptures. It was important to 'rightly divide the Scripture', interpret properly and 'compare scripture with scripture'.[3] This was the same safeguard against the deceptive spirits, which since the days of the Corinthian church, had sought to bring in fanaticism.[4] Reading and studying the Word was to be balanced, however, with prayer and singing of praises. Prayer would keep the one who read too much from being 'too argumentative', while singing would revive the heart. But the saints could not live without the blessed Word.[5] The discipline of the church followed the lines of the discernment of the Spirit. The Spirit took people into the church and turned them out. It was the church's responsibility to discern the condition of the life according to the Spirit and Word, and to restore those who might fall away. Discipline

1.   *AF* 1.12 (January, 1908), p. 3.
2.   *AF* 1.5 (January, 1907), p. 1; 1.6 (February–March, 1907), p. 1; 1.12 (January, 1908), p. 3.
3.   *AF* 1.12 (January, 1908), p. 3.
4.   *AF* 1.12 (January, 1908), p. 3.
5.   *AF* 1.12 (January, 1908), p. 3.

was for the purity of the body. Without purity the unity would be compromised and without unity the mission would be hindered.[1]

Discernment of spirits then seeks to determine the source and evaluate the results of spiritual manifestations and teachings by means of the gift of the Spirit and the Word in the body of believers.[2] The affects of gratitude, compassion and courage serve as the existential prerequisite for being fully open to and benefiting most deeply from the work of the Spirit and the Word in the church. Some spirits must be cast out and the chief protection against them is the Christian character yielded to and sustained by God. The fruit of the Spirit and the gifts of the Spirit belong together. Christ is both a fruit and supreme gift of the Spirit. His life, ministry, death and resurrection were all due to the formation, leading and empowering of the Spirit.

Every spirit from God will testify in word, deed, and character to the incarnate Son who had the Spirit without measure. The Spirit-filled community is the best safeguard against deception of the world, flesh or devil. The Scripture is the story of righteousness and truth. The Spirit creates hunger and thirst for righteousness and leads into all truth. Canon and charisma as given in the Spirit and received in the body of Christ are mutually conditioning. Neither can be explained or benefited from without the other. Ultimately, without the Scripture there is no path; without the Spirit there is no light. The fruit of the Spirit is the character of God and therefore is depicted fully and narratively for believers in the life of Jesus. But the acts of Jesus must be taken together with the acts of the Spirit and the story of God the Father throughout Scripture, for all three of these are parts of the one story which should evoke and shape the Christian life for the kingdom of God. Prayer is the fundamental vocation of the community and each believer. It is the belief and practice which shapes and evokes the affections, and is essential to discernment and every other gift. Out of the heart affected toward God, the Father, through God the Son and in God the Holy Spirit the mouth speaks.

1. Roberts, *Strengths*, pp. 18,19.
2. R. Martin, 'Discernment of Spirits', *DPCM*, pp. 244-47.

Pentecostal Prayer: Shaping and Expressing the Affections

Praying in the Missionary Fellowship

The Pentecostal affections are given shape and expression in prayer which is offered to, through and in God. The traditional way of expressing this is to note the procession of all things from God through Christ in the Holy Spirit. But then all things are offered and returned in the Spirit through Christ to God. Each of the Christian affections is correlated with an attribute of God. All the divine attributes are integrated in the living unity of God who is the ground and source of the unity and continual renewal of Christian character. Thus,

> [each] affection is a facet of the life of prayer and is correlated to various attributes of God... In the final analysis, neither God nor the one who prays can be analyzed into a discrete series of attributes... unlike the being of God, our experiences are always partial and therefore subject to tension and one-sidedness. Fear and love of God may coexist, not because of the strength of our affectional understanding, but because of the nature of God toward whom these emotions are directed. Prayer turns us back again and again to praise and thanksgiving, to awe and confession, to rejoicing and intercession and unifies these in the love of God.[1]

Pentecostal affections are shaped and expressed through the prayers of missionary fellowship. There the heart is formed for worship and witness as mutually conditioning aspects of Christian discipleship. The corporate and individual prayers are shaped by the preaching and teaching of the Word, the singing of songs, the giving and hearing of testimonies and prayer requests, the fellowship of the believers before, during and after the services, the constant praises and thanks offered throughout the service and the operation of the various gifts of the Spirit, and the intercessions of the saints. All these activities shape the prayers and the prayers in turn shape the affections.

Prayer in the missionary fellowship is the primary means of participation in worship and is a rehearsal for witness. One remembers, acknowledges and anticipates the mighty acts and faithfulness of God in prayer. It is this memory and anticipation which evokes gratitude, informs compassion, and undergirds courage. Often the testimonies of the believer, usually offered in regular 'testimony services', will be in the form of a prayerful meditation on the individual's life. These

1.   Saliers, *Soul*, pp. 72, 73.

testimonies usually end with a request that the body pray for certain needs, that the believer's life will be a blessing and that he or she will finally 'make heaven' their home.

The believers give thanks to the Lord continually and enjoy seasons of praise for the excellency and greatness of God toward them. Compassion is expressed through the cries and groaning intercessions commonly heard throughout the sanctuary, through 'holy laughter' believers rejoice in the Lord. As past deliverances, preservations and healings are remembered thanksgiving and praise increase, making the memory, expectation and longing more intense and deeply ingrained.

In seasons of 'concert prayer' it sounds as if the congregation is an orchestra warming up for the concert rather than playing the same musical arrangement. The unity of this sort of prayer derives from the common response to the one Spirit. Believers have a deep sense of joy together. They are flowing together in the same stream, a unifying flow which bears one along, guided by the Spirit and the scriptural narratives.

To use another metaphor, at times it is like a jazz performance with first this and then that one improvising from a common theme; and at other times it is as if all are playing one great symphony of praise. There are praises, silences and periods of waiting on the sovereign Spirit. Sometimes the body will come together for hours to intercede for a special need. Or they will go on an extended fast or vigil,[1] this accentuating the idea of prayer as 'waiting on the Lord'. Such waiting is essential for focus and affective transformation. There is no patience, steadfastness or meekness without 'waiting on the Lord'.

Prayer is the primary theological activity of Pentecostals. All worthwhile knowledge must be gained and retained prayerfully because only the Spirit can lead into all truth. Even correct knowledge will lead to presumption without constant, prayerful thanksgiving, intercession and praise. A church that rejoices, waits and yields in the Spirit, a church that loves the Word and will tarry as long as it takes to pray through to the will of God, the mind of Christ and the leading of the Spirit, that church is Spirit filled.

Prayer, therefore, is the most significant activity of the Pentecostal congregation. It suffuses every other activity and expresses the

---

1.   Central American practice is no doubt influenced by Roman Catholic usage, but also emphasizes 'watching' and 'waiting' in prayer in order to be more sensitive to the leading and discipline of the Lord.

affective richness of the believer and the church. All prayer is in the Spirit, and all who truly pray continually open themselves to and receive what the Spirit is saying and doing in and among them. To receive and to be indwelt by the Spirit of Christ is to be a Christian. This indwelling and constant receptivity constitutes the church as a fellowship or participation in God and, at the same time, a missionary force. All who have the indwelling witness of the Spirit to Jesus Christ are to be witnesses to him. Being a part of the missionary fellowship is

> like being in God's home. It is like learning from an earthly parent who gives you a vision of how things are going to be and leads you in his or her way, rewarding your obedience and chastening your waywardness but through it all nurturing you and giving you peace. There is a spirit that moves in God's home; it is the Spirit of God. And getting possessed by this Spirit is what happens to those who dwell in the home of the Lord all the days of their life—who are nurtured by the environment of hope, compassion, and peace. Because Christian spirituality is a kind of intercourse, prayer and the church are its central foci: prayer as conversation with God, and the church as God's 'home', the place where he especially dwells, his earthly presence, his 'body'.[1]

The Pentecostal Church is very much like a family with fathers and mothers in Zion and sisters and brothers in training for their fundamental Christian vocation—witness. The affections of gratitude, compassion and courage cannot be developed apart from the activity of the Spirit nor can an authentically Christian witness be given without the same Spirit's power. The gospel of the crucified, risen and coming one must be proclaimed in words, power and demonstration of the Spirit. Worship in spirit and truth must be according to the nature and will of the missionary God who constitutes the church a missionary movement of transformation.[2] And prayer, the heart of true worship and witness, must always and continually be in the Spirit.

---

1.   Roberts, *Strengths*, pp. 24, 25.
2.   Gerlach and Hine (*People, Power, Change*) analyze Pentecostalism and the Black Power movements and characterize both as potentially revolutionary. For their more recent consideration of this issue as well as a critique of the deprivation-reductionist model for analyzing and understanding religious movements, see L.P. Gerlach, 'Pentecostalism: Revolution or Counter-Revolution?', and V.H. Hine, 'The Deprivation and Disorganization Theories of Social Movements', both in I.I. Zaretsky and M.P. Leone (eds.), *Religious Movements in Contemporary America* (Princeton, NJ: Princeton University Press, 1974), pp. 669-99, 646-54.

Praying in the Spirit

Pentecostals could agree with most Christians that prayer is the fundamental act of faith, the central act of worship and the deepest meaning of human existence. Humans are made for God and thus for prayer. The human is spirit, made in and for the God who is Spirit. Faith, as the establishment of a proper spiritual responsiveness by grace, believes the promises of God and lives in hope. But the heart of faith and hope is love. The Spirit is traditionally recognized as the bond of love between the Father and the Son and the point of contact between God and humanity. The Spirit of God and not human consciousness or pious feelings is the noetic *ratio* of faith. The Holy Spirit is the knowability of God who gives his self-knowledge to humanity as a gift.[1]

Theology may depart from the Spirit through skepticism, fear of fanaticism, presumption, or the attempted domestication of the Spirit. Persons also may attempt to cultivate Christian character as a self-improvement exercise. But this attempt is as doomed as that of a spouse who tries to develop the requisite affections for a good marriage apart from his or her beloved. The Christian affections are relational and thus spiritual in that they are the fruit of the Spirit. The means must be spiritual if the result or goal is to be spiritual. The goal of the Christian life is not the achievement of a certain personality profile but a participation in the life of God. When the means become the end the believer is susceptible to one of the greatest dangers to the Christian life, spiritual pride.

Central to the Pentecostal practice of prayer is the view of fullness or filling with the Spirit. All Christians pray in the Spirit. But what do Pentecostals means by Spirit-filled prayer? The possibility, some would say inevitability, of spiritual pride is a clear and present danger, because this would seem to imply a greater development of the fruit of the Spirit, and a greater openness to and desire for spiritual gifts. This subsequent experience of filling would seem of necessity to create two classes of Christians: the indwelt and the filled. Perhaps a brief discussion of filling or fullness will show how Pentecostals seek to avoid this danger.

Part of the problem, of course, is the notion of 'filled'. If this refers to an objectivization and quantification of the Spirit, then the believer

1. P.J. Rosato, *The Spirit as Lord: The Pneumatology of Karl Barth* (Edinburgh: T. & T. Clark, 1981); Prologue, p. v., pp. 47-52.

would feel full and satisfied, perhaps something like one feels after a hearty meal. While there is often a deep satisfaction attendant upon spiritual blessing there are no normative feelings. Notions of the Spirit as a force or a substantial quantity have as their primary referent not the Spirit but the effects which the Spirit produces. In a similar manner the biblical words for Spirit which refer to wind or oil, flowing waters, or fire, all are used to refer to some effective property and not the essential nature of the Spirit.

Earlier discussion noted the importance to the early Pentecostals of emptying out, putting off and mortifying the flesh. All these disciplines were not in order to become worthy to receive a blessing from God, to be a kind of spiritual elite. They were designed to give God more of the heart and to eliminate those things contrary to his nature and will. To be filled was to be determined in a decisive way by the Spirit. This is analogous to the idea of being filled, for example, with fear. When this happens one will either flee or fight—or perhaps be totally immobilized. Fear fills the heart and thus decisively orients the entire person. Thus, to be filled with the Spirit is to be decisively determined by and oriented to the things of the Spirit, to what the Spirit is saying and doing. The fruit of the Spirit's indwelling is given a deeper intensity and, in the eschatological community of Pentecostalism, a new urgency.

To be filled with the Spirit and opened to greater fruitfulness has implications for the character and vocation of the believer. Others who claim no such filling or baptism in the Spirit may appear and actually be more stable personalities. Many have made more converts and many have greater Christian knowledge and insight. The first Pentecost, like those subsequently, took what the disciples were and set it on fire.

They still had much to learn and unlearn. There were still going to be differences of opinion, depression and struggles. But there is no denying the dynamic impact and charismatic character of the post-Pentecost community.

Pentecostals testify that they are stronger, more open, more useful than they used to be prior to the baptism and infilling of the Holy Spirit. They continually seek the filling of the Spirit. For, though they speak of one Spirit baptism, they testify to repeated fillings.

Saying that one wants to grow and that one wants to be filled with the Spirit may or may not be the same thing because Spirit baptism is fundamentally for the vocation of the believer as witness in the power of the Holy Spirit. But to say that the fruit of the Spirit has no relation to the witness of the believer would be similar to saying that holiness had nothing to do with the Spirit. The deepening of the believer's life through cultivation of the fruit of the Spirit is directly related to concern for and effectiveness (as a yielded vessel) in witness. Some views of power and gifts tend to ignore this, emphasizing how God used Samson even during his initial compromises, or how God used Balaam and even spoke through an ass (a somewhat humbling observation for all gifted preachers!) But the point of Spirit baptism is not how many or what kind of gifts have been manifested. The point is to walk in and live out of the fullness of God, to exist in radical openness, meek yieldedness and passionate zeal for the things of God.[1]

When the Spirit comes to indwell the believer in regeneration, he brings the Son and the Father.[2] The living of God in the believer and the believer in God—a mutual indwelling—makes of the Christian, and the church as a whole, a habitation of God through the Spirit. Praying in the Spirit is intercourse and deep communion with God. Being filled with the Spirit is being yielded to, directed and empowered by God to give a witness more consistent with his Spirit to Jesus Christ. Sins against the Spirit hinder that witness, divide the missionary fellowship and distort the Christian affections.

Indeed a consideration of sin in relation to the Spirit adds a needed corrective to the one-sided view of sin as transgression with its resultant moralism. In Scripture the Holy Spirit may be resisted (Acts 7.51), grieved (Eph. 4.36), insulted (Heb.10.29), quenched (1 Thess. 5.19), lied to (Acts 5.3, 4) and blasphemed (Mt. 12.31; Lk. 12.10; Mk 3.21, 29). So sin is not only transgressing the law, it is also something deeply personal. To think of opposite kinds of responses would indicate something of what it would mean to be filled with the Spirit. Instead of resisting, yielding; instead of grieving, rejoicing evermore; instead of insulting, revering in honor; instead of quenching, being inflamed and provoking others to love and good works; instead of lying to the Spirit, speaking the truth in love in order to edify and preserve the missionary fellowship; instead of blaspheming, blessing, treasuring and proclaiming the witness of the Spirit as the

---

1. Col. 3.1-3.

2. Jn 17. The Spirit brings the Son and the Father, who by the Spirit makes a habitation in the midst of and within humanity.

witness of God. If these responses were forthcoming in the Spirit, the resultant affections would have God as the source, goal and means of fulfillment, and self-fulfillment would be a by-product.

In the final analysis the fruit of the Spirit cannot be cultivated by anyone but the Spirit in persons who constantly submit to his reminding, leading, searching and enabling. As Karl Barth, who can hardly be accused of promoting enthusiasm, has said, 'Only where the Spirit is sighed, cried and prayed for does He become present and newly active'.[1]

Indeed, the best defense against enthusiasm is the continual filling of the Spirit. In this way humble gratitude, compassionate love and courageous hope will dispose one toward reproof, rebuke, correction or resistance, opposition and rejection of everything that is unscriptural, unedifying and antithetical to Christian witness.

Pentecostals have often used the strategy for detecting counterfeit money as an analogy for discerning spirits: 'Be so familiar with the authentic, that the false is readily detectable'. This can only happen in ongoing yieldedness and openness to the Spirit. It is a life lived in and from the Spirit, in Christian discipleship, in the missionary fellowship that is lived in the truth. The Spirit leads into this reality, this faithfulness of God with us. A relationship with God is only possible actually, continually and ultimately in the Spirit of God. Prayer is the way to acknowledge this means to fruitfulness, and the prerequisite for discernment as the Spirit's gift.

Pentecostal prayer is offered in three forms which shape and express the affections each in its own way. These forms are: with words understood, without words, and with words not understood. One of the three affections discussed earlier will be paired with one of the modes of prayer to illustrate this diversity.

The first and most obvious mode of prayer is with words understood or prayer in the vernacular. Pentecostal prayers have been shaped primarily by the Bible and the understanding of the Christian life which has been mediated through the early Holiness movement. Gratitude has been the most commonly expressed prayer in the Pentecostal congregation. Thanks for what God has done and praise for who God is are continually offered in Pentecostal worship. The presence of the Spirit is most characteristically responded to in this way.

---

1.   Barth, *Evangelical Theology*, p. 58.

But sighs, groans and laughter also express and shape the affections. Compassion is the most obvious example. In intercessory prayers Pentecostals weep over the lost and afflicted and long for the coming of the Lord. Prayer as sighs is evoked by the Spirit who groans and sighs even as all creation for the full and final manifestation of the sons and daughters of God.[1] 'Holy laughter' is also common as believers experience the comfort and joy of the Spirit and meditate upon the eschatological promise and vision. Indeed all of prayer is eschatologically qualified by the already–not yet tension previously discussed in Chapter 2. Thanksgiving, love and confidence are indicative of the 'already' of what God has done, is doing and will do, whereas petitionary longing, rejoicing and praise because of the promised victory, and courageous waiting through hard trials are more indicative of the 'not yet' pole of the affections.

Speaking in tongues, the most studied and discussed aspect of Pentecostal piety, is a form of prayer which is especially edifying to the individual; it gives assurance, confidence and courage. This eschatological speech indicates that the power of the end is breaking in now in this way, though of course it is only one of the ways this is happening. The end began in Jesus Christ and is coming to consummation. This speech creates and sustains a community whose culture is situated simultaneously in the 'already' and 'not yet' of eschatological existence. Tongues, when interpreted, are, like prophecy, good for the whole body.[2] All will not exercise this gift in tongues in the body; but for Pentecostals, all may speak in tongues in self-edification which will, in the unity of the body, ultimately if indirectly edify the whole.

All prayer, as noted earlier, is in the Spirit. The three modes suggest that the whole of the personality is to be engaged in prayerful dialog and communion with God. Further, the threefold shape of prayer indicates that affections are not only complex, cognitive integrations but that they also operate on and are expressions of different levels or dimensions of human consciousness. This is true whether one's culture is oral-narrative or literate. First World and Third World participants are in need of such searching, formative and multidimensional prayer.

1. Rom. 8.26.
2. 1 Cor. 14. Pentecostals never seem to tire of reminding other evangelicals, usually their toughest critics, that tongues plus interpretation is the equivalent of prophecy, thus edifying the body every bit as much.

All three modes of prayer are interdependent and mutually conditioning. In prayer the Holy Spirit continually sanctifies believers so that the structure, content and dynamics of God's holiness are reproduced in Christians as righteousness, love and power. These three correspond to the gratitude, compassion and courage used earlier to characterize Pentecostals.

The modes of prayer are modeled and practiced in the missionary fellowship as the fundamental means to form and express the distinctive affections. The witness, fruit, gifts and filling with the Holy Spirit contribute to a single unifying passion which orders the affections and directs them to a single goal: the kingdom of God.

Pentecostal Passion: Living toward the Kingdom

Just as Pentecost is larger than a single day, so Pentecostalism is larger than a single experience. Pentecost, originally a spring harvest festival (the Feast of Weeks), became a commemoration of the giving of the Law at Sinai. This Law was a way of life, a covenant established by words written on stone by God and the voice of God speaking out of the fire and cloud that covered the mountain. Pentecost, like Sinai, represents a dispensation to live by and not simply a 'kick-off event' inaugurating the church. For one thing, the church as the people of God, the people of faith, hope and love, is much older than Pentecost. For another, the people at Pentecost continued in the apostles' doctrine, fellowship and breaking of bread.[1] The prophetic fulfillment of that day opened history in a new and decisive way for the church's witness to Jesus Christ in the power of the Spirit. In the words of José Comblin, Catholic liberation theologian,

> Christianity has two sources: the 'Jesus event' and experience of the Spirit—Easter and Pentecost... intimately bound up in one another, but neither can absorb or reduce the other. The tradition of Western Christianity has never given enough importance to the Spirit. There was one Easter; there are millions of Pentecosts.[2]

---

1.   See Valliere, *Holy War and Pentecostal Peace*, esp. ch. 1 where the social, moral and cosmic dimensions of Pentecost are delineated along with a call to the church to become a house of prayer for the healing of all nations. Valliere's peace message is timely and carefully argued; Pentecostals would do well to consider it carefully.

2.   J. Comblin, *The Holy Spirit and Liberation* (Maryknoll, NY: Orbis Books, 1989).

The message of millions of Pentecostals today is that the kingdom of
God is breaking in, through the gospel ministry of words, power and
demonstration of the Holy Spirit. For them Pentecost has become a
liturgical paradigm, an existential reality, and a dispensation of the
Spirit in the last days. Earlier in this chapter it was shown how these
Pentecostals have operated out of an implicit correlation between God
as righteous, holy and powerful, and the Christian life as gratitude,
compassion and courage. This was a correlation of divine attributes
and to Christian affections. The Holiness parentage and apocalyptic
orientation of Pentecostalism gives these affections, common to all
Christians, their distinctively Pentecostal configuration. Through
prayer in particular, in the three modes mentioned above, the believer
is shaped for and expresses the foretaste of the kingdom.

A Passion for the Kingdom
For Pentecostals the kingdom, at least their being a victorious part of
it in the future, is by no means inevitable. They remember that the
kingdom was taken from Israel and given to others who brought forth
the proper fruit (Mt. 21.43). This introduces another tension in
Pentecostal spirituality in addition to the characteristic 'already–not
yet'. Seen in this light, the fruit of righteousness, peace and joy and
the correlative affections of gratitude, compassion and courage are
indispensable as dispositions requisite to faithful participation in the
reign of God. Indeed, since for most Pentecostals there is no place of
unqualified or 'eternal security' other than abiding in Christ, there is
therefore no static, abstract vision of the Christian life which will
suffice. They are a goal-oriented or teleological community on the
way to the kingdom. As Robert Roberts has observed concerning the
requisite earnestness of seekers after the kingdom,

> I have to yearn for the kingdom, seek it, treasure it, desire it, before the
> vision it gives me will amount to Christian spirituality—that is will
> amount to hope, peace, joy, compassion and gratitude as genuine emo-
> tions. If I am content with my present worldly life, successfully denying
> the prospect of death and complacent about the evil in the world's heart
> and in my own, then the message of the kingdom will not bear these fruits
> in me even if in some sense I believe it.[1]

1. Roberts, *Strengths*, p. 24.

Therefore, to live before and in the presence of God through Christ is absolutely necessary if all is not to be in vain and fruitless.[1]

The kingdom of God is God's rule or reign. It is that society and situation in which persons, created by God in the divine image, love God and their neighbor with their entire being. The kingdom is 'present and future', 'already and not yet', 'in but not of this world'. The community of Christ acknowledges and agrees to submit joyfully to this reign. The Holy Spirit is the reigning power who forms persons in accordance with the requirements of the kingdom. These requirements correspond to the nature of the king and what it means to be rightly related to the king and others. To be filled with the Spirit, therefore, is to be disposed toward the kingdom with all decisiveness, longing and earnestness. As Paul has said, the kingdom is not a matter of meat and drink (moralism) but of righteousness, peace and joy in the Holy Spirit. These three fruits of the Spirit require and envision a society or community of the king.[2] The representative Pentecostal affections discussed in detail earlier are dynamically and teleologically related to this society on the way to the end. The fellowship of the Holy Spirit and the affections of individuals mutually require and condition each other. But the passion for the kingdom of God is the organizing principle, the integrative center of the affections.

This passion may be construed as a ruling affection in the following manner. Praying for the kingdom of righteousness and walking in the light are ways of shaping and expressing the affection of gratitude. Giving thanks is a fundamental recognition that one's life and the kingdom are God's gift. Praise and gratitude mean living to the praise of God's glory and walking in the works ordained from the foundation of the world to glorify God.[3] Notice that to walk in the light, to be grateful and to long for righteousness in the whole world are what it means to believe in a righteous God. To know this God is to be made righteous by faith, then to become the righteousness of God in

---

1. See Jn 15 for the fate of the 'fruitless' and 1 Cor. 13 for the 'profit margin' of those who express gifts, make offerings, sacrifice themselves and so forth but lack love. The important point is participation in the divine life and mission of God. Salvation is participation—abiding, fruitful love.

2. H.A. Snyder, *The Community of the King* (Downers Grove, IL: IVP, 1977).

3. Eph. 2.10.

the world in anticipation of a consummated kingdom of righteousness. The Spirit guides into all truth and empowers the believer to proclaim the gospel message. Righteousness means missionary faithfulness. Righteousness speaks of the ordering of all of life according to the will of God. It describes the structure, limits and contours of that relationship. There can be no peace with God and no true joy without righteousness. But righteousness will never be perfectly realized in this world because of human fallibility and worldly rebellion. The interim fulfillment of the Law and thus of all righteousness is love.

The heart of Pentecostal spirituality is love. A passion for the kingdom is a passion for the king; it is a longing, as has been shown already, to see God and to be at home. When the heart is whole in its love for God there is a profound peace. It is the peace purchased on Calvary and applied through the blood of Jesus to the believer to cleanse from all filthiness of flesh and spirit, perfecting holiness in the fear of God.[1] This deep fear and reverence for God, with the realization that salvation is a dynamic relationship and not a static inevitability, gives an edge to Pentecostal spirituality. There is little peace and rest for the double-minded person who regards iniquity or resistance in his or her heart. The awareness of this struggle, the vigilance, consecration and the travail of praying through to peace, all contribute to the compassionate drive of Pentecostals toward the world; their neighbors are not only transgressors, but also, like themselves, are defiled and inwardly alienated from the life of holiness and happiness. This peace borne of perfect love and reverence, is a moment-by-moment abiding in Christ through the Spirit and the Word. The saints at Azusa were deeply aware of this dimension of spirituality.

> When men and women are saved and sanctified, they need the Blood just as much as they ever did. We should not trust ourselves a half a second; we need the Blood every moment.[2]

In the Spirit, the blood, or life given and being given, keeps on cleansing daily as believers submitted themselves to God in confession and repentance. The kingdom is for those who pursue peace and

1. 2 Cor. 7.1.
2. Those at Azusa emphasized the necessity of the blood every moment. One should trust God, and not the arm of flesh, at all times. Sanctification, then was no static condition of presumption or self-help.

holiness without which no one will see the Lord.[1] The passion for the kingdom means yielding to the Spirit as he searches, fills with love and sighs and groans for the kingdom. When one sighs with the Spirit in longing expectation, then one is disposed rightly.

Several times it has been noted that living in the presence of God was crucial to Christian spirituality and especially Pentecostal piety. This does not entail living with certain constant sensations, nor is it merely a mental exercise. There is a daily vital experience of placing one's self at the disposal of the Spirit as the source of and direction of life.[2] The disciplines of private and corporate prayer, living in the Scriptures, walking in fellowship, the Lord's Supper, fasting, all are ways of learning to attend to the Spirit in following Christ. Living in the presence of God, walking in the light and delighting in the Lord are all aspects of the same thing. This is what it means to know God.

For Pentecostals being baptized in or filled with the Spirit is a way of speaking of the integration of these aspects of the Christian life. The joy of the Lord is a strength, encouragement and source of hope. This joy is the fruit of the Spirit who gives the believer a 'taste' of the power of the age to come. Sometimes even a taste will cause the believer almost to lose consciousness. The ecstasy of Pentecostals is not a possession or loss of self-control. It is a relinquishment of control in a trust that believes that the kingdom-like salvation is a gift of God that has nothing to do with self-willed and technique-manipulated progress but has everything to do with the power of the God who raised Jesus and sends the Spirit with witness and wonders into the community of hope. The enjoyment is most often a quiet, constant, abiding sense of God's leading and providence. But it is also—and the two are mutually reinforcing—characterized by moments of unspeakable joy.

All gifts of the Spirit are eschatological, proleptic signs of a kingdom of joy where sorrow, death and sin are put down and banished once and for all and banished. Speaking in tongues may express the painful longing of joy or its exultant victory, but true joy always instills courage to press on to the kingdom. Healings, from a headache to a heart attack, are provisional, temporary inducements to rejoice because the Father is going to give the kingdom to the poor who seek first the kingdom and his righteousness. When it is kept in mind that

1. Heb. 12.14.
2. Gal. 5.25.

most Pentecostals are poor, non-white, Third World, young adults, it is no wonder that this renewal in the Spirit, this anticipatory celebration of the kingdom, is so often characterized by laughing, leaping and praising God. They believe the kingdom is theirs. They could heartily agree with Wesley who, in his comments on Rom. 14.17 and 1 Cor. 4.20, proclaimed that

> The kingdom of God... that is true religion, does not consist in external observances but in righteousness... the image of God stamped on the heart; the love of God and man, accompanied with the peace that passeth all understanding, and joy in the Holy Ghost... For the kingdom of God... real religion does not consist in words, but in the power of God ruling the heart.[1]

The passion for the kingdom is the ruling affection of Pentecostal spirituality and not the mere love of experience for experience's sake. There are several ways of justifying this statement, but for now the most important one is to observe that Pentecostal spirituality is not developed in solitude but requires a Pentecostal community of witnesses.

The Community of the King
The Pentecostal passion for the kingdom of God is formed and expressed in and through a Pentecostal community. This community exists in the pronounced eschatological tension of the already–not yet. The strategy of the Holy Spirit in announcing and previewing the kingdom is to form and sustain the community of the king. This strong tension explains why Pentecostals to this day have no strongly developed ecclesiology. In some way the church as a human organization, a polity with policies and procedures, is a great disappointment. This is a strength and a weakness.

It is a strength because it is an ongoing critique of the tendency of the church toward an involuted institutionalism. The church is a church on the way to the kingdom and is thus more a movement of the Spirit than a structure wedded to the present age. It is an obvious weakness, because it means that there are often not sufficient biblical and theological controls and directives worked out for the church's life outside the worship and witness settings. Pentecostals have often

---

1. J. Wesley, *Explanatory Notes on The New Testament* (London: Epworth Press, 1976 [1754]), pp. 575, 598.

divided over minor points of doctrine and personality clashes. They are serious about doctrine but often lack the interest and will to give sustained attention to the 'politics' of the church. The community, in its desire to be separate from the world, often uncritically takes on elements of its culture. This is even more true as Pentecostals experience 'redemption and lift' into a higher socio-economic status.

But my purpose here is to note the relation of the church to the kingdom in the Spirit's strategy. Pentecostals do not believe that worldly politics, manipulation and coercion will ever bring in the kingdom. They are often criticized for their lack of social consciousness and responsibility. There are historical, social and theological reasons for this.

From the revivalism and social reform of the nineteenth-century Holiness movement to the great reversal among evangelicals of the late nineteenth and early twentieth century there was a complex shift culturally, socially and theologically which influenced Pentecostals.[1] There was a shift from cultural optimism to pessimism, from postmillennial optimism to premillennial pessimism, from sanctification as purity to sanctification as Spirit baptism for power. Coupled with these shifts was the rise of the radical, historical-critical approach to Scripture, the assertion of evolutionary progress and the devastating aftermath of the Civil War. Many Pentecostals at the beginning of the twentieth century were a part of the proletarian masses of people who had joined the more radical Holiness groups. Faced with the choice of liberal, social-gospel activism or conservative fundamentalism the latter seemed more socially and theologically appropriate. This was unfortunate for both the liberals and the Pentecostals—to say nothing of the fundamentalists!

1. T. Smith, *Revivalism and Social Reform* (Gloucester, MA: Peter Smith, 1957); D. Moberg, *The Great Reversal: Evangelism versus Social Concern* (Philadelphia: Lippincott, 1972). Smith chronicles the wide-ranging and deep social involvement of the early holiness movement, while Moberg charts the great evangelical reversal or turn to the individual. This reversal occurred because of the crushing effects of the Civil War on all optimistic plans to build a utopia. But it also developed among evangelicals with a holiness heritage because of the association of social reform with liberalism and evolutionary progress by the turn of the century. Pentecostals, isolated at first, gradually became more and more associated with the more conservative, individualistic evangelicals. The really strict fundamentalists never did and do not now embrace Pentecostals.

At any rate, given that kind of historical, social and theological location, Pentecostals eschewed politics. After all, why should those of the disenfranchised masses, then or now, try to play the game of the power elites? Jesus would reward covenant faithfulness to his Word and to the neighbor, but the world would never do this. The church was a community on the way to the kingdom; this world was not home. This did not mean that Pentecostals had no social significance however. They, of course, were and are very much involved in rescue missions, medical help, orphanages, schools, feeding the hungry and clothing the naked. They cared for each other and those around them who needed the love and care of the Lord. The church was to spread the gospel, relieve suffering, and prepare the faithful for the coming of the Lord, not crush social injustice. Many early Pentecostals were pacifists and quite critical of society. The mixing of the races, leveling of persons in the 'democracy' of the Spirit and his gifts, and the ministry of women, all were countercultural, to say nothing of the practices of dress, speech and behavior which further manifested the social ethic and narrative of holiness that characterized them!

Nevertheless, this counterculture trained men and women to be courageous, articulate and patient. The community was the Spirit's strategy for transforming the world and them with it. As such the 'works of the flesh' were destructive of unity, therefore of mission. Those who practiced these things could not inherit the kingdom of God. The world, the flesh and the devil were enemies of the kingdom of God. The fruit of the Spirit, on the other hand, tended to unify and, coupled with the gifts, build up the community and qualify it for effective witness.

In later years, as economic fortunes and the social location of North American Pentecostals have risen, their sense of eschatological passion has often declined.[1] If the tendency of the early years was toward rejecting society or ignoring it, the tendency of later years has been to accommodate. With respectability has come new perils. But now many Pentecostals are becoming interested in the roots of the movement. They are in dialog with other theological traditions and, with some evangelicals, are rediscovering something of the apocalyptic and

1.   G.B. McGee, 'Apostolic Power for End-Times Evangelism: A Historical Review of Pentecostal Mission Theology' (unpublished paper presented to the International Roman Catholic and Classical Pentecostal Dialogue in Emmetten, Switzerland, 1990).

revolutionary potential of Pentecostalism. The eschatological tensions (already–not yet, church–kingdom, church–world) must be heightened and given new theological direction if the spirituality is to recover something of the original radical vision, deepen affectively and open out to give to and receive from the richness of the larger body of Christ. Even more importantly for Pentecostals, the missionary expansion, so stunning in the twentieth century, is in danger of stalling out and being betrayed by a strictly pragmatic lust for quantity and effectiveness which lacks the theological concern for quality—that is, for a responsible Christian discipleship and ecclesiology.

The passion for the kingdom of God with the attendant attention to affective transformation and integration could offer one way to move forward. But first, attention must be given to certain crucial internal tensions and external criticisms; new theological paradigms need to be constructed to address these tensions and criticisms and to unify elements of the spirituality which tend toward individual fragmentation, ecumenical isolation and missionary narrowness. This will be the agenda of the fourth and final chapter.

Chapter 4

PENTECOSTAL SPIRITUALITY AS TRINITARIAN TRANSFORMATION:
A THEOLOGICAL RE-VISION

The Breakup of the Pentecostal Synthesis:
Internal Problems and External Criticisms

The Logic of the Argument
Perhaps it would be helpful now to step back and look not only at the structure but also, and especially, at the logic of this presentation. The following chart may be referred to as the explanation unfolds.

The Logic of the Argument

Chapter

1   THESIS

        Theological Task   and Spirituality
        Perspective   and Purposes

2   APOCALYPTIC

            Beliefs   Practices

3   AFFECTIONS

        Divine Attributes   Apocalyptic Affections

4   PASSION FOR THE KINGDOM

        Reaching In   Reaching Out

This study has sought to demonstrate a certain correlation, implicit at least, between a particular view of God (divine attributes) and a distinctive Pentecostal spirituality whose integrating core is found in certain apocalyptic affections. These affections are shaped and

Appendix
versions
of them

son chhas heals
saved
baptizes king

4. *Pentecostal Spirituality as Trinitarian Transformation*   183

expressed by certain beliefs and practices, and represent the existential integration of those beliefs and practices. It was shown that this spirituality is Christocentric (the fivefold gospel) because of its pneumatic starting point. In the Spirit Christ saves, sanctifies, heals, baptizes in the Holy Spirit and is coming soon as king. It was asserted and demonstrated that, given the nature and history of Pentecostalism, the theological task is best understood as a discerning reflection by the eschatological missionary community upon the living reality of God with us.

Since spirituality, the fundament of all theology, was construed as the integration of beliefs and practices in the affections, and further, since these affections were characterized as 'apocalyptic', it was important to portray the apocalyptic ethos which is the immediate context and horizon of believer and doer of the Word. The good and bad elements of this apocalyptic were assessed. Next the fivefold gospel, and three-blessing scheme of salvation were seen to constitute the core of early Pentecostal orthodoxy. Salvation was a narrative journey and pilgrims practiced their faith, in the light of the inbreaking kingdom through worshipping, walking (ethics) and witnessing in the Spirit of the end. The walk was a living out of a cosmic drama in which the testimony to Christ and the testimony about one's daily life were processed in and with the eschatological community.

The orthodoxy and orthopraxy of the Pentecostal community were shown to be interdependent in Chapter 2, and integrated in the affections (orthopathy) in Chapter 3. It was at this point that the divine attributes of righteousness, love, and power—sometimes implicit, sometimes explicit in the previous chapter—were seen to be correlated with the salvation testimony (saved, sanctified and filled with the Spirit) and the biblical understanding of the kingdom of God as righteousness, peace and joy in the Holy Spirit. Following a discussion of the fundamental characteristics of affections (objective, relational, dispositional), the apocalyptic affections of Pentecostal spirituality were explicated in such a way that their correlation with the divine attributes was made explicit. The affections were shown to be shaped by and expressive of the beliefs and practices. Though not the only ones, gratitude, compassion and courage were selected as central Pentecostal affections. Connectedness with each other and some other affections were shown in order to indicate the kind of 'grammar' necessary to speak the language of Pentecostal spirituality or, better still, to understand something of the 'rulishness' of the way Pentecostals speak the language of the Christian faith. Pentecostal prayer was shown to evoke and express the affections, and its various modes were explored. Prayer was seen to be the primary and essential theological act of the community as well as the continual milieu of its worship and witness.

The beliefs and practices are integrated in the affections, which are correlated with God and salvation. But then the affections are focused toward the kingdom of God which was shown to be the ruling affection or passion of Pentecostal spirituality. This passion at the heart of the beliefs and practices gave definite direction, depth and intensity to the affections.

The view that Christianity is fundamentally, though not exclusively, a matter of certain affections, which form the existential core of the spirituality but are not merely self-generated pious feelings—the view held more or less by Jonathan Edwards and John Wesley, with ample biblical precedent—is especially appropriate for the study of Pentecostalism whose corporate-individual spirituality is marked by living in and from the eschatological presence of God. In addition to the claim that this is an especially appropriate approach to Pentecostalism there was, in Chapters 1 and 2, an argument that this was true for Christianity in general and crucially important in a consideration of the theological and pastoral task of the church. Though not central to the argument itself, this theological claim underlies everything done herein. Theology is the reflective, prayerful business of working at the interrelationship of orthodoxy, orthopraxy and orthopathy, or beliefs, actions and affections, respectively. This view is taken to be over against that of an overly rationalistic fundamentalism or a liberalism, rooted in human reason or experience, which is not decisively shaped by Scripture.

For the early Pentecostals the inbreaking of the kingdom with all the signs of the Latter Rain required a re-vision of the Christian life, the church and missionary priorities. This was in continuity with the nineteenth-century Holiness and revivalist themes but represented an eschatological intensification of those restorationist, perfectionist, premillennial motifs. The resulting Pentecostal synthesis with the attendant signs, wonders, holy affections, and missionary explosiveness was vibrant, powerful and widely influential. But it was not yet established. Within five to ten years of the Azusa Street Revival problems would arise which were so severe and so deep that they would mark and fragment the movement for the rest of the century.

The Nature of the Problem

Into the 'Pentecostal pot' of the first decade of the twentieth century were added several different and potentially explosive ingredients which needed careful, slow cooking. Persons of different racial, regional and theological backgrounds were brought together in prayer, renewal and communal care. Men and women, African American and Caucasian, north and south, east and west, all converged in 'upper rooms' in Topeka, Kansas, Los Angeles, California (Azusa), Dunn, North Carolina and Atlanta, Georgia. Their suspicion of organization and naiveté concerning the revivification of the church through a deeper sanctification and last days' empowerment set them up for trouble. In addition, there was an excitement and hunger for new insights and experiences. While not bad in itself and almost always qualified by seeking biblical precedent for everything, it was nevertheless contributory to the entire volatile ethos which developed. Like the book of Acts there was no developed ecclesiology or polity for adjudicating differences—especially those that might require more than a few days or weeks to consider. Although there were many periodicals, and people gathered to discuss matters in a Christian conference reminiscent of Acts 15, nevertheless, the fact remained that the new movement, though strong on transforming experiences, lacked experience in adjudicating theological and interpersonal differences and moving toward a consensus.

In 1910 William H. Durham began to challenge the predominant three-blessing view of salvation and within four years the movement was split along soteriological, theological (doctrine of the nature of God) and racial lines.[1] Durham held that sanctification began in regeneration and continued as growth. The second crisis was Spirit baptism and not sanctification. He could not find a second work of sanctification in Acts nor did he experience one before his Spirit baptism. He rested upon the 'finished work of Calvary'. This, of

1.   Faupel, 'Everlasting Gospel', pp. 265, 332; 33-393; A.L. Clayton, 'The Significance of William H. Durham for Pentecostal Historiography', *Pneuma* (Fall, 1979), pp. 27-42; Reed, 'Origins and Development'; R.M. Riss, 'Finished Work Controversy', *DPCM*, pp. 306-309; *idem*, 'Latter Rain Movement', *DPCM*, pp. 532-34.

course, was more acceptable to many fundamentalists; but neverthe-less, not enough to cause the more conservative elements among them to embrace or even tolerate the Pentecostals. When the controversy became 'carnal' some persons, like Frank Bartleman, parted company with Durham even though they agreed with most of his concerns.

Durham's rejection of subsequence and eradication in relation to sanctification put Pentecostals even more at odds with the Wesleyan Holiness movement which had been its cradle. Sanctification now became positional (imputed) and progressive. Holiness would continue as a concern, a consecration in readiness for the return of Christ and an ideal to be sought. And indeed much of the altar theology of Phoebe Palmer could be embraced by Finished Work advocates, at least the emphasis on claiming one's sanctification in faith. But there was no real consideration of what in fact Wesley had taught, and Wesley's safeguards against Pharisaism and moral complacency had not been carefully considered.

Denying the attainability of entire sanctification there was a tendency

> to accept some compromised ideal as the goal itself. For denial of the attainability of an enjoined moral ideal leads inevitably to the practical repudiation of that ideal. If realism determines that only compromise is possible, then compromise becomes the goal. It is sought for, acceded to, enshrined; acquiescence displaces aspiration.[1]

The fivefold gospel became the fourfold once again, with Christ as sanctifier dropping out, and the possibility of a new soteriological integration vis-à-vis a reappropriation of deep Wesleyan insights was lost. It seemed to many Wesleyan-Holiness Pentecostals to be a betrayal of the original vision and tantamount to a disastrous disjoining of purity and power. This was ironic since the Holiness movement had seen purity and power as two sides of the same coin; for them sanctification *was* Spirit baptism. Many of the Wesleyan Pentecostals had become Wesleyan before receiving the Spirit baptism and had been persecuted because of it (e.g. R.G. Spurling and N.J. Holmes); thus they were very disturbed over abandoning a spiritual reality which they had earlier maintained in the face of opposition. C.H. Mason, the bishop of the Church of God in Christ (Wesleyan-Pentecostal body), nevertheless did not see this as a reason

---

1.   Peters, *Christian Perfection*, p.187.

to disfellowship the Finished Work proponents or divide the movement. Others were not so sure. J.H. King of the Pentecostal Holiness Church pronounced the Finished Work to be 'Antinomianism, Darbyism dressed up in a Zinzendorfian garb and going throughout the land doing its old destructive work among believers'.[1]

Within weeks of Durham's death in July of 1912, the new Issue or 'Jesus Only' controversy erupted. This was a unitarianism of the second person of the trinity which sought to establish, in order, the correct baptismal formula (Acts 2.38 over Mt. 18.19), the correct name (Jesus = Joshua = Jehovah saves, therefore Jesus is Jehovah and all the names of God are unified in him) and the correct nature of God (Jesus as united designation for Father, Son, Holy Spirit). Three factors contributed to the rapid development of this doctrine, in addition to the immediately precipitating historical events:[2] the already prevailing Jesucentric experientialism, the openness to and search for special revelations, and the intense focus on the book of Acts.

The Finished Work and New Issue controversy, along with a desire to unify the many scattered missions, storefronts and churches of the movement, led to a call for an assembly in Hot Springs, Arkansas, 2–12 April 1914. The group assembled was almost entirely white; though C.H. Mason attended, he had not been invited. The opening address by M.M. Pinson was entitled 'The Finished Work of Calvary', and the preamble to the Bases of Union, while mentioning redemption and Spirit baptism, was explicitly silent on entire sanctification. Though the words 'entire sanctification' would later appear as a doctrinal heading in the 1916 Statement of Fundamental Truths, its wording and the memory of the 1914 meeting clearly signaled that the movement was divided. The Finished Work, New Issue, racial controversies, all were swirling around in the air at the birth of what was to become the largest Pentecostal denomination.

Women were not prominent in all these controversies as protagonists, adjudicators or (with the exception of Florence Crawford and later Aimee Semple McPherson) as formers of new movements. For the most part women, though continuing to found churches, pastor, prophesy, missionize and so forth, were increasingly left out of polity and leadership matters. They had been elders at Azusa. In the ensuing

1.   J.H. King, *From Passover to Pentecost* (Memphis, TN: H.W. Dixon, 1914), p. 106.
2.   Faupel, 'Everlasting Gospel', pp. 33-393.

years their numbers in the ministry were to decrease though their spiritual influence and importance to the movement was immeasurably great.[1]

The Force of the Criticisms

In addition to the fierce internal debates over doctrine and the frequent personality clashes, there was, from the beginning, severe criticism of the style and substance of Pentecostalism.[2] The criticism of the revivalistic, emotional activity was nothing new really. Dancing, yelling, leaping, prostration, crying out to and waiting upon the Lord were all part of the revivalism of the previous centuries. The prominence of African Americans, poor whites and women was a source of shock and embarrassment to many. The combination was startling, to say nothing of the gifts of the Spirit. Speaking in tongues was especially targeted and used to label the movement. The Pentecostals were, to use the kinder, gentler terms, 'Holy Rollers' and 'tongue talkers'; the less kind referred to the movement as the 'last vomit of Satan' before the end of the age. Pentecostals were variously characterized as demonized, deranged, regressive, orgiastic, divisive, elitist, escapist and anti-intellectual.[3]

With the rise in socio-economic and educational standing, the emergence of Pentecostals into the Evangelical mainstream through the national Association of Evangelicals in the 1940s, and the explosion of the charismatic renewal from the 1960s onward, some of the criticisms have softened. But other more pointed theological criticisms have emerged[4] having to do with subsequence, works-righteousness, and the alleged exegesis of experiences; the old criticisms are still around in North America and the Third World. Richard Quebedeaux, though making his critique a little less severe in a later work,

1. R.M. Riss, 'The Role of Women', *DPCM*, pp. 893-89.
2. Anderson, *Vision of the Disinherited*, pp. 153-94.
3. H. Ward, 'The Anti-Pentecostal Argument', in Synan (ed.), *Aspects*, pp. 99-122.
4. For the most vigorous anti-Pentecostal arguments (though Dunn is supportive of part of the argument Pentecostals make), see Bruner, *A Theology of the Holy Spirit*; and Dunn, *Baptism*. For strong Pentecostal replies, see Ervin, *Conversion-Initiation*; idem, *Spirit Baptism*; Stronstad, *Charismatic Theology*; J.B. Shelton, *Mighty in Word and Deed* (Peabody, MA: Hendrickson, 1991); R.P. Menzies, *The Development of Early Christian Pneumatology* (JSNTSup, 54; Sheffield: JSOT Press, 1991).

nevertheless contrasted classical Pentecostalism and the charismatic renewal, respectively, in the following manner:

Theology	Fundamentalism versus Progressive Evangelicalism
Worship	'Spirit of Confusion' versus 'The Quiet Spirit'
Ecclesiastical Stance	Sectarianism versus Ecumenism
Mind and Spirit	Anti-Intellectualism versus Intellectual Motivation
Religion and Society	Social Unconcern versus Social Conscience
Christ and Culture	Culture Rejection versus Culture Affirmation
Constituency	Working Class versus Middle Class Standing[1]

Of the seven criteria above the last is probably the most telling: class location contributed to his negative and one-sided analysis of Pentecostalism. Early Pentecostals and those in the Third World would evaluate themselves using different categories. He ameliorated the severity of his analysis after conferring with some more formally educated Pentecostals.[2]

In North America, though accommodation is not the total picture (giving of time, talents and treasures usually exceeds that of most other Christian bodies), there has, nevertheless, been a price to pay as Pentecostals move into the middle and upper classes. Movie stars, money and megachurches have often eclipsed tongues as evidence of spiritual fullness and blessings. Though denominational officials lament the changes and condemn the 'name it and claim it' prosperity gospel, nevertheless, from Jim and Tammy Bakker to Jimmy Swaggart,

> the record leaves little doubt that Pentecostals have not tried very hard to resist the temptations of the good life... Describing this latter aspect of contemporary Pentecostalism as a 'veritable Amway movement', historian Harrell notes that it offers not healing for the sick, but security for the well; not consolation for the poor, but confirmation to the successful... as Martin Marty perceptively noted... in times past Pentecostalism 'was "true" because it was small and pure but now it is "true" because so many are drawn to it'.[3]

Grant Wacker believes that even though the trend may be toward accommodation, now the first- and second-generation pioneers are best understood, not in terms of theories of compensation for low

---

1. *The New Charismatics: The Origins, Development and Significance of New-Pentecostalism* (Garden City, New York: Doubleday, 1976).
2. *The New Charismatics II* (New York: Harper & Row, 1983), pp. 190-92.
3. G. Wacker, 'Wild Theories and Mad Excitement', in H.B. Smith (ed.), *Pentecostals from the Inside Out* (Wheaton, IL: Scripture Press), p. 27.

social status or poverty, but in terms of a radical perfectionism which was not a means of escape from but a means of transcending life's difficulties. They 'tried to cope with sin and suffering by forging a new vision of what the gospel was all about'. Wacker goes on to observe,

> In crucial respects, the Pentecostal movement is less mature today than it was in the early years. Modern Pentecostals do not need to romanticize their past in order to learn from it. The first generation resisted the blandishments of secular society in order to preach a gospel that challenged the culture in more than superficial ways. Modern Pentecostals might recover that vision. They might discover as church historian George Marsden has put it, that grace is not cheap and forgiveness is more than good manners. They might discover that in the beginning, the movement survived not in spite of the fact that it was out of step with the times, but precisely because it was.[1]

The logic of the initial spirituality of Pentecostalism (still present though distorted), the nature and number of internal problems and external criticisms, as well as the emerging class differences and accommodations of modern Pentecostalism all point toward the need to reconsider Pentecostal spirituality.

The Need for Re-vision
The Pentecostal movement is in a period of theological adolescence. Tempted to forget or selectively remember the past, dangerously accommodated to North American middle- and upper-class culture, and having its supposedly distinctive experience, the baptism in the Spirit, marketed in every church or induced for the bored and impatient, Pentecostals are being asked to choose whom they will be. It is neither possible nor desirable merely to repeat the past, and pragmatism soon leads to cynical detachment and withdrawal.

The call for re-vision is coming from various quarters. Some speak of the movement as being at a 'crossroads'.[2] Margaret Poloma in her detailed sociological analysis of the Assemblies of God, one of the largest Pentecostal denominations, asserts that Pentecostals should pay attention to their core values (she focuses on the 'holiness ideal' or the closing of the 'ideal-real gap'). She notes that power and success

---

1. Wacker, 'Wild Theories', p. 28.
2. C.M. Robeck, Jr, 'Where Do we Go from here?', *Pneuma* 7.1 (Spring, 1985), pp. 1-4.

rather than simplicity and sacrifice are now looked upon as synonymous with holiness. She concludes that if they abandon 'dynamism for relativism, the supernatural for the natural, the ideal for the real, and ambiguity for rigidity' the church's distinctive identity will be destroyed.[1] These observations could easily apply to most North American Pentecostals who have moved into the middle and upper classes and are third- and fourth-generation members. Along with several inside observers, she believes that charisma or Pentecostal distinctiveness will be diminished in the marriage of the movement to the powerful and famous or to conservative fundamentalism. As the charismatic movement begins to lose its novelty, the mainline denominations work to 'conservatize' and accomodate it; and while the independent charismatic movement is growing, there may be a decline in overall growth in North America.[2] Meanwhile, as the explosive growth of the Third World continues, new and urgent questions of theology, discipleship and suffering press for a careful response.

While personal televangelism kingdoms fall in public view and private despair, there is a growing desire to re-vision the past, to look with realism and respect upon the fathers and mothers of the movement. Those who share this concern are convinced that Pentecostalism is more than a feeling, more than an episode in church or individual history, more than an added option for Christians whose personality profile happens to match. They seek a second naiveté, and a rekindling of the apocalyptical vision—expanded so as not to be so individualistic—of the kingdom of God.[3] Along with Roman Catholics, Eastern Orthodox and Protestants, Pentecostals too are being called to a renewed vision which addresses global and local pastoral issues.

The Pentecostal spirituality which has been the concern of this monograph represents one of the most significant and far-reaching developments in the modern church. On one level gifted, careful leadership is needed more than ever, but on an even deeper level theological work alone will bring unity, focus and renewed power so that the movement can both give and receive gifts in the body of Christ. The pioneers were not afraid to risk and to sacrifice. If sons

1. Poloma, *The Assemblies of God*, pp. 232-41.
2. Poloma, *The Assemblies of God*, pp. 242, 243.
3. McGee, 'Apostolic Power'. McGee highlights the importance of eschatology for Pentecostal missiology, then worries about the declining power and urgency of the North American Pentecostal eschatological vision.

and daughters are going to prophesy and not merely speculate they must do likewise. And part of that risk will be in the area of serious, sustained theological discussion within and without the movement. If apocalyptic is in some sense the mother of theology and especially of this spirituality, then it is time to get to know her better; it is time to wait for fresh interpretations of what the Spirit of the end is saying to the church.

The Re-visioning of Pentecostal Spirituality: The Eschatological Trinity

Let us recall the definition of the theological task put forward in Chapter 1 and illustrated in Pentecostal history with varying degrees of faithfulness: theology, for Pentecostals, is a discerning reflection by the eschatological misssionary community upon lived reality. The story and testimony of this community lives by the power of the Spirit within and all around the believer. The Spirit of the end groans, sighs and pressed within in order to drive out toward the world in witness and toward God in worship. Prayer is the first act of discerning reflection, engaging the whole person and involving the whole community as context and example. The living reality of God and the kingdom calls forth a holistic response which in turn leads to deeper reflection and further response. The spirituality of the community as an integration of beliefs, practices and affections is the precondition and ongoing result of this discerning reflection. When the integration begins to fragment there are intellectual struggles, affective distortions and practical dilemmas which cry out not merely to be solved one at a time but also to be interpreted as symptomatic of deeper need.

Unification and Fragmentation

The Apostolic Faith Mission at Azusa Street stood 'for the restoration of the faith once delivered to the saints—the old time religion, camp meetings, revivals, missions, street and prison work and Christian unity everywhere'.[1] From the Christian Union of 1886 to the Azusa Street Mission there was a cry for unity as they sought to 'displace dead forms and creeds and wild fanaticisms with living, practical Christianity'.[2] But as seen earlier in this chapter the disagreements and

---

1. *AF* 1.1 (September, 1906), p. 2.
2. *AF* 1.1 (September, 1906), p. 2.

divisions over the number of crucial salvation experiences, the name and nature of God, and the unity of all peoples and races throughout the body, globally and locally, was soon at issue. Splits over doctrine, personalities, race and regionalism were common. Along with the fusion of Christian love was the fission into varying groups as the power and impact of the movement intensified and swept all outward to the world and forward toward the end.

In spite of attempts at unity, a polity and process for consensus did not emerge. Things were moving too fast; the pressures were too great. And perhaps also there was a need for greater sanctification in terms of love and patience. But the concern for truth in every part of faith's formulation placed strain on the best of motives. If unity could not be assured by 'man-made' creeds, neither could it be guaranteed by good intentions.

Everyone agreed that unity as love and biblical belief was crucial for carrying out the last days' mission of the church. But with so much emphasis on revival and the church as an event, there was not much inclination or interest in building the kind of organization that could serve the vibrant organism. Having rejected not only 'man-made' creeds, but also being suspicious of 'man-made' organizations, they were left to the improvisations, imitations and pragmatism of leaders of varying ability and maturity who often fought each other as much as they fought the devil.

In addition to ecclesiastical fragmentation there was a splitting or lack of integration of the stages of salvation. They became almost like the strict dispensational divisions which the Pentecostals had inherited (and read about in their Scofield Bibles) from the Fundamentalists.

Speculation and Determinism
Although Pentecostals generally had a different kind of dispensationalism than Fundamentalists, they were nevertheless influenced by their use of Fundamentalist publications and speculations concerning end-time events and characters. Pentecostal dispensationalism was more like that of John Fletcher or Joachim of Fiore (they were familiar with Fletcher but not Joachim). According to this schema there were three overlapping interrelated ages of the Father, Son and Spirit respectively. They were living in the age of the Spirit before the final day of glory following the return of Christ and the making of all things new. As the first decade of the twentieth century passed and the

first generation began to die out, so too the apocalyptic fervor began
to wane and interest in detailed charts grew to an all time high.[1]
Speculation as to 'who', 'when' and 'how' in Daniel, Ezekiel,
Revelation and Matthew increased, and sermons and paperback books
on prophecy proliferated.

Along with the continuing missionary concern there was, among the
Pentecostals who stayed home, a longing for heaven and a strong
prayer and financial support for missions which continues unabated to
this day. But, because of their association with the evangelicals who
had rejected the modernist social gospel, the Pentecostals and others
with nineteenth-century Holiness roots were in many ways cut off
from that century's social witness and larger view of the kingdom of
God.

Renewal or Realization
In the 1940s the renewal of apocalyptic ardor and desire for apostolic
order returned with great force in a movement competitive with and
condemned by most Pentecostal groups: the New Order of the Latter
Rain.[2] It was premillennial and, arising basically among the lower
middle- and working-class poor, was a protest against the *embourgeoisement* of Pentecostalism. In addition to new apocalyptic zeal there
was a renewed emphasis on healing and other gifts, and on the fivefold
ministry gifts of apostles, prophets, evangelists, pastors and teachers.
These had been in some decline in the decade before this revitalization
occurred. Many of those involved in the Latter Rain of the mid-
century went on to contribute to the genesis of the charismatic
movement of the 1960s and 1970s.

In contradistinction to the New Order of the Latter Rain which was
working class, premillenial and pessimistic concerning bringing in the
kingdom of God on earth, the Kingdom Now movement of the
1980s is optimistic, postmillenial and socially located more in the
middle to upper class. While similar in many ways to the Christian
Reconstructionist movement which wants to apply the law of God to

1.   The books of Clarence Larkin, famous dispensational illustrator, are still
being sold in Pentecostal 'camp meetings' and bookstores. C. Larkin, *Dispensational
Truth or God's Plan and Purpose in the Ages* (Philadelphia: Rev. Clarence Larkin
Est., 1920).
2.   R.M. Riss, 'Latter Rain Movement', *DPCM*, pp. 532-34; Faupel,
'Everlasting Gospel', pp. 394-518.

society so as to compel righteousness, the rationale of the Kingdom Now movement is the infiltration of the structures of the world so as to transform them from within. Coupled with a strong emphasis on pragmatic faith or principles of kingdom living (in the K-Dimension), this movement represents the other end of the spectrum of response to Pentecostal apocalypticism. It is activist but thus far not revolutionary. It is more often than not a part or reflection of the 'can-do' optimism and 'positive thinking' which pervades much of conservative American piety.

In addition to the Kingdom Now move toward realization of the kingdom there is yet another significant movement challenging Pentecostalism with a form of realized eschatology; that is the 'faith-formula' or 'name it—claim it' approaches associated with, but by no means limited to, Kenneth Hagin and Kenneth Copeland.[1] Although divine healing in the atonement was taught before, during and after the Azusa revival there were qualifications, explanations and retractions of extreme statements occurring as early as 1910 in the *Apostolic Faith* paper. While the movement would continue to be assaulted by 'hyper-faith' healers, there would also always be a pastoral temperament which countered these extreme claims. Just as they had to admit that they were wrong about tongues as missionary languages so the early Pentecostals had to admit that God did not always, immediately, heal, and certainly that all die in Adam.

Nevertheless, healing as a crucially important gift, sign and ministry became yet another focus for the tendency toward human as

---

1.   For reviews and critiques of prosperity or 'faith' theology, see C. Farah, *From the Pinnacle of the Temple: Faith versus Presumption* (Plainfield, NJ: Logos, n.d.); *idem*, 'A Critical Analysis: The "Roots and Fruit" of Faith-Formula Theology', *Pneuma* 3.1 (Spring, 1981), pp. 3-21; D. Gee, *Trophimus I Left Sick: Our Problems of Divine Healing* (London: Elim Publishing, 1952). For an overview followed by a brief bibliography of prosperity and non-prosperity sources, see R. Jackson, 'Prosperity Theology and the Faith Movement', *Themelios* 15.1 (October, 1989), pp. 16-24. Pentecostals developed pastoral responses to these 'hyper-faith' views early in the century. To critics who charge that they encourage such extremes, they would reply that it is better to err on the side of what God can and may do than to say what he cannot and will not do—at least with regard to miracles, signs and wonders. But it would seem that both positions need each other in a way analogous to the way faith needs works, fruit needs gifts and all need patient, humble love if magical techniques and 'creeping naturalism' are both to be avoided and the mission of the church advanced in the modern world.

opposed to divine sovereignty, toward technique as opposed to waiting upon the Lord, and toward inducement as opposed to gift. Enough healings occurred to keep the hope and joy alive; enough did not occur to keep the faithful questioning, struggling hopeful and compassionate. Although some built clienteles, the pastors who lived among the people built communities of those who suffered, were healed, were sick and died together.

The resolution of the renewal–realization tension evident in the New Order, Kingdom Now and 'faith formula' strategies are indicators of what happens when the 'already–not yet' tensions of the kingdom are pushed too far in either direction, toward the imminent end or the realizable present. What is needed is a revision of the old models, a reappraisal of dispensational association, an integration of soteriological 'experiences', a concerted effort toward unity and inclusiveness and an expanded definition of mission which will move Pentecostalism away from some of the more individualistic understandings of the past.

Correlation and Transformation
It is evident that there was and is a distinct apocalyptic, Pentecostal spirituality, but it is equally clear that it needs some fresh attention. What is offered here can and should be only a suggestive, programmatic statement which, while having continuity with the past, will nevertheless offer the possibility for future developments and innovation. Theology is concerned with the relation between God and creation, and Pentecostal theology conceives that relation to be a living dynamic, requiring discerning discursive reflection, that is gifted by and attuned to the things of the Spirit. Since Pentecostalism is an apocalyptic movement of the Spirit, it will want to have the eschatological context and horizon prominently displayed in its approach. In this sense Pentecostal theologizing is not only a reflection *upon* but also a reflection *of* and *within* reality. The God–salvation correlation with its attendant affective transformation was discussed in Chapter 3. What was implicit in Pentecostal history and thought must now be made explicit, but grounded in a slightly different way. What follows are five interrelated loci for a new correlation and expanded view of transformation. These loci are God, history, salvation, church and mission.

God. God is the last thing. Therefore Pentecostals should focus their attention and theological efforts on an understanding of God as the eschatological trinitarian presence and not on speculative end-time sequences.[1] This does not necessarily mean giving up on premillennialism; but it does entail a shift of focus.

There is one presence but three persons whose unity and identity consists and is given in perichoretic interrelatedness, in which each person fully participates in the life of the others; the unity is in the community. But the distinctiveness is seen in the appropriation of certain works to each, though all by virtue of their coinherence are involved in each work. Thus, the work of creation is sovereignly appropriated to the Father; the work of reconciliation, to the Son; and the work of sustaining and unification unto glory, to the Spirit.

Appropriation and perichoresis are ancient doctrines of the church which were formulated to be faithful to the biblical narratives and the lived reality of the redeemed. Today they may serve the re-visioning of the Pentecostal spirituality as a way to guarantee the unity and diversity of the church, the crisis and development of soteriological transformation and the recognition of the eventfulness of the one work of God in creation revealed from Eden to the end: redemption from beginning to end.

To live in the presence of the God of redemption is to live as a participant in the divine drama; to be created in God's image is to be made for love and fellowship with God and each other. God is a communion who creates us for communion and moves us toward ultimate full participation in the divine life. Heaven is theocentric and therefore anthropocentric; in the Pentecostal imagination it is home, reunion and family celebration with all the redeemed around God's throne.

1.   The trinitarian perspective of this chapter emerged during the last ten years of teaching with my colleague R.H. Gause in the Church of God School of Theology in Cleveland, Tennessee. It has been deepened and extended by the following: J. Moltmann, 'The Fellowship of the Holy Spirit—A Trinitarian Pneumatology', *SJT* 37 (1984), pp. 287-300; P. Hocken, 'The Meaning and Purpose of "Baptism in the Spirit"', *Pneuma* 7.2 (Fall, 1985), pp. 125-34; D.A. Dorman, 'The Purpose of Empowerment in the Christian Life', *Pneuma* (Fall, 1985), pp. 147-65; M. Duggan, 'The Cross and the Holy Spirit in Paul: Implications for Baptism in the Holy Spirit', *Pneuma* 7.2 (Fall, 1985), pp. 135-46.

History. But revelation is not of some idea or static reality. It is a revelation (like the last book of the Bible) of the God who speaks to the churches, works in all things, and brings all things before his throne. History, then, is eschatological trinitarian process.

This does not mean that God, in Hegelian fashion, is dissolved into history; it means that history is in God. God works in history, in the world, for the good of those called according to his purpose. As God is the eschatological trinitarian presence who is the goal and limit of all things, so history, as God's great theater, moves *by* God *in* God *to* God. A dispensational understanding of history like that of Joachim of Fiore,[1] the Cappadocians, John Fletcher and Jürgen Moltmann is more compatible with and suitable for Pentecostal theologizing and spiritual formation.[2]

It is fascinating to find an association of trinitarian 'deepening' or revelation with Spirit baptism in the early Pentecostal writers B.H. Irwin (1896) to D. Wesley Myland (1906), and Bishop J.H. King (1914). Irwin testified that the 'blessed baptism [of the Holy Spirit and fire] deepens and intensifies our love toward God and...gives us a clearer insight into the nature of the adorable Trinity'.[3] Myland showed perichoretic sensibilities when he exhorted believers,

> Do not think that all these displays are of the Spirit alone; the Father is there, the Son is there, and the Holy Spirit is there. Whenever God has come to anyone, the whole Godhead is manifested therein; it is the dynamic of the Godhead; the things of the Spirit are displayed in His

1.   For accessible primary source reading in Joachim of Fiore, see B. McGinn (ed.), *Apocalyptic Spirituality* (New York: Paulist Press, 1979). Joachim has proven suggestive to Jürgen Moltmann and his 'constantly present interacting strata' approach to the trinitarian dispensations: Melvin Dieter relates Moltmann and Joachim to John Fletcher, 'Wesley's early systematizer', and Fletcher's dispensational development of sanctification as baptism in the Holy Spirit. See Dieter's excellent article, 'The Development of Nineteenth Century Holiness Theology'. Dieter goes to the heart of the theological predispositions and hermeneutics separating the more Reformed understandings of history and pneumatology from that of Holiness and Pentecostal approaches.

2.   Dieter, 'Holiness Theology'.

3.   Critics are quick to point out Irwin's theological eccentricities and later moral failure ('open and gross sin'), but his creativity and early leadership led eventually to the formation of the Pentecostal Holiness Church under his assistant, J.H. King. See B.H. Irwin, 'Pyrophobia', *The Way of Faith* (28 October 1896), p. 2; and H.V. Synan, 'Benjamin Hardin Irwin', *DPCM*, pp. 471-72.

sovereign working. This movement must be saved from saying that there
is never any Spirit until there is Pentecostal fulness, and also after we get
Pentecost, from saying it is the Spirit only. It is God! The Father, the Son
and the Holy Spirit.[1]

The outpouring of the Holy Spirit on the day of Pentecost was a
decisive revelation of the Trinity according to Bishop J.H. King of the
Pentecostal Holiness Church. This revelation he took to be essential
for the 'Church's message and self-understanding'. His personal
Pentecost was an '*inward* revelation of the Trinity which was
unknowable to anyone outside of the Pentecostal experience...this
knowledge of the Trinity was essential, in order for the Church as a
whole and the believer in particular, to be truly apostolic'.[2]

God acts in and is affected by history. Jesus and the Spirit 'sigh and
groan' as do creation and the believer who share in the eschatological
trinitarian process. God creates, gathers in Christ and leads forward
in a process that is in actuality a processional into the new heaven and
new earth. Pentecostal spirituality narrates this journey and acts in
God in the light of the goal of the consummated kingdom reign begun
in Jesus and carried forward in the Spirit. This procession

has two sources: the 'Jesus Event' and the experience of the Spirit—
Easter and Pentecost. The two events are intimately bound-up in one
another, but neither can absorb or reduce the other... There was one
Easter; there are millions of Pentecosts.[3]

1.   D.W. Myland, 'The Latter Rain Covenant and Pentecostal Power', in *Three
Early Pentecostal Tracts* (The Higher Life Series; New York: Garland Publishing,
1985) is cited in Hocken, '"Baptism in the Holy Spirit"'.

2.   D.A. Alexander, 'Bishop J.H. King and the Emergence of Holiness
Pentecostalism', *Pneuma* 8.2 (Fall, 1986), pp. 159-83. More work needs to be done
on King's integration. My work represents a step in that direction. See also
H.V. Synan, 'Joseph Hillery King', *DPCM*, pp. 520-21. H.A. Snyder (*The
Divided Flame* [Grand Rapids: Zondervan, 1986]) is coming at the Holiness-
Pentecostal construction from the Holiness side. In my opinion, we are not that far
apart. Snyder's work is all the more important, since he too seeks to correlate
soteriology with ecclesiology and missiology. Our only difference may be in the
nuancing of eschatology.

3.   The most creative recent Roman Catholic appreciation of the positive
theological and pastoral benefits of Pentecostalism is José Comblin's, *The Holy
Spirit and Liberation* (Maryknoll, NY: Orbis Books, 1989). Although there will still
be differences over the Marian and ecclesiological views, there is much agreement on
the importance of pneumatology, spirituality and experience for the life and mission

Thus salvation history is a progression from the Father through the Son in the Spirit, then in the Spirit through the Son to the Father. But then God is all in all and the Godhead opens as we 'know as we are known'. Moltmann calls the three movements the monarchical, eucharistic and doxological respectively; all refer to God as the trinitarian origin, presence and goal of Christian existence. This is no modalistic interpretation of history because the kingdom sovereignty of the Father, Son and Holy Spirit are 'continually present strata and transitions in the kingdom's history'.[1]

This means that the Spirit is not limited to inspiration of Scripture and illumination and empowerment of the believer. The Spirit is also creator, and is intimately involved in all things, providentially sustaining and directing them toward their goal in God. The goal of creation is not annihilation but transformation; just as the goal for humans is new creation.[2] By the Spirit the creative intention of the Father and the redeeming passion of the Son are communicated to all creation in a prevenient grace which is the source of all that is good and true and beautiful.

Pentecostals, it will be recalled, spoke of a restoration of apostolic faith. This approach acknowledges that through Luther, Wesley and then the Pentecostal movement, things vital and good were restored to the church. But this process of restoration is part of the larger

of the church. For creative interactions from the Pentecostal side with liberation perspectives see *Pastoralia* 7.15 (December, 1985), pp. 55-68, articles resulting from a consultation held in Puerto Rico in 1984. See especially the articles by Hector Comacho, Aida Gaetan, Rudolfo Giron, and Ricardo Waldrop. The conclusions are preserved in this issue of *Pastoralia* in the 'Declaracion de la consulta de lideres educacionales de la iglesia de Dios: Dessarrollo de un modelo pastoral pentecostal frente a la teología de la liberación', pp. 99-106. See also the brief suggestive analysis by D.W. Dayton in 'Pentecostal/Charismatic Renewal and Social Change: A Western Perspective', *Transformation* 5.4 (October/December, 1988), pp. 7-13. Miroslav Volf has compared Pentecostal and Liberation approaches to salvation to find some surprising commonalities as points for further development in 'Materiality of Salvation: An Investigation in the Soteriologies of Liberation and Pentecostal Theologies', *JES* 26.3 (Summer, 1989), pp. 447-67.

1. See Moltmann, *Trinity and Kingdom*, p. 208.

2. M. Volf in 'On Loving with Hope: Eschatology and Social Responsibility', *Transformation* 7.3 (July–September, 1990), pp. 28-31, urges Pentecostals to keep the hope in love by remembering that creation is to be transformed, not annihilated, by the Spirit. His article shows how works are significant in the kingdom without sacrificing the sovereignty of God.

restoration of all things which will finally issue in that which is greater than the initial creation. It is a 'restoration plus', for God will be 'all in all'.

According to this understanding of history as eschatological trinitarian process, all of history is missionary history, and to become a Spirit-filled Christian is to become a part of the teleological process of suffering, healing, hope and victory which presses toward the kingdom in God.

Salvation. Even as history may be characterized in terms of a kind of crisis-development eventfulness in which new possibilities are created by God, so also the individual Christian live is a crisis-development process which moves forward, not passively but passionately.

Eschatological salvation as participation in the divine life of historical mission requires affective transformation. Salvation is not fundamentally an accomplished event, though it is grounded in what God has done for us. But the 'for us' is grounded in the 'in himself', the *pro nobis* in the *a se*. Because God is trinitarian eschatological presence in history, and because humans are made for love and fellowship with God and each other, what God has done for us in Christ he accomplishes in us through Christ in the Spirit. Salvation is a passion for the God who is at work in all things moving history toward the consummation.

The holiness of God speaks of the fact that God's presence is like no other in that he alone is the source of the divine order, the divine unity and the divine power to reveal and effectuate, both in creation and redemption. Therefore, the structure of holiness is righteousness, the content of holiness is love, and the dynamic of holiness is the power of the Spirit who enables the giving of one's self to justice and love in the world. To be filled with the Spirit is to delight in the will, love and service of God.

This salvation means first of all the giving and the ordering of life. The resurrection was the justification of the life of Christ and thus the world of sinners. This was the vindication of the life, teaching and death of Christ and the setting right of human life. To be born anew is to live from this new source of life which has overcome sin, death and hell. He declares righteous those who turn and acknowledge by grace his Lordship that they may become the righteousness of God in him. To receive a declaration of righteousness requires a declaration for

righteousness. Since the Spirit is at work ordering all things according
to this word of righteousness and moving all things in judgment and
grace toward the end, therefore to be saved is to receive the Spirit
of righteousness and to be led into all truth as it comes to be unto
the end.

But to be saved is also to love. This is the integrating center,
because salvation as participation requires that all be done in love or it
profits nothing. Love is the center of affective transformation. There
is no question of eradication of an evil substance, no question of the
sentence of death still in effect because of the Fall and fallenness of
humanity. Love as union means all will die in God and therefore live;
as one lives, one dies. Death is the final validation of the direction of a
life. It is the acknowledgment of solidarity with all creation under the
curse; but, because it is also solidarity with Christ in the Spirit who
groans, it is a filling up of what remains of Christ's suffering.

The question of entire sanctification then is not so much a question
of subsequence or eradication. Rather, it becomes a question of the
kind of measure of love appropriate or adequate to one who 'so loved'
the world. Nothing but a wholehearted love is adequate to this.
Resistances seen in this light are confessed as they come into
consciousness. The 'flesh' is mortified as thoughts and desires come to
light in a participatory following of Christ and are renounced as 'not
I' but the 'old I', which found its integrating center in the 'flesh' and
not the Spirit.[1] In this sense Wesley's instinct was correct. If God is
love, the love of one who 'so loved', then the fulfillment of the Law
and all righteousness in Christ was unto holiness, which is in this life
essentially wholehearted devotion to God and one's neighbor.

This requires an affective transformation. Without this the
righteousness received and declared for will be resisted and the
unrighteousness not fully and deeply repented—since love wounds and
heals. Sin in the believer is not, in its most serious guise, some lack of
perfect conformity to all the will of God as God knows and acts. That
is the ultimate goal. But penultimately (and crucially for Pentecostal
spirituality) sin is a betrayal, a willful resistance of that purpose for
which we were called. The passion of Christ on the cross is finished.
The passion of the believer and the church in Christ is not. In him that
passion becomes compassion, a wholehearted longing to see all and

1.   See Mt. 16.24; Lk. 14.26, 27, 33; Jn 8.31; Phil. 2.12, 13; Gal. 2.20;
5.16-24.

everyone redeemed, and a pursuit of peace and holiness without which no one will see the Lord.

To speak of power without the integrating center of love is to run the risk of becoming a 'sounding brass and a tinkling cymbal' or worse to pursue justice to the letter while excluding mercy and humility born of wholeheartedness toward God. Wholeheartedness as simplicity of intention and desire will direct power toward self-offering witness rather than domination or presumption.[1]

The power of Pentecost should be seen as historical, existential, habitual and extraordinary. The power of the Spirit forms a life for God as Christ was formed in Mary's womb. This power is a person, the Holy Spirit who must then be existentially invoked, received and welcomed. To receive the Spirit is to receive the Spirit's witness and accede to the Spirit's leading, fruit-production and empowering for witness. The Spirit's filling must be invoked daily because the point is to live out of his fulness and by his direction and not that of the world, the flesh or the devil. The Spirit's continual filling is a penultimate and proleptic realization of the filling of all things when all confess that Jesus Christ is Lord to the glory of God the Father. This filling means that the Spirit's life and power and fruit unto holiness are decisive. One is filled with the Spirit, not fear, lust or greed. Extraordinary filling is analogous to the Gethsemane crisis of Jesus' life. He who had the Spirit without measure cried out for strength to offer himself as he struggled and suffered. So there are extraordinary times of suffering which many Pentecostals have had to endure, when an extraordinary filling and enabling of the Spirit is necessary to make an offering of one's self. This is the gift and witness of martyrdom.

For fourth- and fifth-generation Pentecostal children and new converts in Pentecostal churches perhaps this view of salvation as eschatological trinitarian passion could be thought of simply as a developmental process with three dimensions. Each of the three may become a moment of crisis or be a source of continuing direction and inspiration or judgment, depending on one's background, knowledge and present spiritual condition.

The new believer or child is received into the community and belongs to God and the family of God. Whether baptism or dedication

---

1. Heb. 9.14.

is used (and Pentecostals have done both) to indicate this reception and claiming of the child and God's reception and claiming of him or her, it is still a time that looks forward to an existential saying of 'yes', and turning toward God in repentance and love with full assurance of forgiveness of sins. But as the new believer grows or the child enters adolescence, new situations and temptations present themselves. A new awareness of self and the world, coupled with, in the new believer, an acknowledgment perhaps of known hold-outs or resistances to the love and will of God, call for the internalization of the righteousness by which one was received and in which one has been directed. Now is the time to become affectively, wholeheartedly identified with Christ and the mission of the spiritual community. Moral integration will be an ongoing, daily gift of grace through all the means of grace (prayer, Scripture, worship, fellowship, counsel, confession, Lord's Supper, footwashing and so on). It is this abiding in Christ wholeheartedly in love that is the core of the spirituality.

But if the righteous path toward the kingdom is to be followed in love in the world, one must be empowered daily not only to will and to walk but also to wage war against the principalities and powers. Pentecostals desire the filling of the Spirit because they understand the present age or world to be under the spell of evil: the demon spirits must be fought with spiritual weapons, spiritual strategy and in spiritual might and power. In order to fill the earth with the gospel, in order to do justice, in order to love and defend others, believers need the continual filling of the Spirit. As they speak in tongues in the eschatological missionary fellowship, the praise of the kingdom that has come joins with that which is coming in a proleptic celebration of God's victorious grace. But, and this is equally as spiritual, one will also sigh, cry and groan as that very joy and victory makes the lostness and need of the world stand out in bolder relief.

This development is a progression from *belonging* to a community ordered by and for righteousness, to *being identified* with Christ wholeheartedly in order to fulfill all righteousness, to *being empowered* to actualize the missionary purpose of God in the world as led and filled by the Holy Spirit who gives his fruit (character of the witness) and gifts (special equipment for the witness). This is a movement which emphasizes the new people of covenant righteousness by grace through faith, the new heart of wholehearted integration by grace through faith and the new vocation as witness by grace through faith. These three dimensions of salvation are constantly present and interrelated in a way analogous to the perichoretic trinitarian relations. These dimensions correspond to the resurrection, the cross and Pentecost. As these are central events of continuing significance, so these dimensions are ongoing crises or landmarks of the faith development of Pentecostal believers. As Calvary is central in salvation history so sanctification as moral integration or wholehearted love is central in salvation as participation in the divine life.[1]

The Church. The Church is a communion of diversity and unity in the Spirit. Just as God is one in three so the church is one and many in God. The church as eschatological trinitarian fellowship is a communion in God—a people of God, a body of Christ and thus a communion in the Holy Spirit. What is fellowship but participation? In this fellowship gifts and office coincide and theology is the discerning reflection of the whole as each offers his or her gift, recognizes the other's gifts and is built up to disciple and love the neighbor.

The fruit of the Spirit is one because the Spirit is the sole source and the fruit is the character of God. But the church is the milieu or garden for that cultivation. The fruit is cultivated by the Spirit so that the church as a whole and each believer may be witnesses who represent something of the divine character and care of God in the world.

The gifts are diverse, differently applied, sovereignly distributed (not 'discovered' or 'cultivated' or 'operated at will'), and different in each manifestation. But the gifts are for the whole body which is for the kingdom. Thus the gifts simultaneously serve an 'inner' edificatory function and an 'outer' evangelistic one.

The church that is caught up in the divine fellowship is one because of the same divine presence from whom it lives; the church is holy because that presence is the holy and only presence which sanctifies. To be set apart unto God, for believer and church, is to be set apart for union, for that which is joined to God is holy. To treat the church anywhere as profane is to profane the church everywhere. The holiness of the church demands unity. All who pray to and in the same

1.   1 Cor. 13, cited frequently in this study, is the model of integration for spirituality. Beliefs and practices express, shape, strengthen and are rooted in the love which is the integrating core of Christian spirituality. Entire satisfaction as wholeheartedness is the only appropriate response to one who has and does *so* love.

presence are one, are holy and thus should strive to show the world how they love one another. But this church that is one in the divine presence and holy in divine union is apostolic and catholic in its power and universal mandate, respectively. The church in the trinitarian eschatological presence of God moves into all the world in the power of the Spirit who is moving all the world toward the end. The apostolic power is authority and strength to proclaim the one gospel in word and demonstration of the Spirit.

All believers are part of one another as they are part of Christ's body. They coinhere as children of God. God is the divine mother who has begotten them and brought them forth as dear children in the same family by creation and redemption and destination.[1] The church lives from God through Christ in the Spirit, and in the Spirit exalts Christ to the glory of the Father.

Mission. The mission of the church in the light of all that has been said is, therefore, eschatological trinitarian transformation. The church is being transformed by and for God and thus bears witness in what it is and what it does to the kingdom.

The mission is to do justice, love mercy and walk humbly with God. In keeping with what was said before, the church is to recognize the divine presence at work in creation and providence as well as in the more immediate soteriological dimensions. This means that the sanctification of the believer and of the church is to be the motive and analog for the sanctification of the world, not by dissolving the church into the world but by calling the world to repentance and to righteousness. The church, where possible, must work to make structures more adequate to the life as righteously ordered and intended by God. Structures cannot be sanctified in the same way as individuals, but, since the Spirit is at work in all creation, discerning action of the church can bear witness to and participate in those activities which more nearly embody righteousness, dignity and love for people.

Defense of the weak and prophetic denunciation of sin and oppression are part of the church's mission to love the neighbor. There is no dichotomy between the command to love one's neighbor and the Great Commission to disciple the nations. These commands are to be neither confounded nor dichotomized, because love is the character of God

1.   See Moltmann, 'The Fellowship of the Holy Spirit'.

and of the Christian in God. On the other hand, to refuse the mandate to disciple is to hate, or worse, to be indifferent. To seek to disciple only those who seem to be likely candidates for church membership is to deny the global care and providence of the Spirit. In this regard also the Spirit is not to be grieved or quenched. The personal, social and cosmic implications of Pentecost are only now beginning to be grasped in the movement, especially in the Third World and among some North American Pentecostals.[1]

The love which pursues righteousness and presses the demands of God on all structures and people faithfully is the love which, full of hope, seeks to liberate the captives, because the Spirit of the Lord is poured out upon the church.[2] Thus Pentecostal liberation brings great joy because peace, not violent coercive manipulation, is the means and the goal as fruit and gift of the Spirit, respectively.[3] The early Pentecostal pacifism, in a nuclear age of extensive poverty, is the best strategy for the church today.[4] The vast needs of Third, First and

1.   Pentecostalism represents a major new approach in Christianity which is both supplementary and complementary. It is an indigenized folk religion which overwhelmingly has a black and brown majority in its constituency. Although there are theological, ethical and political differences I have argued that there is a core, a spiritual fundament present in the first part of the century with roots in the nineteenth and eighteenth centuries and, through Wesley, all the way back through eastern and western sources to the early church. This is an important point which an exclusive focus on phenomenological or external similarities may obscure. It is also important for the theological revisioning and cooperative praxis—a simultaneous operation—of the future. See Walter Hollenweger's foreword, pp. vii and viii to C.E. Jones, *A Guide to the Study of the Pentecostal Movement* (2 vols; Metuchen, NJ: Scarecrow Press, 1983), pp. vii, viii. See Valliere, *Holy War*; J. Moltmann, *The Church in the Power of the Spirit* (New York: Harper & Row, 1977), pp. 289-336.

2.   Note R.J. Cassidy, *Society and Politics in the Acts of the Apostles* (Maryknoll, NY: Orbis Books, 1988). It is this countercultural, potentially transformative, leavening influence that Pentecostals and others are just beginning to see and work out in terms of political and missionary implications.

3.   Valliere, *Holy War*, pp. 46-86.

4.   Jay Beaman traces the early pacifist stance of several Pentecostal bodies; this was all but abandoned as the twentieth century progressed into more and more horrible global and regional conflicts and Pentecostals moved more into the mainstream of North American culture. They still represent a 'third way' of peace in many Third World countries, as in Guatemala, for example, where they are often killed by the right and the left. But Pentecostals are also now fielding candidates in Chile, Brazil, South Africa and parts of Asia.

Second World believers alone would stagger the church to its knees, much less the affliction, hatred and bondage of millions of others. The original vision of unity through sanctified hearts for last-days mission in the power of the Spirit is still valid. And the end is as near and as imminent as God; it is as urgent as God's passion. But before the unity of the whole church can be addressed, Pentecostals, drawing upon the resources of their spiritual journey and God's way with them thus far, must themselves come together in a new way. After all, the church cannot very well ask the world to consider the justice, peace, unity and love of God if it is not itself living out of practising these things with visible zeal.

Reaching in to One Another: Remembrance and Repentance

Based on the foregoing suggestive sketch of a new direction or revision of Pentecostal spirituality, the following observations are offered in order to show what possible impact such a programmatic endeavor might make on the contemporary Pentecostal scene.

The Vision and the Disinherited

From Niebuhr's work on the *Social Sources of Denominationalism* to Robert Mapes Anderson's classic social history of Pentecostalism, *The Vision of the Disinherited*, it has been accepted that the movement was of and by the poor and working class.[1] Although there were educated persons and members of the middle class present at Azusa and scattered throughout the early movement (e.g. J.H. King and N.J. Holmes) it is nevertheless true that the greatest part of the constituency then and now has been drawn from the poor and working classes. This is very much true in the Third World today although there, of course, the overwhelming majority of the people are poor. So, in the beginning of the movement in North America and in other parts of the world the liturgy has been of, by and for the people[2] and characterized by

1. H.R. Niebuhr, *The Social Sources of Denominationalism* (New York: World Publishing, 1929); Anderson, *Vision of the Disinherited*. See the perceptive critique of Anderson by Grant Wacker and Timothy Smith (*Religious Studies Review* 8.1 [January, 1982], pp. 15-28) from Pentecostal and Holiness perspectives, respectively.

2. J.F. White, *Protestant Worship: Traditions in Transition* (Louisville, KY: Westminster/John Knox, 1989).

maximum participation of races, sexes and classes. There was thus racial integration and the full ministry of women in a church of the poor and working classes.

The reason for this overcoming of social and economic barriers was the eschatological perspective which accompanied the fall of the Latter Rain. Such an understanding was already found in the nineteenth-century Holiness movement, where writers such as Phoebe Palmer (*The Promise of the Father*) defended the ministry of women. Now women had a vital ministry as elders, pastors, missionaries, teachers and so forth. And for a while it did seem as if the color line had been washed away in the blood. Everyone was needed and appreciated in the great task of world evangelization: whosoever was called and gifted by the Spirit was acceptable as long as they evidenced the fruit of a godly life.

Due to the work of C.H. Mason and W.J. Seymour, Pentecostalism was, in the beginning, one of the 'most powerful expressions of Black religion in the world', a movement in which black piety had exerted its greater direct influence on American religious history. But very soon there was an accommodation to the racism of American culture instigated by the Whites, leading to racial separation among Pentecostals. Although Mason maintained, and usually initiated, close fellowship and preaching assignments within the Church of God and the Pentecostal Holiness Church, Pentecostals worshipped and fellowshipped in increasingly segregated flocks.

As the decades passed the increasing association with fundamentalist evangelicals meant that it seemed less plausible to ordain women. Although they still could pastor or evangelize, their ministry was classed at a lower rank than men and the polities were careful to indicate that they were under the supervision of men, thus not 'usurping authority'.

Today the racial divisions continue inter- and intra-denominationally. The Church of God in Christ, for example, is almost completely black while the Assemblies of God in North America is mostly white. There are denominations with more African Americans and other ethnic representations, but they are not really equal in terms of access to leadership ministries. The gifts of leadership distributed by the Spirit are not yet reflected in the politics of most North American Pentecostal churches. Pentecostals have moved into middle-class respectability but they are still ambiguous about the ministry of women.[1]

A restoration of the eschatological missionary vision wedded to vigorous common study of the relevant Scriptures would go a long way to a reunifying of what has been fragmented and stratified. Challenges are very great in terms of mission fields and human need. In the last days the curse and divisions of the Fall are having to be overcome in anticipation of the coming kingdom. The unity and distinctiveness of the Godhead reflected in the male/female atonement bound in Christ means that each has a distinctive and equally important part to play in ministry. Ordination becomes recognition of the Spirit's assignment for the ministry which one is set apart to accomplish.

The Doctrines of Division
In the beginning of the movement there was a rather unified view of salvation, the Godhead and the kingdom. Salvation was understood in terms of the fivefold gospel and three blessings. The triune presence was manifested in gifts and wonders which signaled a fresh inbreaking of the kingdom of God.

With the emergence of the Finished Work view, the fivefold gospel was effectively reduced to fourfold again, leaving out the distinctive emphasis on sanctification. Victory replaced sanctification, and power categories were dominant over purity and cleansing ones. But there was an ongoing ambiguity regarding holiness. The Assemblies of God retained a statement on 'entire sanctification' in their initial 'Declaration of Fundamental Truths' and continued to emphasize consecration for greater service, effectiveness and readiness for the Rapture of the saints.

When the Pentecostal Fellowship of North America (PFNA) was formed, the 'Statement of Faith' was exactly that of the earlier National Association of Evangelicals with the exception of Article 5: 'We believe that the full gospel includes holiness of heart and life,

---

1.   I.C. Clemmons, 'Charles Harrison Mason', *DPCM*, pp. 585-88. Clemmons cites Gayraud Wilmore and Sidney Ahlstrom in support of his claim of the place of honor and significance for Seymour and Mason in particular and Blacks in general in Pentecostal origins. R.M. Riss, 'The Role of Women', *DPCM*, pp. 893-94. See also the entries in *DPCM* for Phoebe Palmer, Pandita Ramabai, Aimee Semple McPherson, Maria Woodworth-Etter, *et al.*

healing for the body and the baptism in the Holy Spirit with the initial evidence of speaking in other tongues as the Spirit gives utterance'. It is perhaps significant that there was an ongoing struggle and ambiguity concerning holiness. The holiness codes of conduct remained in effect for decades, with the Assemblies of God being one of the first groups to modify their statements and the Church of God being one of the last.

In keeping with the roots and spirit of the PFNA 'Statement of Faith', Pentecostals need to retain the fivefold gospel and something like the three-dimensional understanding of salvation developed previously in this chapter under 'Correlation and Transformation'. The use of three dimensions affirms the necessity of crisis experience in the development of a morally committed, integrated and empowered life while avoiding the necessity of choosing between two or three crises.

Sanctification as moral integration within a lifelong process of discipleship and growth may offer a way to begin to address this long-standing impasse. Moral integration would make desirable but would not imply maturity. It would help guard against moralism and presumption by centering the spirituality not in righteous deeds or in powerful manifestations but in humble love through abiding in Christ. Moral integration under these circumstances, though requiring struggle and mortification, would nevertheless be neither a works-righteousness, nor a sentimental episode. If the demands of New Testament discipleship as found in the Gospels are taken seriously, then it will be seen that nothing short of revolutionary, affective transformation is called for if one is to deny the self, take up the cross daily, follow, love as he loved and walk as he walked (Mt. 16.24-26; Mk 8.34-38; Lk. 14.26-35). By considering the demands of radical discipleship and the shape of the Christian life, Pentecostals could develop a spirituality which correlates more closely with the fivefold gospel's emphasis on Jesus.

The issues raised by the New Issue or Jesus Only movement are more difficult and complex because they go to the heart of the original and especially the re-visioned spirituality. To their credit, the Jesus Only churches warn against tritheism. But by following the Jesu-centric emphasis of early Pentecostalism to its logical conclusion, this modern form of modalistic monarchianism undoes the logic of the progressive revelation of salvation history and violates the plain sense of Scripture. These Scriptures are given special interpretation by the

Oneness Pentecostals when perspicacity would seem to demand otherwise (for example Jn 17 or the passages dealing with the baptism of Jesus). Unity is not identity. An ongoing, indepth dialog on the pastoral, soteriological and missional dangers of tritheism and modalism is needed between Oneness and other Pentecostals. This dialog has begun in the Society for Pentecostal Studies but needs further denominational sanction and support.

The New Order of the Latter Rain and the Kingdom Now movements represent, respectively, the protest against and evidence of the *embourgeoisement* of Pentecostalism.[1] They are representative of the pessimism of nature and optimism of grace present in the broader Pentecostal movement. But over against both, the tension between the 'already–not yet' of the kingdom must be maintained. Premillennialists have never, at least in Pentecostal circles, sat around and wanted to escape in a secret Rapture; they have been anything but passive. But sometimes their expectations of grace were overblown and they forgot they were still in this world. The kingdom is breaking in but still to be consummated, thus combining optimism and pessimism in an active missionary waiting—as in John Wesley, who is claimed by the pre- and postmillenialists!

Passion and Polity

A passion for the kingdom of God was the unifying center of the movement. Even in their divisiveness the Pentecostals still share this passion. With the exception of the Oneness groups, the differences have not prevented contemporary cooperation and pulpit exchanges. They have had a shared passion but not a shared polity.

Ironically, following the initial divisiveness of the earlier part of the century, Pentecostals only began talking officially to one another again in 1943 when they, along with several Holiness and Protestant groups were invited to join the National Association of Evangelicals

---

1. P.D. Stockard, 'Modern Kingdom Theology: A Brief Review and Critique of the Book, *Held in the Heavens Until: God's Strategy for Planet Earth* by Earl Paulk' (Term Paper, Church of God School of Theology, 1989). Stockard conducted interviews and reviewed the essential primary and secondary materials. See also the more stinging critique of Robert Bourman, Gary S. Hawkins and Dan Schlesinger in 'The Gospel According to Paulk: A Critique of "Kingdom Now Theology"', *Christian Research Journal* (Winter/Spring 1988), pp. 9-13, and (Summer/Fall, 1988), pp. 15-20.

(NAE) in 1943. The first World Pentecostal Conference (WPC) was organized in 1947 and the Pentecostal Fellowship of North America (PFNA) came into being the next year. African Americans are not participants in the PFNA but they are involved in the WPC. But the WPC is nothing like a really representative or inclusive body of Pentecostals worldwide. It is dominated by North American and European Pentecostals who are now in the minority in terms of the global movement.[1]

Pentecostals are, nevertheless, beginning to talk to one another and to cooperate somewhat in the areas of mission strategy, publishing, chaplaincy and academic interchange. The latter was initiated in 1970 with the formation of what is now quite an ecumenical, scholarly group, the Society for Pentecostal Studies.[2]

With the great number of Pentecostal Bible Schools, several liberal arts colleges and a few seminaries, there should be a greater exchange taking place in the future, if there is to be a genuine re-visioned revitalization of Pentecostalism in North America. The Third World membership is burgeoning and still there is no polity to bring representatives together with administrators and Pentecostal theologians to reflect on their common praxis and to re-envision their spirituality. The traditional Pentecostal suspicion of organizations and the protection of 'turf' by the existing bureaucracies make competition, redundancy and 're-inventing the wheel' a problem. What is need is for something like the WPC to become a more vigorously inclusive forum for theological, pastoral, and missional concerns.

Pentecostal missionaries are coming now from all over the world and going to all parts of the world. Increased leadership and participation of Third World Pentecostals and mergers or close association with First and Second World Pentecostals is encouraging greater effectiveness and theological deepening of one another through narrative exchange and common worship. These promising dialogues

1. D. Barrett, 'Global Statistics', *DPCM*, pp. 810-29. See also J.W. Sheppard, 'Sociology of Pentecostalism', *DPCM*, pp. 794-99; especially intriguing is Sheppard's comments on p. 799 that 'the assumption that Pentecostals are likely to be politically conservative has left another segment of the population—namely politically liberal or radical Pentecostals whose concern is with social justice and with liberation—under researched'.

2. See R.P. Spittler, 'Society for Pentecostal Studies', *DPCM*, pp. 793-94, and C.M. Robeck, Jr, 'Seminaries and Graduate Schools', *DPCM*, pp. 722-26.

and mergers could go a long way toward healing more of the divisions of the past and avoiding further needless fragmentation or fanaticism.

Until recently there was no single international publication in which Pentecostals could speak to each other across cultures and socio-economic, racial and national boundaries. A re-visioned Pentecostal spirituality requires such a global interchange. A common end in the consummated kingdom of God requires a common process of shared hopes. A spiritual result (unity) requires a spiritual process, a shared praxis of witness, fellowship, testimony and searching the Scriptures. These are old Pentecostal strategies which once worked locally and made the movement strong. To emphasize the merely quantitative aspects of growth to the neglect of the qualitative issues of identity and contribution to the larger body of Christ grieves the Spirit of unity.

Reaching out Together: Learning with the Critics

Subsequence and Sectarianism

The charges of subsequence, elitism and divisiveness have been lodged against Pentecostals from the beginning. And, as we noted earlier, these were some of the milder charges! It is said, for example, that Pentecostals disintegrate the unity of Christian initiation, especially through their lack of understanding of baptism, the rite of initiation in mainline churches. All this is laid to the account of the subsequence doctrine.

As a result of claims to subsequent blessing—whether of entire sanctification, Spirit baptism or both—Pentecostals are further charged with an elitism which divides Christians into before and after or the 'haves' and the 'have nots' of redemptive experiences. Special claims have been made by Pentecostals concerning the preparation of the Bride (having on the spotless wedding garment and/or having oil in the lamp) and those who are 'sealed' by the Spirit for the Rapture.

Finally the critics said that all of this leads naturally, if ungracefully, to division by encouraging people to leave 'dead, formal churches' for the free and lively worship of Pentecostal communities of faith. The divisive spirit is also seen in continuing subdivisions of Pentecostals.

To understand subsequence, one needs to consider the eventfulness of salvation history itself. Why Pentecost after Calvary and the resurrection? Was it just a formal inaugural event for the new church which was waiting for its birthday to arrive? No, just as in salvation history, so in personal history there are crises or events which make possible new developments or intensify the development in a way unimagined before the event.

Christian initiation is not generally understood as terminal, and even the critics admit to subsequent sacramental actions and events which, however continuous with the initiation, are nevertheless decisive for ongoing development. Here Pentecostals, still very immature theologically, could learn with the critics in a discussion of the meaning and significance of confirmation, theosis and Spirit baptism, for example. What is the difference in remembering one's baptism and remembering one's new birth? What are the similarities? How might they be construed together? These questions and others need to be a part of a common spiritual project.

It might also be helpful to realize that whereas God is received in Christian initiation, one does not receive all that one needs from God. That requires a walking in the light and prayerfully seeking fuller understanding and development—both chronologically and spiritually.

When the bored, cynical and unfruitful become renewed, joyful and fruitful, does that make them elitist? Or does that occur only if they testify to it? Surely not. It is only when exclusivist claims are made which make it incumbent on all to receive just what others have and just the way they have. Grace is a many splendored and multi-faceted reality, at least in the application to and transformation of lives by the Spirit. The hard claim to a particular experiential filling with the Spirit is still not a claim to greater spiritual maturity nor greater scriptural understanding. Surely here there is room for discussion and learning together.

All churches have special claims and believe that their distinctive gift is important enough to justify their corporate existence and individual efforts. Each must first recognize the church in his or her own church and then in other churches. The presence of God made known through a confession to Jesus Christ in word, deed and fruit is the basis for such a mutual recognition. In that recognition and the ensuing mutual exchange, one can discover what is 'better' or 'worse' in each.

Finally, it should be remembered that in addition to 'come-outers', there were just as many Pentecostals who were 'crushed out' or 'pushed out' of their churches because of their testimony and claims to sanctifying and empowering experiences. Associated with these departures were, of course, theological differences, but there were also at the same time race, class and cultural conflicts and often a perception that the church existed for and was ruled by a clerical elite who saw themselves as not needing to learn anything new with the people. These clergy would neither weep nor rejoice with others in their spiritual struggles and victories. Such actions by the clergy too often gave the impression that the church was a 'closed shop' whose non-negotiable rules and liturgies existed for the benefit of the few. This is to say nothing of the lack of missionary sacrifice and concern or compassionate involvement in the needs of the hurting and the hungry. Quick judgment, misunderstanding and lack of communication led to many needless divisions.

The rediscovery in each age of the radical discipleship of Jesus and the potency of the Holy Spirit makes it necessary for the church to accommodate its own Pentecostal brothers and sisters with at least as much patience and attention as it gives to the accommodation of its culture. When the disinherited and powerless who have become enfranchised and enabled by the gospel in the power of the Spirit hear from non-Pentecostals that they are elitist for teaching a subsequent work of grace, they gladly reply, 'Yes, of course!', or simply, 'Hallelujah!'

Mission and Unity

For Pentecostals, it is consistent with their spirituality and their distinctive way of being Christian to say that shared missionary passion is the means to unity today. Pentecostals could heartily agree with the perspective of Harry Boer, who in his influential work *Pentecost and Mission* reminded all Christians that the Spirit was not given to church organizations, 'to many desperate individuals' or even to the organism. No, the Spirit has been given 'to the organization as it serves the organism, and to the organism as it comes to expression in the organization'. Boer further observed concerning the Great Commission that the 'outpouring of the Spirit is in and by reason of its very nature the effectuation of the Great Commission in the life of the Church... It is not, like the commands of the law, a command which men are impotent to obey'. And rather than preaching it as a command to obey, Boer asserted that the Great Commission must be presented 'as a law that expresses the nature and that governs the life of the church'. Boer further warned that if the church was

> seen as a body that meets for edification and praise which *also* has the task of obeying the missionary command, no great deployment of missionary power is to be expected. Nor can the Spirit enter upon a full exercise of His function in the Church so long as He is regarded as the Spirit of regeneration and sanctification who must *also* provide the Church with a missionary *donum superadditum*.[1]

Pentecostals do not feel that their movement or the baptism in the Holy Spirit is a *donum superadditum*. All authentic Pentecostals are witnesses who can start meaningful ecumenical exchange at the point of that missionary concern. There is a growing need for expanded contacts through structures and practices that will allow and enable a merging of horizons of hope in the context of narrative exchange and reflection on missionary praxis.

In this regard there are many hopeful signs today which would have been unheard of a few decades ago. These signs include an ongoing and rich Roman Catholic–Pentecostal dialog;[2] a National Council of Churches of Christ in the United States–Pentecostal Dialog; several Pentecostal Churches that have joined the World Council of Churches (primarily from the Third World);[3] large Pentecostal-Charismatic National Conferences in Kansas City and New Orleans during the past decade;[4] ongoing Pentecostal participation in the National Association of Evangelicals;[5] Pentecostal participation in the World Evangelical

---

1. Boer, *Pentecost and Missions*, pp. 215-17.
2. Jerry Sandidge, a long-time participant in and careful researcher of Pentecostal ecumenical endeavors, has provided a concise, useful summary of the 'Roman Catholic/Classical Pentecostal Dialogue' in *DPCM*, pp. 240-44.
3. See J.L. Sandidge, 'World Council of Churches', *DPCM*, pp. 901-903.
4. See C.M. Robeck, Jr, 'Pentecostal World Conference', *DPCM*, pp. 707-10.
5. See C.M. Robeck, Jr, 'National Association of Evangelicals', *DPCM*, pp. 634-36. Along with Donald Dayton, I question the *taxonomy* (a narrow understanding of 'evangelical') and *historiography* (a one-dimensional, dichotomized understanding of 'reason' and 'emotion'—'reason', standing for the evangelical establishment in North America and 'emotion', for the Holiness, Pentecostal and ethnic faith communities) of modern, North American evanglical writers. When this approach is taken, what Dayton has called the 'presbyterian paradigm' takes the field as the only player. See, for example, Dayton's 'Yet Another Layer of the Onion', pp. 87-110. Dayton's historiographical and theological work should encourage Pentecostals to begin to overcome their theological 'inferiority complex', but in ways

Fellowship; and innumerable smaller but equally significant grass-roots efforts.

In all this there are practices arising out of Pentecostal spirituality which have facilitated and will advance future ecumenical encounters. If the large conciliar organizations want to dialog with Pentecostal leaders representing millions of believers today, then testimony, intercessory prayer and praise, and some common missionary praxis is the way to proceed. There can be a merging of horizons and a shared hope as each person narrates his or her faith journey. Catholics often complain that they do not have the dramatic crises and events reported by Pentecostals, but as they narrate their journey new mutual insights are gained, making the encounter itself an event if not a crisis! Praying together, and not just for one another, bearing burdens and confessing to one another is essential for any Christian community and especially for meaningful ecunemical fellowship.

Finally, with regard to missionary praxis, perhaps a fruitful, specific place to start would be with a shared healing ministry. In prayer for and ministry to the sick, oppressed, demonized and suffering, Pentecostals could participate with other Christians in a missionary praxis which would be at once a sign of the last days' ministry, a gift of the Holy Spirit, a sacrament symbolizing the mystery of redemption by the wounded healer and an expression of the most central and most needed of the affections for the time between the times, compassion.

As Pentecostals reflect on these practices of testimony, prayer and healing with other believers, new insights and openness can emerge as God's gift. This is the presupposition for any meaningful progress in other areas. A shared spiritual formation is the fundament of a shared theology, at least from the Pentecostal perspective.

Theology and Passion

This study has claimed that there is a distinctive Pentecostal spirituality which should be reflected in the process and results of the theological task. Prayer is necessary and not a mere 'pious addition' if that task is taken to be a discerning reflection upon lived reality by the

faithful to their folk, narrative traditions and essential spirituality. The evangelical-ization of Pentecostalism could become the pentecostalization of evangelicalism thus moving both to consider alternatives to the Princeton theology of Warfield *et al.* and its common sense philosophical underpinnings.

eschatological, missionary community. Prayer expresses and evokes the apocalyptic affections which integrate and motivate the beliefs and practices of the community.

What is given to the Pentecostal community in Scripture is opened to the future in God and 'set on fire' with a passion for the kingdom which precludes those private experiences or involuted corporate indulgences which only invite the judgment of God.[1] This means that faith and love are opened to the world and strain forward in hope. Spirit baptism and ongoing filling intensify and focus that hope which saves even as it reaches to lift, save and encourage others.[2] This hope gives courage in the face of the world and the devil, and confidence toward the God of all hope. The Pentecostal outpouring in the first and twentieth centuries resulted in the increase of faith, hope and love for millions of disinherited but not abandoned men, women and children.

But Pentecostals must see the connection between this passion for the kingdom and theology lest they lose both through neglect or dissipation. Theology itself is a kind of passion for God, and passion for God requires ongoing theological work as part of its inner logic and worldy vocation. The merging of the two is the mark of a true theologian—one who truly prays for the kingdom.

There arose in Israel during the several hundred years of the intertestamental period an apocalyptic movement which sought to recapitulate the concerns of the priests, prophets and sages for cultic, social and personal holiness within their eschatological horizon of hope for cosmic transformation. Perhaps God has raised up the rough-hewn, largely immature but passionate Pentecostals in this century to remind the church of the apocalyptic power and force of the gospel of the kingdom and to prepare the world for the end—the triune God who is to be 'all in all'. The church which is filled with the Spirit and immersed in the compassionate care of a lost and afflicted humanity has one common longing, one unfiying cry, one joyful shout: Come, Lord Jesus!

1. 1 Pet. 4.17; Rev. 1–3; Heb. 12.
2. Rom. 8.24.

AFTERWORD

mu

It is time to say what must be said of all such interpretive-constructive studies: this is a work begun but unfinished. In the writing of this monograph I have often had the sense of being borne along, as if in a mighty river. Having come ashore and had an opportunity to look back, there are at least seven tributaries that need to be explored further.

First of all, Pentecostalism raises anew the question of the relation of theology and spirituality. That issue, discussed in Chapter 1 but implicit throughout, is not a merely sectarian or parochial concern. It has to do with theology's object, objective, context and goal. By starting with the Holy Spirit, the living reality of God with us, certain methodological and hermeneutical commitments and presuppositions are laid on the table. These need to be drawn together in a separate piece using the work of the new Pentecostal theologians of North America to be sure, but especially taking account of the Third World majority who are only just beginning to be published.

Central to these hermeneutical, methodological concerns is the matter of the role and meaning of experience. If Edwards's and Wesley's approaches to the reason–emotion debate are taken as offering a primal evangelical paradigm, what new light might that throw upon the current evangelical debates over balance, cognitive structure and the role of the Holy Spirit? Will fundamentalists continue to see the concern with affections discussed in this study as a dead-end approach which is hopelessly mired with feelings? If so, should not Pentecostals begin at least to question the labels 'fundamentalist' or 'evangelical' when applied to themselves?

Perhaps Pentecostals would be well advised to construct their own distinctive rendition of the Wesleyan quadrilateral (Scripture, reason, tradition and experience). This third line of inquiry is related to the second but is more comprehensive. It would afford a means to re-establish contact with the Wesleyan roots of the movement. If the word 'integration' not 'balance' is more appropriate for Pentecostals, how can this be demonstrated using the quadrilateral? What are the implications of the Spirit-Word formulation used in this presentation for a fresh understanding of the meaning of Scripture and how should the hermeneutic take into account and reflect the apocalyptic context and horizon with its attendant already–not yet tension? With regard to reason in such an eschatological fellowship, it would be important to explore what has been implicit in this work: the critical, communal discernment of a Pentecostal community.

Surprising to some will be the use made of tradition. Contemporary Pentecostals should explore what it would mean to be in experiential continuity with the early movement in light of the claim to be in continuity with the apostolic church. Apostolic succession takes on new meaning in this light. Luther and Wesley, often mentioned in the early literature, are vitally important today. Of the two traditions, why are Lutherans almost always the most vociferous critics? Why do they find it so hard to accept the Pentecostal denials of Pelagianism and enthusiasm? Here the Wesleyan connection is extremely important; the two traditions should make common cause. Pentecostals should examine Wesley's creative Protestant-Catholic construction and then follow Wesley's sources, both Eastern and Western, back into his main source, Scripture. Wesleyans and Pentecostals seem to be in agreement with regard to a particular integration of Scripture, tradition and reason in the sanctified, Spirit-filled life. Further work on the Christian affections would perhaps enable Pentecostals to appreciate more and more their sectarian distinctiveness and ecumenical import.

But this raises a third matter for consideration. Given the vast expansion and diversity of Pentecostalism today and the importance of narrative to the tradition, is there some common, foundational narrative which might serve to identify, unify and direct the future development of at least a majority of its adherents? Such a common narrative might serve in much the same way as the 'canonic' narrative of the first ten years; that is, it would unify those who differ in terms of geography, race, class, culture and gender. The biblical account of Pentecost, the present reality, the apocalyptic goal; all would be elements in such a contemporary reformulation of the Pentecostal testimony.

A fourth set of issues clusters around the doctrine of the church. Pentecostals have been clear enough in their rejection of institutionalism but have failed to produce a viable ecclesiology which could allow for ongoing change and debate without schisms. A polity for the development of consensus has yet to be constructed (perhaps the World Pentecostal Conference, the European Pentecostal Theological Association, the Pentecostal Fellowship of North America or the Society for Pentecostal Studies could pursue this). Some way must be found to talk and study with the Independent and Oneness groups; this is vital for Pentecostal self-understanding as well as the reunifying of the movement. Can Pentecostals, among themselves and in dialog with other churches, discover another model for ecumenical discussion, development and mission?

Another internal ecclesiological issue will be a consideration of what structure of the church is best correlated to the shape of the Christian life. If Pentecostal faith development is to proceed, what is there about exclusively hierarchical, mass revivalist, or autonomous congregational approaches which is either inadequate or inimical to the health of the church or the individual believer? If the logic of Pentecostal affections and gifts is followed, how would that alter traditional ecclesiological formulations?

There is, fifthly, an acute need for new metaphors for crisis experience. Eschewing the exclusively substantialist, supplementing the exclusively relational and working toward an affirmation of a truly ontological change in the believer, can a soteriology be developed which reflects the eventfulness of the biblical narratives, historical and human development? Perhaps affective transformation and integration will prove to be new and useful metaphors for crises within and with a view toward a certain eschatological development. This work is a step in that direction.

If Pentecostal theology is a discerning reflection upon living reality in the light of the end, then the shape of the eschatological expectation is crucially important. The sixth area of further research would center on the question of how Pentecostals can live within the tensed dynamic of the already–not yet while avoiding the fragmentation of a wholistic, integral mission to souls, bodies and structures on the one hand, and accommodation to the optimistic, seemingly omnicompetent technological society on the other.

Pentecostal eschatology, while premillennial and apocalyptic, is qualified by the Latter Rain doctrine. There is an emphasis on the power and sovereignty of God, but because the Holy Spirit brings the life of the kingdom of God into the present, passivity and cultural pessimism are minimized as people are empowered for ministry. It is not postmillennial; it avoids presumption and cultural accommodation. The kingdom of God is larger than the church and therefore there is an implicit 'post-millennial' activism contained within the premillennial expectancy. Indeed the expectancy of the coming fulness of righteousness, peace and joy feeds the activism. This can, by means of further development of the trinitarian perspective of Chapter 4, be expanded to include socio-cultural concerns without a loss of evangelistic commitment.

As a work begun but unfinished and a movement approaching its first centennial, Pentecostalism holds much promise for the future, if it remains open to the Spirit who indwells the people of God and moves all things toward their consummation in Jesus Christ.

BIBLIOGRAPHY

Abel, T.D., *Better Felt Than Said: Pentecostal Experience in Southern Appalachia* (Waco, TX: Markham Press, 1982).

Abraham, W., *The Logic of Evangelism* (Grand Rapids: Eerdmans, 1989).

Albrecht, D.E., 'An Investigation of the Sociocultural Characteristics and Dynamics of Wallace's "Revitalization Movements": A Comparative Analysis of the Works of Four Social Scientists' (unpublished paper, Graduate Theological Union and The University of California at Berkeley, 1989).

Aldana, R., D. Munguia and R. Waldrop. Interview with author. Centro Guatemalteco de teologica Practica, Quetzaltenango, Guatemala. 3 October 1989.

Alexander, D.A., 'Bishop J.H. King and the Emergence of Holiness Pentecostalism', *Pneuma* (Fall, 1986), pp. 159-83.

Alexander, D.L., (ed.), *Christian Spirituality: Five Views of Sanctification* (Downers Grove, IL: IVP, 1988).

Alvarez, C.E., *Santidad y compromiso* (Mexico: Casa Unida de Publicaciones, n.d.).

Anderson, R.M., *Vision of the Disinherited: The Making of American Pentecostalism* (New York: Oxford University Press, 1979).

Arrington, F.L., *The Acts of the Apostles: An Introduciton and Commentary* (Peabody, MA: Hendrickson, 1988).

Arthur, W., *The Tongue of Fire; or the True Power of Christianity* (New York: Harper, 1856).

Barrett, D.B., *Cosmos, Chaos, and Gospel: A Chronology of World Evangelization from Creation to New Creation* (Birmingham, AL: New Hope–Foreign Mission Board of Southern Baptist Convention, 1987).

Barrett, T.B., *In the Days of the Latter Rain* (London: Simpkin, Marshall, Hamilton, Kent and Co., 1909).

Barrios, Magdalena de, and Elizabeth de Gomez. Interview with author. Centro Guatemalteco de teologia Practica, Quatzaltenango, Guatemala, October 1989.

Barth, K., *Evangelical Theology: An Introduction* (New York: Holt, Rinehart & Winston, 1963).

—*Church Dogmatics* (Edinburgh: T. & T. Clark, 1975–1977).

—*Prayer* (ed. D.E. Saliers; trans. S. Terrien; Philadelphia: Westminster Press, 1985).

Bartleman, F., *Azusa Street* (South Plainfield, NJ: Bridge Publishing, 1980).

Beaman, J., *Pentecostal Pacifism* (Hillsboro, KS: Center for Mennonite Brethren Studies, 1989).

Beasley-Murray, G.R., *Jesus and the Kingdom of God* (Grand Rapids: Eerdmans, 1986).

Bell, R.H., (ed.), *The Grammar of the Heart* (San Fransisco: Harper and Row, 1988).

Berkhof, H., *Christian Faith: An Introduction to the Study of the Faith* (Grand Rapids: Eerdmans, 1979).

Boer, H.R., *Pentecost and Missions* (Grand Rapids: Eerdmans, 1961).

Bourman, R., G.S. Hawkins and D. Schlesinger, 'The Gospel according to Paulk: A Critique of "Kingdom Now Theology"', *Christian Research Journal* (Winter/Spring, 1988), pp. 9-13, and (Summer/Fall, 1988), pp. 15-20.

Bowdle, D.N. (ed.), *The Promise and the Power* (Cleveland, TN: Pathway Press, 1980).

Bowers, J.P., 'Sanctification in the Church of God: A Shift from the Three Blessing Paradigm' (unpublished paper, Southern Baptist Theological Seminary, 1985).

Brewster, P.S., (ed.), *Pentecostal Doctrine* (Gloucestershire: Grenehurst Press, 1976).

Bridges-Johns, C., *Pentecostal Formation: A Pedagogy among the Oppressed* (JPTSup 2; Sheffield: JSOT Press, 1993).

Brown, D., *Understanding Pietism* (Grand Rapids: Eerdmans, 1978).

Brueggeman, W., 'II Kings 18–19: The Legitimacy of a Sectarian Hermeneutic', *HBT* 8 (1985), pp. 1-42.

—*Hope within History* (Atlanta: John Knox, 1987).

Bruner, F.D., *A Theology of the Holy Spirit: The Pentecostal Experience and the New Testament Witness* (Grand Rapids: Eerdmans, 1970).

Burgess, S.M., (ed.), *Reaching Beyond: Chapters in the History of Perfectionism* (Peabody, MA: Hendrickson, 1986).

Burgess, S.M., and G.B. McGee (eds.), *Dictionary of Pentecostal and Charismatic Movements* (Grand Rapids: Zondervan, 1988).

Campos, B.L., 'From Experience to Pentecostal Theology' (unpublished paper, trans. J. Beaty and S.J. Land, paper presented to the Encuentro Pentecostal Latinoamericano, Buenos Aires, Argentina, 1989).

Carr, W., 'Towards a Contemporary Theology of the Holy Spirit', *SJT* 28 (1975), pp. 501-16.

Cassidy, M., *Bursting the Wineskins: The Holy Spirit's Transforming Work in a Peacemaker and His World* (Wheaton, IL: Harold Shaw Pub., 1983).

Cassidy, R.J., *Society and Politics in the Acts of the Apostles* (Maryknoll, NY: Orbis Books, 1988).

Castegeda, J.M. Interview with author. Centro Guatemalteco de Teológica Practica, Quetzaltenango, Guatemala. October 1989.

Castillo, P., Interview with author. Managua, Nicaragua. 15 October 1989.

Chikane, F., *No Life of my Own: An Autobiography* (London: Catholic Institute of International Relations, 1988).

Christenson, L., *Speaking in Tongues and its Significance for the Church* (Minneapolis, MN: Bethany Fellowship, 1968).

Clapper, G.S., *John Wesley on Religious Affections: His Views on Experience and Emotion and their Role in the Christian Life* (Metuchen, NJ: Scarecrow Press, 1989).

—'Orthokardia: The Practical Theology of John Wesley's Heart Religion'., *Quarterly Review* 10.1 (Spring, 1990), pp. 49-66.

Clark, S.B., *Confirmation and the 'Baptism of the Holy Spirit'* (Pecos, NM: Dove Publications, 1969).

Clayton, A.L., 'The Significance of W.H. Durham for Pentecostal Historiography', *Pneuma: JPT* 1 (Fall, 1979), pp. 27-42.

Collins, J.J., *The Apocalyptic Imagination: An Introduction to the Jewish Matrix of Christianity* (New York: Crossroad, 1989).

Comacho, H., 'Involucramiento del laico en la revitalización de la vida congregacional', *Pastoralia* 7.15 (December, 1985), pp. 55-68.

Comblin, J., *The Holy Spirit and Liberation* (Mary Knoll, NY: Orbis Books, 1989).

Conn, C.W., *A Balanced Church* (Cleveland, TN: Pathway Press, 1975).

Cooey, P., *Jonathan Edwards on Nature and Destiny* (Lewiston, NY: Edwin Mellen, 1985).

Cook, G., at the Latin American Biblical Seminary, San Jose, Costa Rica. 17 October 1989.

Corum, F.T., (ed.), *Like As of Fire*, a collection of *The Apostolic Faith*, 1906–1908 (Wilmington, MA: F.T. Corum, 1981).

Cottle, R., 'Tongues Shall Cease'. *Pneuma: The Journal of the Society for Pentecostal Studies* 1 (Fall, 1979), pp. 43-49.

Crews, E.M., Jr, 'From the Back Alleys to Uptown: A History of the Church of God (Cleveland, Tenessee)' (PhD dissertation, Harvard University, 1988).

Dayton, D.W., *Discovering an Evangelical Heritage* (Peabody, MA: Hendrickson, 1976).

—'Declaración de la consulta de líderes educacionales de la Iglesia de Dios: Desarrollo de un modelo pastoral pentecostal frente a la teología de la liberación', *Pastoralia* 7.15 (December, 1985), pp. 99-106.

—'The Holiness Witness in the Ecumenical Church' (unpublished paper, Wesleyan Theological Society, 1987).

—*The Theological Roots of Pentecostalism* (Grand Rapids: Zondervan, 1987).

—'Yet Another Layer of the Onion: Or Opening the Ecumenical Door to Let the Riffraff in', *The Ecumenical Review* 40.1 (January, 1988), pp. 87-110.

—'Pentecostal/Charismatic Renewal and Social Change: A Western Perspective', *Transformation* 5.4 (October/December, 1988), pp. 7-13.

D'Epinay, C.L., *Haven of the Masses* (London: Lutterworth Press, 1969).

Dieter, M.E., *The Holiness Revival of the Nineteenth Century* (Metuchen, NJ: Scarecrow Press, 1980).

—'The Development of Nineteenth Century Holiness Theology', *Wesleyan Theological Journal* 20.1 (Spring, 1985), pp. 61-77.

—'The Wesleyan-Holiness and Pentecostal Movements: Commonalities Confrontation, and Dialogue' (unpublished paper, Society for Pentecostal Studies, 1988).

Dorman, D.A., 'The Purpose of Empowerment in the Christian Life', *Pneuma* 7.2 (Fall, 1985), pp. 147-65.

Dowd, M.B., 'Contours of a Narrative Pentecostal Theology and Practice' (unpublished paper, Society for Pentecostal Studies, 1985).

Drayer, J.R., 'The Significance of Apocalypticism in Contemporary British Eschatology' (ThD dissertation, Southern Baptist Theological Seminary, 1970).

Duffield, G.P., and N.M. Van Cleave, *Foundations of Pentecostal Theology* (Los Angeles: L.I.F.E. Bible College, 1983).

Duggan, M.W., 'The Cross and the Holy Spirit in Paul: Implications for Baptism in the Holy Spirit', *Pneuma* 7.2 (Fall, 1985), pp. 135-46.

—'Implications for Pentecostal–Charismatic Theology' (unpublished paper, Society for Pentecostal Studies, Gaithersburg, MD, 1985).

Dunn, J.D.G., *Baptism in the Holy Spirit* (Philadelphia: Westminster Press, 1970).

—*Jesus and the Spirit* (Philadelphia: Westminster Press, 1975).

Dupree, S.S. (ed.), *Biographical Dictionary of African-American, Holiness-Pentecostals 1880–1990* (Washington, DC: Middle Atlantic Regional Press, 1989).

Durnbaugh, D.F., *The Believers Church: The History and Character of Radical Protestantism* (New York: Macmillan, 1968).

Elbert, P., (ed.), *Faces of Renewal* (Peabody, MA: Hendrickson, 1988).

Elliott, W., 'Continuity/Discontinuity Between Protestantism and Pentecostalism' (unpublished paper, Society for Pentecostal Studies, 1989).

Ervin, H.M., 'Hermeneutics: A Pentecostal Option', *Pneuma* 3.2 (Fall, 1981), pp. 11-25.

— *Conversion-Initiation and the Baptism in the Holy Spirit* (Peabody, MA: Hendrickson, 1984).

—*Spirit Baptism: A Biblical Investigation* (Peabody, MA: Hendrickson, 1987).

Fahey, S.McM., *Charismatic Social Action* (New York: Paulist Press, 1987).

Farah, C., *From the Pinnacle of the Temple: Faith Versus Presumption* (Plainfield, NJ: Logos, n.d.).

Farah, C., Jr, 'A Critical Analysis: The "Roots and Fruits" of Faith-Formula Theology'. *Pneuma* 3.1 (Spring, 1981), pp. 3-21.

Faupel, D.W., *The American Pentecostal Movement: A Bibliographical Introduction* (Society for Pentecostal Studies, 1972).

—'The Function of "Models" in the Interpretation of Pentecostal Thought', *Pneuma* 2.1 (Spring, 1980), pp. 45-71.

—'The Everlasting Gospel: The Significance of Eschatology in the Development of Pentecostal Thought' (PhD dissertation, University of Birmingham, 1989).

Fedotov, I. and V. Fedotov. Interview with author. Maloyaroslavits, Russia. October 1989.

Fee, G.D., 'Baptism in the Holy Spirit: The Issue of Separability and Subsequence', *Pneuma* 2.1 (Fall, 1985), pp. 87-99.

Finger, T.N., *Christian Theology: An Eschatological Approach* (2 vols; Scottsdale, PA: Herald Press, 1985).

Fletcher, J., *The Portrait of St Paul* (New York: Hunt and Eaton, 1889).

Gaetan, A., 'Teologia de la liberacion: Perspectiva de una majer pentecostal'. *Pastoralia* 7.15 (December, 1985), pp. 87-98.

Gammie, J.G., *Holiness in Israel* (Minneapolis: Fortress Press, 1989).

Garcia, P. Interview with author. Guatemala City, Guatemala. October 1989.

'Gathering of Latin American Pentecostals: Summary Report' (unpublished paper, Salvador, Brazil, 6–9 January, 1988).

Gee, D., *Trophimus I Left Sick: Our Problems of Divine Healing* (London: Elim Publishing, 1952).

Gerlach, L.P., 'Pentecostalism: Revolution or Counter-Revolution?', in I.I. Zaretsky and M.P. Leone (eds.), *Religious Movements in Contemporary America* (Princeton, NJ: Princeton University Press, 1974), pp. 669-99.

Gerlach, L.P., and V.H. Hine, *People, Power, Change: Movements of Social Transformation* (New York: The Bobbs-Merrill Co., 1970).

Giron, R., 'Analisis de la pastoral pentecostal en América Latina', *Pastoralia* 7.15 (December, 1985), pp. 55-68.

Goff, J.R., Jr, 'Fields White unto Harvest: Charles F. Parham and the Missionary Origins of Pentecostalism (PhD dissertation, University of Arkansas, 1987).

—'The Faith that Claims', *Christianity Today* (February 19, 1990), pp. 18-21.

Hamilton, M.P., (ed.), *The Charismatic Movement* (Grand Rapids: Eerdmans, 1975).

Hanson, P.D., (ed.), *Visionaries and their Apocalypses* (Philadelphia: Fortress Press, 1983).

Haynes, E., and M.S. Lemons, *Church of God Songs No. 3* (Cleveland, Tennessee: Church of God Publishing House, n.d.).

—*Church of God Songs No. 4* (Cleveland, TN: Church of God Publishing House, n.d.).

—*Church of God Songs: Tears of Joy* (Cleveland, TN: Church of God Publishing House, 1920).

Hine, V.H., 'The Deprivation and Disorganization Theories of Social Movements', in Zaretsky and Leone (eds.), *Religious Movements*, pp. 646-64.

Hocken, P., 'The Pentecostal-Charismatic Movement as Revival and Renewal', *Pneuma* 3.1 (Spring, 1981), pp. 31-47.'

—'The Meaning and Purpose of "Baptism in the Spirit"', *Pneuma* 7.2 (Fall, 1985), pp. 125-34.

—Signs and Evidence: The Need for Catholic–Pentecostal Dialogue on the Relationship between the Physical and the Spiritual' (unpublished paper, Society for Pentecostal Studies, 1989).

Hollenweger, W.J., *The Pentecostals* (Peabody, MA: Hendrickson, 1972).

—*New Wine in Old Wineskins* (Gloucester: Fellowship Press, 1973).

—*Pentecost between Black and White* (Belfast: Christian Journals, 1974).

—'After Twenty Years' Research on Pentecostalism', *International Review of Mission* 75.297 (January, 1986), pp. 3-12.

—Interview with author. Asbury Theological Seminary, Wilmore, Kentucky. February 1990.

—'The Critical Tradition of Pentecostalism', *JPT* 2 (1992), pp. 7-17.

Holmes, N.J., and L.S. Holmes, *Life Sketches and Sermons: The Story of Pentecostal Pioneer N.J. Holmes* (Royston, GA: Press of the Pentecostal Holiness Church, 1920).

Howell, J.H., 'The People of the Name: Oneness Pentecostalism in the United States' (PhD dissertation, Florida State University, 1985).

Hunter, H.D., *Spirit Baptism: A Pentecostal Alternative* (Lanham, MD: University Press of America, 1983).

—'Reflections by a Pentecostal on Aspects of *BEM*' (unpublished paper, prepared for the NCCUSA Dialogue, 1990).

Irwin, B.H., 'Pyrophobia', *The Way of Faith* (28 October 1896).

Jackson, R., 'Prosperity Theology and the Faith Movement', *Themelios* 15.1 (October, 1989), pp. 16-24.

Johns, J.D., and C.B. Johns, 'Yielding to the Spirit: A Pentecostal Approach to Bible Study', *JPT* 1 (1992), pp. 109-34.

Jones, C., G. Wainwright and E. Yarnold (eds.), *The Study of Spirituality* (New York: Oxford University Press, 1986).

Jones, C.E., *A Guide to the Study of the Holiness Movement* (Metuchen, NJ: Scarecrow Press, 1974).

—*Perfectionist Persuasion: The Holiness Movement and American Methodism, 1867–1936* (ATLA Monograph, 5; Metuchen, NJ: Scarecrow Press, 1974).

—*A Guide to the Study of the Pentecostal Movement* (Metuchen, NJ: Scarecrow Press, 1983).

—*Black Holiness: A Guide to the Study of Black Participation in Wesleyan Perfectionist and Glossolalic Pentecostal Movements* (Metuchen, NJ: ATLA, 1987).

Käsemann, E., *New Testament Questions of Today* (London: SCM Press, 1969).

Kenyon, H.N., 'An Analysis of Racial Separation within Early Pentecostalism' (MA thesis, Baylor University, 1978).

King, J.H., *From Passover to Pentecost* (Memphis, TN: H.W. Dixon Printing Co., 1914).

Kirkpatrick, D., (ed.), *Faith Born in the Struggle for Life* (Grand Rapids: Eerdmans, 1988).

Knight, H.H., III, 'The Relation of Narrative to Christian Affections' (unpublished paper, Emory University, 1987).

—*The Presence of God in the Christian Life* (Metuchen, NJ: Scarecrow Press, 1992).

König, A., *The Eclipse of Christ in Eschatology: Toward a Christ Centered Approach* (Grand Rapids: Eerdmans, 1989).

Ladd, G.E., *The Presence of the Future* (Grand Rapids: Eerdmans, 1974).

Land, S.J., 'Pentecostal Spirituality and Disciplines' (unpublished paper, Guatemala Center for Practical Theology, 1989).

—'Pentecostal Spirituality', in L. Dupré and D. Saliers (eds.), *Christian Spirituality: Post-Reformation and Modern* (New York: Crossroad, 1989), pp. 484-90.

Larkin, C., *Dispensational Truth or God's Plan and Purpose in the Ages* (Philadelphia: Rev. C. Larkin Est., 1920).

Lawrence, B.F., *The Apostolic Faith Restored*, in D.W. Dayton (ed.), *Three Early Pentecostal Tracts* (The Higher Christian Life Series; New York: Garland Publishing, 1985).

Lederle, H.I., 'An Ecumenical Investigation into the Proprium or Distinctive element of Pentecostal Theology', *Theologica Evangelica* 21.2 (June, 1988), pp. 34-41.

—*Treasures Old and New: Interpretations of Spirit-Baptism in the Charismatic Renewal Movement* (Peabody, MA: Hendrickson, 1988).

Lovelace, R., 'Baptism in the Holy Spirit and the Evangelical Tradition', *Pneuma* 7.2 (Fall, 1985), pp. 101-23.

Lovett, L., 'Black Holiness-Pentecostalism: Implications for Ethics and Social Transformation' (PhD dissertation, Emory University, 1979).

MacArthur, J., Jr, *The Charismatics: A Doctrinal Perspective* (Grand Rapids: Zondervan, 1978).

—*Speaking in Tongues* (Chicago: Moody Press, 1988).

McClendon, J.W., Jr, *Systematic Theology: Ethics* (Nashville: Abingdon Press, 1986).

McClung, L.G., (ed.), *Azusa Street and beyond: Pentecostal Missions and Church Growth in the Twentieth Century* (South Plainfield, NJ: Bridge Publishing, 1986).

MacDonald, W.G., 'The Cross versus Personal Kingdoms', *Pneuma* 3.2 (Fall, 1981), pp. 26-37.

McDonnell, C., and B. Lang, *Heaven: A History* (New Haven: Yale University Press, 1988).

McDonnell, K., 'The Experiential and the Social: New Models From the Pentecostal/Roman Catholic Dialogue', *One in Christ* 9 (1973), pp. 43-58.

—'The Distinguishing Characteristics of the Charismatic-Pentecostal Spirituality', *One in Christ* 10.2 (1974), pp. 117-28.

—*Presence, Power, Praise: Documents on Charismatic Renewal* (Collegeville, MN.: Liturgical Press, 1980), I–III.

—'The Determinative Doctrine of the Holy Spirit', *TTod* 39.2 (July, 1982), pp. 142-61.

McGee, G.B., 'Apostolic Power for End-Times Evangelism: A Historical Review of Pentecostal Mission Theology' (unpublished paper, presented to the International Roman Catholic and Classical Pentecostal Dialogue, 1990).

McGinn, B., (ed. and trans.), *Apocalyptic Spirituality* (New York: Harper & Row, 1977).

McLean, M.D., 'Toward a Pentecostal Hermeneutic', *Pneuma* 6:2 (Fall, 1984); pp. 35-56.

MacRobert, I., *The Black Roots and White Racism of Early Pentecostalism in the U.S.* (New York: St. Martin's Press, 1988).

Maddox, R., (ed.), *Aldersgate Reconsidered* (Nashville: Abingdon Press, 1990).

Marshall, I.H., (ed.), *Christian Experience in Theology and Life* (Edinburgh: Rutherford House, 1988).

Masserano, F.C., 'A Study of Worship Forms in the Assemblies of God Denomination' (MTh thesis, Princeton Theological Seminary, 1966).

Menzies, R.P., The Development of Early Christian Pneumatology (JSNTSup, 54; Sheffield: JSOT Press, 1991).

Mills, W.E., *Speaking in Tongues: A Classified Bibliography* (Franklin Springs, GA: Society for Pentecostal Studies, 1974).

Moberg, D.O., *The Great Reversal: Evangelism versus Social Concern* (Philadelphia: Lippincott, 1972).

Moltmann, J., *The Church in the Power of the Spirit* (New York: Harper & Row, 1977).

—*The Trinity and the Kingdom* (New York: Harper & Row, 1981).

—'The Fellowship of the Holy Spirit—A Trinitarian Pneumatology', *SJT* 37 (1984), pp. 287-300.

Moonie, P.M., ''The Significance of Neo-Pentecostalism for the Renewal and Unity of the Church in the United States' (ThD dissertation, Boston University School of Theology, 1954).

Moore, E. LeR., 'Handbook of Pentecostal Denomiantions in the United States' (MA thesis, Pasadena College, 1954).

Moore, R.D., 'Approaching God's Word Biblically: A Pentecostal Perspective' (unpublished paper, Society for Pentecostal Studies, 1989).

—'Canon and Charisma in the Book of Deuteronomy', *JPT* 1 (1992), pp. 75-92.

Morris, P.C., 'The Holy Spirit in the Music of the Church of God' (unpublished paper, term paper, Church of God School of Theology, 1989).

Myland, D.W., *The Latter Rain Covenant and Pentecostal Power*, in D.W. Dayton (ed.), *Three Early Pentecostal Tracts*.

Nelson, D.J., 'For such a Time as this: The Story of William J. Seymour and the Azusa Street Revival' (PhD dissertation, University of Birmingham, England, 1981).

Newbigin, L., *The Household of God* (London: SCM Press, 1953).

Nichols, D.R., 'The Search for a Pentecostal Structure in Systematic Theology',. *Pneuma* 6.2 (Fall, 1984), pp. 57-76.

Niebuhr, H.R., *The Social Sources of Denominationalism* (New York: World Publishing, 1929).

—*Christ and Culture* (New York: Harper & Row, 1951).

—'Theological Unitarianisms', *TTod* 40.2 (July, 1983), pp. 150-57.

O'Connor, E., *The Pentecostal Movement in the Catholic Church* (Notre Dame: Ave Maria Press, 1971).

Oosthuizen, G.C., *Moving to the Waters: Fifty Years of Pentecostal Revival in Bethesda, 1925-75* (Durban, South Africa: Bethesda, 1975).

Palmer, P., *The Promise of the Father* (Boston, MA: H.V. Degen, 1859; reprs. Salem, Ohio: Schmul, 1981, and New York: Garland, 1986).

Pearlman, M., *Knowing the Doctrines of the Bible* (Springfield, MO: Gospel Publishing House, 1937).

Peters, J.L., *Christian Perfection and American Methodism* (Grand Rapids: Zondervan, 1985).

Plüss, J.-D., *Therapeutic and Prophetic Narratives in Worship: A Hermeneutic Study of Testimony and Vision* (Bern: Peter Lang, 1988).

—'Pentecostal Visions of Peace between Ecclesial Authority and Secular Society' (unpublished paper, Society for Pentecostal Studies, 1989).

Poewe, K., 'Links and Parallels between Black and White Charismatic Churches in South Africa and the States: Potential for Cultural Transformation', *Pneuma* 10.2 (Fall, 1984), pp. 141-58.

Poloma, M., *The Assemblies of God at the Crossroads: Charisma and Institutional Dilemmas* (Knoxville: University of Tennessee Press, 1989).

Pomerville, P.A., *The Third Force in Mission* (Peabody, MA: Hendrickson, 1985).

Poythress, V.S., *Understanding Dispensationalists* (Grand Rapids: Zondervan, 1987).

Quebedeaux, R., *The New Charismatics II* (New York: Harper & Row, 1983).

Ranaghan, K.M., 'Rites of Initiation in Representative Pentecostal Churches in the United States, 1901-1972' (PhD dissertation, University of Notre Dame, 1974).

Reed, D.A , 'Origins and Development of the Theology of Oneness Pentecostalism in the United States' (PhD dissertation, Boston University, 1978).

Reeves, M., and W. Gould, *Joachim of Fiore and the Myth of the Eternal Evangel in the Nineteenth Century* (Oxford: Clarendon Press, 1987).

Reid, D.G., (ed.), *Dictionary of Christianity in America* (Downers Grove, IL: IVP, 1990).

Rhodes, J.S., 'Karl Barth and the Base Communities: A Dialogue on Praxis and Interpretation' (PhD dissertation, Emory University, 1987).

Robeck, C.M., Jr, 'Pentecostalism and Ecumenical Dialogue: A Potential Agenda', *Ecumenical Trends* 16.11 (December, 1987), pp. 185-88.

—'Pentecostal Perspectives on the Ecumenical Challenge' (unpublished paper, prepared for the Pentecostal/COFO dialogue, 1989).

Robeck, C.M., Jr, (ed.), *Charismatic Experiences in History* (Peabody, MA: Hendrickson, 1985).

Roberts, R.C., *Spirituality and Human Emotion* (Grand Rapids: Eerdmans, 1982).

—*The Strengths of a Christian* (Philadelphia: Westminster Press, 1984).

Roebuck, D., 'From Extraordinary Call to Spirit-Baptism: Phoebe Palmer's Use of Pentecostal Language to Justify Women in Ministry' (unpublished paper, Society for Pentecostal Studies, 1989).

Rosato, P.J., *The Spirit as Lord: The Pneumatology of Karl Barth* (Edinburgh: T. & T. Clark, 1981).

Runyon, T., 'System and Method in Wesley's Theology' (unpublished paper, American Academy of Religion, 1982).

Runyon, T., (ed.), *What the Spirit is Saying to the Churches* (New York: Hawthorne Books, 1975).

—*Sanctificaton and Liberation* (Nashville: Abingdon Press, 1981).

Saliers, D.E., and L. Dupre (eds.), *Christian Spirituality*. III. *Post-Reformation and Modern* (World Spirituality, 18; New York: Crossroad, 1989).

Sandidge, J.L., *Roman Catholic/Pentedostal Dialogue, 1977–1982: A Study in Developing Ecumenism* (Studies in the Inter-cultural History of Christianity, 44; Frankfurt: Peter Lang, 1987).

Sauls, N.D., *Pentecostal Doctrines: A Wesleyan Approach* (Dunn, NC: The Heritage Press, 1979), I.

Sepúlveda, J., 'Reflections on the Pentecostal Contribution to the Mission of the Church in Latin America', trans. J. Beaty and S.J. Land, *JPT* 1 (1992), pp. 93-108.

Sheppard, G.T., 'Pentecostalism and the Hermeneutics of Dispensationalism: Anatomy of an Uneasy Relationship', *Pneuma* 6.2 (Fall, 1984), pp. 5-34.

Shopshire, J.M., 'A Socio-Historical Characterization of the Black Pentecostal Movement in North America' (PhD dissertaion, Northwestern University, 1975).

Showalter, A.J., *The Best Gospel Songs and their Composers* (Dalton, GA: A.J. Showalter, 1904).

Smeeton, D.M., 'Perfection or Pentecost: Historical Comparison of Charismatic and Holiness Theologies' (MA thesis, Trinity Evangelical Divinity School, 1971).

Smith, H.B., (ed.), *Pentecostals from the Inside Out* (Wheaton, IL: Scripture Press, 1990).

Smith, T., *Revivalism and Social Reform* (Gloucester, MA: Peter Smith, 1957).

Snyder, H.A., *The Community of the King* (Downers Grove, IL: IVP, 1977).

—*The Divided Flame* (Grand Rapids: Zondervan, 1986).

Spittler, R., (ed.), *Perspectives on the New Pentecostalism* (Grand Rapids: Baker, 1976).

Spurling, R.G., 'The Evening Light and Church of God', *Evangel* 1.1 (1 March 1910); *Evangel* 1.6 (15 May 1910).

—*The Lost Link* (Turtletown, TN: Farner Church of God, 1920).

Stafford, G.W., 'Experiential Salvation and Christian Unity in the Thought of Seven Theologians of the Church of God, Anderson Indiana' (ThD dissertation, Boston University School of Theology, 1986).

Stockard, P.D., 'Modern Kingdom Theology: A Brief Review and Critique of the book, *Held in the Heavens Until: God's Strategy for Planet Earth* by Earl Paulk' (unpublished term paper, Church of God School of Theology, 1989).

Stockwell, E.L., 'Pentecostal Consultation' (unpublished paper, Salvador, Brazil, 6–9 January 1988).

Stoll, D., *Is Latin America Turning Protestant?*(Los Angeles: University of California Press, 1990).

Stronstad, R., *The Charismatic Theology of St Luke* (Peabody, MA: Hendrickson, 1984).

—'Pentecostalism, Experiential Presuppositions and Hermeneutics' (unpublished paper, Society for Pentecostal Studies, 1990).

Stroup, G.W., *The Promise of Narrative Theology* (Atlanta: John Knox, 1981).

Stylianopoulos, T., and S.M. Heim (eds.), *Spirit of Truth: Ecumenical Perspectives on the Holy Spirit* (Brookline, MA: Holy Cross Orthodox Press, 1986).

Swaggart, J., 'The Coming Kingdom', *The Evangelist* (September, 1986), pp. 4-12.

Synan, V., 'The Role of the Holy Spirit and the Gifts of the Spirit in the Mystical Tradition', *One in Christ* 9 (1973), pp. 193-202.

—'Theological Boundaries: The Arminian Tradition', *Pneuma* 3.2 (Fall, 1981), pp. 38-53.

—'Holiness and Pentecostal Traditions in Dialogue' (unpublished paper, Society for Pentecostal Studies, 1988).

Synan, V., (ed.), *The Holiness-Pentecostal Movement in the United States* (Grand Rapids: Eerdmans, 1971).

—*Aspects of Pentecostal-Charismatic Origins* (Plainfield, NJ: Logos, 1975).

—*In the Latter Days* (Ann Arbor, MI: Servant Books, 1984).

Taylor, G.F., *The Spirit and the Bride*, in D.W. Dayton (ed.), *Three Early Pentecostal Tracts*.

Thielicke, H., *The Evangelical Faith*(Grand Rapids: Eerdmans, 1974), I.

Thomas, J.C., 'The Spiritual Situation of the Disciples Before Pentecost' (unpublished paper, Society for Pentecostal Studies, 1984).

—*Footwashing in John 13 and the Johannine Community* (JSNTSup, 61; Sheffield: JSOT Press, 1991).

Toon, P., *Justification and Sanctification* (Westchester, IL: Crossway Books, 1983).

Torrance, T.F., *God and Rationality* (New York: Oxford University Press, 1971).

—*The Trinitarian Faith* (Edinburgh: T. & T. Clark, 1988).

Tugwell, S., G. Every, J.O. Mills and P. Hocken, *New Heaven? New Earth? An Encounter with Pentecostalism* (London: Darton, Longman, & Todd, 1976).

Turner, W.C., Jr, 'The United Holy Church of America: A Study in Black Holiness Pentecostalism' (PhD dissertation, Duke University, 1984).

Tuttle, R.G., *Mysticism and the Wesleyan Tradition* (Grand Rapids: Zondervan, 1989).

Ulanov, A., and B. Ulanov, *Primary Speech: A Psychology of Prayer* (Atlanta: John Knox, 1982).

Vaccaro, G., *Identidad Pentecostal* (Quito: Consejo Latinoamericano De Iglesias, 1988).

Valliere, P., *Holy War and Pentecostal Peace* (New York: Seabury Press, 1983).

Vaughan, J.D., *The Silver Trumpet* (Lawrenceburg, TN: James D. Vaughan, 1908).

Volf, M., 'Materiality of Salvation: An Investigation in the Soteriologies of Liberation and Pentecostal Theologies', *JES* 26.3 (Summer, 1989), pp. 447-67.

—'On Loving with Hope: Eschatology and Social Responsibility', *Transformation* 7.3 (July/September, 1990), pp. 28-31.

Wacker, G., 'Taking Another Look at the *Vision of the Disinherited*', *RSR* 8.1 (January, 1982), pp. 15-22.

—Review of *Vision of the Disinherited* by R.M. Anderson, *Pneuma* 4.2 (Fall, 1982), pp. 53-62.

—'The Functions of Faith in Primitive Pentecostalism', *HTR* 77 (July/October, 1984), pp. 353-75.

Wagner, C.P., *Spiritual Power and Church Growth* (Altamont Springs, FL.: Strang Communicatons, 1986).

Wainwright, G., *Doxology* (New York: Oxford University Press, 1980).

Waldner, M.M., 'Christian Mission in Eschatological Perspective: Promoting the Dynamic of Eschatology for Missionary Motivation (DMiss dissertation, Fuller Theological Seminary, School of World Mission, 1987).

Waldrop, R., 'La teologia de la liberacion: Enfoque critico'. *Pastoralia* 7.15 (December, 1985), pp. 31-44.

Waldvogel, E.L., 'The "Overcoming Life": A Study in the Reformed Evangelical Origins of Pentecostalism' (PhD dissertation, Harvard University, 1977).

—'The "Overcoming" Life: A Study in the Reformed Evangelical Contribution to Pentecostalism', *Pneuma* 1.1 (Spring, 1979), pp. 7-9.

Walvoord, J.F., *The Rapture Question* (Grand Rapids: Zondervan, 1979).

Ware, K., *The Orthodox Way* (Crestwood, NY: St Vladimir's Seminary Press, 1980).

Wheelock, D.R., 'Spirit-Baptism in American Pentecostal Thought' (PhD dissertation, Emory University, 1983).

White, J.F., *Protestant Worship: Traditions in Transition* (Louisville, KY: Westminster Press/John Knox, 1989).

Williams, J.R., *The Era of the Spirit* (Plainfield, NJ: Logos, 1971).

—*The Pentecostal Reality* (Plainfield, NJ: Logos, 1972).

—'Pentecostal Spirituality', *One in Christ* 10.12 (1974), pp. 180-92.

—'The Holy Spirit and Eschatology', *Pneuma* 3.2 (Fall, 1981), pp. 54-58.

—*Renewal Theology* (Grand Rapids: Zondervan, 1990), II.

Willis, W., (ed.), *The Kingdom of God in 20th Century Interpretation* (Peabody, MA: Hendrickson, 1987).

Winsett, R.E., (ed.), *Gospel Song Messenger* Memphis TN: R.E. Winsett, n.d.).

—*Songs of Pentecostal Power* (Dayton, TN: R.E. Winsett, 1908).

—*Songs of Perennial Glory* (Chattanooga, TN: R.E. Winsett, 1916).

Wood, L.W., 'Thoughts upon the Wesleyan Doctrine of Entire Sanctification with Special Reference to some similarities with Roman Catholic Doctrine of Confirmation', *Wesleyan Theological Journal* 15.1 (Spring, 1980), pp. 88-99.

—*Pentecostal Grace* (Grand Rapids: Zondervan, 1980).

Yoder, J.H., *The Politics of Jesus* (Grand Rapids: Eerdmans, 1972).

Yoder, P.B., *Shalom: The Bible's Word for Salvation, Justice, and Peace* (Newton, KS: Faith and Life Press, 1987).

Zegwaart, H., 'Apocalyptic Eschatology and Pentecostalism: The Relevance of John's Millenium for Today', *Pneuma* 10.1 (Spring, 1988), pp. 3-25.

INDEXES

INDEX OF BIBLICAL REFERENCES

INDEX OF NAMES

Index of Names

Pomerville, P.A. 25, 120

Quebedeaux, R. 188, 189

Ranaghan, K.M. 34, 75, 94, 148, 149
Reed, D.A. 24, 185
Riss, R.M. 53, 185, 188, 194, 209
Robeck, C.M., Jr 27, 105, 190, 213, 217
Roberts, O. 81
Roberts, R.C. 133, 134, 138, 143, 164, 167, 174
Rogers, W.J. 87
Rosato, P.J. 168
Runyon, T. 42, 43, 82

Saliers, D.E. 36, 37, 43, 133, 134, 165
Sandford, F.W. 19, 20
Sandidge, J.L. 27, 217
Sauls, N.D. 24
Schleiermacher, F.D.E. 37
Schlesinger, D. 212
Sepúlveda, J. 30, 45
Seymour, W.J. 16, 17, 24, 51, 74, 77, 78, 90, 107, 109, 110, 116, 124, 151, 209
Shedd, C. 38
Shelton, J.B. 188
Sheppard, G.T. 27
Shepperd, J.W. 25, 213
Shopshire, J.M. 24
Showalter, A.J. 144
Smith, H.B. 189
Smith, H.W. 47
Smith, T. 17, 179, 208
Snyder, H.A. 175, 199
Spittler, R.P. 25, 78, 213
Spurling, R.G., Jr 107, 186
Stockard, P.D. 212
Stoll, D. 22, 31
Stronstad, R. 58, 188
Swaggart, J. 81, 189

Symeon, St 29
Synan, H.V. 49, 61, 161, 188, 198, 199

Taylor, G.F. 64
Thomas, J.C. 25, 101
Tomlinson, A.J. 18
Torrance, T.F. 32
Tugwell, S. 62
Turner, W.C., Jr 24

Unamuno, M. de 45

Vaccaro, G. 30
Valliere, P. 31, 173, 207
Van Cleave, N.M. 24
Vaughan, J.D. 158
Volf, M. 199, 200

Wacker, G. 27, 63, 67, 189, 190, 208
Wainwright, G. 25
Waldrop, R. 199
Waldvogel, E.L. 24
Ward, H. 61, 161, 188
Warfield, B.B. 38, 51, 79, 217
Warner, W.E. 21
Wesley, C. 88
Wesley, J. 33-35, 41, 42, 44, 47, 54, 55, 95, 106, 118, 132, 143, 144, 178, 184, 186, 200, 202, 207, 212, 220, 221
Wheelock, D.R. 24, 34, 35, 49, 50
White, J.F. 208
Williams, J.R. 25, 46
Wilmore, G. 209
Wilson, L.F. 105
Winsett, R.E. 86, 87, 114, 116, 121, 141, 144, 150, 151, 158
Woodworth-Etter, M. 209

Yarnold, E. 25

Zaretsky, I.I. 167